Dear Sujata,

with warm
regards,

Vivek

(01-10-21)

# RAJIV JAYARAMAN

# CLEARING THE
# DIGITAL
# BLUR

## How Organizations Can Transform Themselves at the Speed of Digital

Foreword by Sangeet Paul Choudary
Best Selling Author of *Platform Revolution*

# WILEY

**Clearing The Digital BLUR: How Organizations Can Transform Themselves At The Speed of Digital**

*Other Wiley Editorial Offices*
John Wiley & Sons, Inc. 111 River Street, Hoboken, NJ 07030, USA
Wiley-VCH Verlag GmbH, Pappellaee 3, D-69469 Weinheim, Germany
John Wiley & Sons Australia Ltd, 42 McDougall Street, Milton, Queensland 4064, Australia
John Wiley & Sons (Asia) Pte Ltd, 1 Fusionpolis Walk #07-01 Solaris, South Tower Singapore 138628
John Wiley & Sons Canada Ltd, 22 Worcester Road, Etobicoke, Ontario, Canada, M9W ILI

First Edition: 2019

ISBN: 978-81-265-7816-0

www.wileyindia.com

Printed at: Sanat Printers

To my parents,
My wife Anu,
My kids Aadita and Agastya
And all the Knollies

# Praise for
# Clearing The Digital BLUR

"This book is an easy yet comprehensive read to educate the rookie about Digital, as well as help the digital native get a holistic picture of the disruption. The interviews with leaders from different industries are fascinating as they show the boundary-less nature of all things Digital. Rajiv does a great job in not just simplifying the complexities, but also gives an action plan to start with across various dimensions – strategy, talent, structure, culture and ecosystem."

—*NS Parthasarathy*
*COO and Executive Vice Chairman,*
*Mindtree*

"If software is eating the world, Clearing The Digital BLUR offers a manual for the thousands of companies that can either eat or be eaten. In this must-read book Rajiv Jayaraman lays out the burning platform for companies in all industries facing disruption and competition from digital upstarts, and a clear step-by-step guide to avoid the fate of companies such as Blockbuster, Borders and Blackberry. Senior managers will find here the solutions they have been seeking and will ignore Jayaraman's advice at their peril."

—*Niraj Dawar*
*Professor of Marketing, Ivey Business School and author of 'TILT:*
*Shifting Your Strategy from Products to Customers'*

"This book helps the reader understand how the industrial age is morphing into a blur. What can managers and leaders do to cope with the inevitable digital transformations? With structured frameworks and actionable insights, the book stimulates thinking and responses."

*—R. Gopalakrishnan*
*CEO, The Mindworks, Ex–Director, Tata Sons*
*Author of 'What the CEO Really Wants From You'*

"Clearing The Digital BLUR makes for easy and exciting reading. Rajiv has made a half-understood but much-voiced over subject accessible, and successfully demystified it! From getting the basic concepts and the history right, to providing advice on the model and the possible approach-prototype, the book unravels itself to the reader. The BLUR, LEAPFROG, and 5A frameworks, as well as the many real-life examples of digital transformation take the reader through a step-by-step journey, in the form of a narrative. Succinct and easily comprehensible, the book is a treat to read and learn from. I thank Rajiv for this book and the effort he has made in putting his thoughts and learnings together. I believe this book has the potential to shape thinking, beyond the obvious impact of educating the reader. It energizes and kindles interest and propels the reader to action."

*—Ashok Ramchandran*
*Group Executive President - Group Human Resources,*
*Aditya Birla Group*

"Clearing the Digital BLUR by Rajiv Jayaraman provides us with the 'why, what and how' of digital transformation. Rajiv begins with elucidating why it is necessary to focus on this very crucial lever of business strategy, and the consequence for businesses in not doing so. The BLUR framework is extremely insightful and immediately connects with the reader. Next, he goes on to explain in vivid detail how one can apply the conceptual elements to real life, with plenty of real-world examples. All in all, Clearing the Digital BLUR is a powerful guidebook to winning in the digital world, that no business executive can afford to miss."

*—V. (Paddy) Padmanabhan*
*The Unilever Chaired Professor of Marketing and Academic Director,*
*Emerging Markets Institute, INSEAD*

"Organizations everywhere are struggling to cope with the digital transformation that is happening all around us. Managers are in search of a unifying framework that will help take the right decisions in this context. Rajiv Jayaraman's new book is a significant contribution towards filling this gap."

—*Rishikesha T Krishnan*
*Director, IIM-Indore and Co-author of '8 Steps to Innovation:*
*Going from Jugaad to Excellence'*

# Contents

# Foreword

A significant shift is underway at the heart of how businesses create and deliver value. Businesses have always thought of the 'value-chain' in a linear manner, that is, the producer generates value which is then delivered to the end consumer. This linear visual of business flow is one we are intimately familiar with. In my work, I call this the *pipeline business model* to illustrate the linear flow of value. However, a new form of business model is emerging, and is already the mainstay of some of the most valuable global companies today. Firms such as Google, Amazon, Facebook, Apple and many others rely on the *platform business model*, enabling interactions between connected producers and consumers. Leaders today need to consider the platform business model, and capitalize on the opportunities that platforms carry with them (or risk being commoditized by them).

In *Platform Revolution: How Networked Markets Are Transforming The Economy And How To Make Them Work For You,* my co-authors and I discussed how organizations can prepare for the economic, social and technological forces that are transforming our world. We introduced the impact that platforms have on our lives today, how platform businesses have swiftly disrupted traditional industries, and driven the successes and failures of companies such as Apple and Nokia respectively.

In this compelling new book, *Clearing The Digital BLUR: How Organizations Can Transform Themselves At The Speed of Digital,* Rajiv Jayaraman introduces the reader to the perils of ignoring key trends related to the digital economy. Rajiv's central framework explains the consequences of technological impact on business. The acronym BLUR serves simultaneously as a metaphor for the speed of change as well as an acronym for the four shifts every company needs to be aware of. With anecdotes, trends and data, the book presents the case for analyzing digital strategy holistically.

Moving from theory to practice, the book also lays out a step-by-step guide for leaders to move from a linear approach to business modelling, to one that can leverage network effects. Business leaders will derive a lot of value in applying these principles to how they define and evolve their business strategies in a digital first world.

This book is an important read for executives looking to transform their organizations to be digital-ready, especially for those daring to think beyond and emerge as leaders in the new connected landscape of business.

—Sangeet Paul Choudary
Best-selling author of *Platform Revolution* and *HBR Top 10 Must-Reads of 2017.*

# Prologue

What do Google, Amazon, Facebook and Alibaba have in common?

Collectively referred to as 'GAFA', these companies represent a new breed of competitors who are disrupting one industry after another using a playbook that most incumbent companies fail to understand. This book will help you understand how these digital born organizations look at the world around them, and more importantly, help you transform your own organization to compete and ultimately, thrive in the digital age.

Do not be misled that digital disruption is just another business buzzword. It is a very real phenomenon that is playing out in every industry. The rapid mortality rate of companies in the digital age is nothing short of shocking. More than 50 percent of global Fortune 500 companies have fallen off the list since the year 2000, because of digital disruption.

Everything that can be digitized is being digitized, to the advantage of disruptors that have the digital edge. Incumbents, on the other hand, are left with no choice but to respond in an accelerated fashion or risk irrelevance and painful obsolescence.

The digital transformation journey is fraught with uncertainties and risks that traditional organizations and its leaders are not familiar with. With management playbooks from the industrial age offering very little meaningful guidance, we need a fresh perspective to respond to the challenge. *Clearing the Digital BLUR* fills the gap by providing a handbook for leaders and managers to navigate the strategic challenges of the digital age.

This book brings to sharp focus the four crucial business lines that are blurring away in the digital age. It describes how traditional organizations are clinging to lines that no longer matter. As a result, these organizations that once powered through the industrial age are now falling by the wayside in the digital age.

The book presents a holistic approach by going beyond strategic frameworks to include practical insights on strategy execution, leadership and culture. Filled with actionable frameworks, worksheets, case studies and interviews from leaders, the book offers a proven pathway to improve the odds of success for organizations undergoing digital transformation.

The Digital BLUR methodology has been embraced by many leading organizations in industries ranging from Oil and Gas to Pharma to Banking, where leaders and managers have been equipped with the frameworks, skillsets and mindsets needed to transform their organizations.

This book is by no means only for large organizations. Even startups can learn from the case studies of other successful digital leaders and turbocharge their growth by applying the Digital BLUR methodology to their ideas.

## Structure of the Book

Section 1, 'Understanding Digital BLUR', focuses on case studies of companies that have been disrupted by digital born organizations. The chapters in this section provide an in-depth understanding of the forces behind digital disruption and crucial lessons that traditional companies can learn about the nature of the new game played by digital born organizations. This section delves deep into the lines from the industrial age that have morphed into a blur in the digital age causing deep disorientation to leaders and managers in traditional organizations.

In Section 2, 'Impact of Digital BLUR', we will analyze the impact of the blurring lines in the retail and banking industries. This section also includes the interview of Tan Sri Tony Fernandes, the CEO of Air Asia Group. He provides deep insights on the impact of Digital BLUR in the airline industry.

Section 3, 'Digital LEAPFROG Framework', we will focus on a 7-step process to clear the Digital BLUR and to transform the traditional business model of an organization into a digital-ready networked business model. Using a series of structured frameworks and worksheets, the Digital LEAPFROG framework allows you to apply key learnings in the context of your business. If you are part of a digital born organization, you will find inspiration from many other organizations to innovate fearlessly and shape new opportunities.

In Section 4, 'Digital Fault Lines', we will turn our attention to the issues that an organization must deal with while clearing the Digital BLUR. This section will take you through both internal as well as external fault lines that come in the way of successful digital transformation. This section also focuses on a couple of very important transformations that an organization must take seriously: leadership and culture.

Section 5, 'Reflections on Digital BLUR', includes interviews of industry leaders on Digital BLUR. The idea of this section is to provide interesting perspectives of leaders from different industries, functions and geographies.

Towards the end of the book, you will find a 90-day action plan to clear the Digital BLUR that you can put to great use at your organization. Hope this book helps you transform your organization at the speed of digital.

Happy reading!
Rajiv Jayaraman

# SECTION 1

# UNDERSTANDING DIGITAL BLUR

# CHAPTER 1

# DIAL D FOR DISRUPTION

"More than 50 percent of global Fortune 500 companies have fallen out of the list since the year 2000 because of digital."

—Pierre Nanterme, ex-CEO, Accenture

*"What do you mean you don't have an
Instagram account?"*

# Blockbusted

*"Investor concern over the threat of new technologies is overstated."*
**—Blockbuster Analyst Report** (1999)

Blockbuster, the iconic provider of home movie and video game rental services, had USD 5 billion in revenues, employed 84,300 employees worldwide and had more than 9,000 stores, while at its peak, in the early 2000s.[1]

Around the same time, a company called Netflix, founded by Reed Hastings and Marc Randolph in 1997, was reimagining the entertainment industry. Capitalizing on the proliferation of the Internet and growing popularity of DVDs, Hastings and Randolph launched Netflix on April 14, 1998, as the world's first online DVD rental store where the users rented movies online and the DVDs were delivered by mail.[2]

# Founding Story of Netflix

Reed Hastings has an interesting founding story to share. "I had a big late fee for *Apollo 13*", says Hastings. "It was six weeks late and I owed the video store USD 40. I had misplaced the cassette. It was all my fault. I didn't want to tell my wife about it. And I said to myself, 'I'm going to compromise the integrity of my marriage over a late fee?' Later, on my way to the gym, I realized they had a much better business model. You could pay USD 30 or USD 40 a month and work out as little or as much as you wanted".[3] This insight is supposed to have sparked the idea for an online subscription-based business model at Netflix, one without any late fee. Incidentally, in the year 2000, Blockbuster was making USD 800 million in late fees, contributing to a whopping 16 percent of their annual revenues.[4]

Legend has it that Hastings met with the then-Blockbuster CEO, John Antioco, to pitch for Blockbuster to become a strategic partner and investor in Netflix. In what would later be cited as one of the biggest misses in business history, Antioco passed up on an opportunity to acquire Netflix for USD 50 million. Bitter rivalry between the two companies ensued and continued well into the mid-2000s. So much so that when in one of the interviews, Reed Hastings said that Blockbuster was throwing everything but the kitchen sink at Netflix to beat them, leaders at Blockbuster promptly sent him a kitchen sink the very next day.[5]

Long story short, while Blockbuster was struggling to get its online and brick-and-mortar story right, Netflix continued to reinvent itself by getting into on-demand shows and online streaming movies, leveraging the power of the Internet, and serving customers to meet their needs for choice and instant gratification. Blockbuster declared bankruptcy in 2010 and was acquired by Dish Network, while Netflix is ranked among the top 10 Internet companies by revenue as of 2018. Figure 1.1 shows the revenues of Netflix and Blockbuster between the years 2004 and 2010.

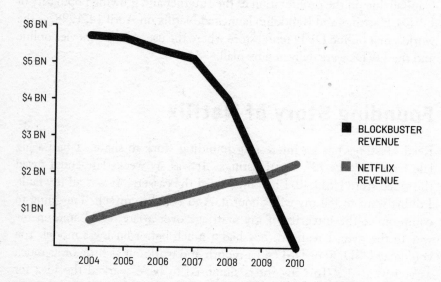

**Figure 1.1** Netflix vs. Blockbuster revenues from the year 2004 to 2010

# The Smartphone Disruption

*"Not everyone can type on a piece of glass."*

—**Mike Lazaridis, co-CEO, Research in Motion**

Research in Motion (RIM) can be safely credited with creating the smartphone category in 1999 when it first launched the Blackberry. The Canadian phone maker focused primarily on business professionals who cared about ease of typing, secure communication, and superior battery life. RIM's product-market fitment worked wonders for them. Blackberry's QWERTY keyboard made it easy for professionals to communicate on the go, making it a feature that users swore by. Blackberry messenger became a killer app that propelled the product not just into the hands of CEOs and business professionals but also heads of state and hollywood celebrities. Blackberry quickly acquired iconic status. At its peak, Blackberry had more than 40 percent market share in the US.[6] While RIM was enjoying its dream run with relentless focus on the core product and its features, a couple of companies were changing the rules of the game.

## Apple Makes a Grand Entry

On January 9, 2007, Steve Jobs made an impressive announcement to launch the iPhone. Considering how inferior the product was compared to the Blackberry on the traditional metrics valuable to corporate users back then, the RIM leadership dismissed the iPhone initially. Looking back, we can see that their arguments did have a lot of merit. The iPhone did not have great battery life, did not support a messenger app and above all, it lacked the QWERTY keyboard. Blackberry was quite certain that business users would not switch to a product that did not hold up to the needs of its power users. Blackberry was right. Corporates did not switch immediately to the iPhone. The executives in these companies, however, did. The stunning design of the iPhone attracted individuals in droves. These individuals increasingly asked their companies to switch to iPhones for their corporate use. The moat that RIM had built around its core segment started falling apart.

## Google Joins the Party

Close on the heels of Apple's runaway success, Google launched its Android Operating System on November 5, 2007. Android was touted to be 'the first truly open and comprehensive platform for mobile devices'.[7] Google also announced the Open Handset Alliance (OHA), a consortium of leading mobile manufacturers such as Samsung, HTC, Motorola, and a group of mobile operators such as T-Mobile, Sprint, and Nextel. Google built Android as an open ecosystem, an industry standard for mobile operating systems. Most importantly, it was free.

Whereas RIM and Apple had closed, proprietary systems, Google entered the market with a radically open approach, one that attracted the entire ecosystem of mobile manufacturers and operators. Not to be left behind in their wake, Apple launched its App Store on July 10, 2008. With over 10 million app downloads in the first weekend of its launch, the app store helped Apple leapfrogged into a completely new business model. The deal with AT&T that allowed Apple to sell apps through its own store in return for exclusive availability of the phone on AT&T's network proved to be a master stroke. Apple managed to create incredible value by inviting developers from across the world to create apps that delighted the users. By unleashing the power of the app ecosystem, Apple quickly amassed a huge variety of apps from mobile games to language apps to fitness apps on its platform. Apple's tagline captured the power of the value proposition to the user: 'There's an app for that'. Apple created a revenue model wherein app developers took 70 percent of all in-app purchases and Apple took a 30 percent share.

Google promptly launched the Android Market in March 2009 (now called Google Play Store) to incredible success. However, RIM continued to fight the battle based on product features and specs. Blackberry Storm, RIM's first touch screen phone, was launched as an iPhone killer at the end of 2008. Smartphone users, however, did not find this feature to be unique or compelling. Storm generated mixed reviews and mediocre revenues. When RIM finally tried to join the party with the Blackberry App World in April 2009, it was a distant third option in a crowded marketplace. By then, developers had started engaging with Apple and Android app ecosystems. Blackberry's aging operating system did not help their cause. It was exasperatingly difficult to develop apps for Blackberry compared to the shiny new systems developed by Apple and Google. Mobile app developers started playing a huge role in the success of a mobile phone brand.

## Downfall of an Iconic Brand

It is shocking how little time Apple and Google took to disrupt Blackberry. By the end of 2011, Blackberry's market share had steadily declined to under 15 percent whereas Apple and Google were experiencing stratospheric success. In less than 4 years, irreparable damage had been done.

It is also interesting to note that RIM's revenue grew at a rapid pace from 2007 to 2011, alongside the growth of Apple's revenues at the same time. This led their leadership team to believe that there was nothing wrong with their strategy. Imagine being a leader at RIM from 2007 to 2011 when things are going fantastically well. Revenues are growing at a furious pace. Buyers are loving your products. The company doubles down on its focus on features and specs. Post-2011, however, the story takes a sharp downward turn. The company slips quickly into irrelevance post its high of 2011.[8]

How did Blackberry fail so catastrophically? It failed to recognize that the rules of the game had changed. The game had changed from courting core professional users to nurturing a thriving ecosystem of app developers. It had changed from product specs and features to ecosystems. Figure 1.2 shows Blackberry's revenues from 2004 to 2017.[9]

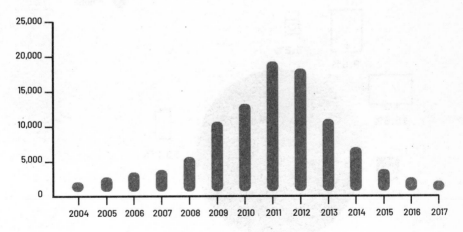

**Figure 1.2** Blackberry's revenues from 2004 to 2017

As a contrast, Figure 1.3 shows the phenomenal growth of Apple's iPhone revenues. iPhone accounted for 53.3 percent of Apple's overall revenue of USD 215.6 billion in 2016.

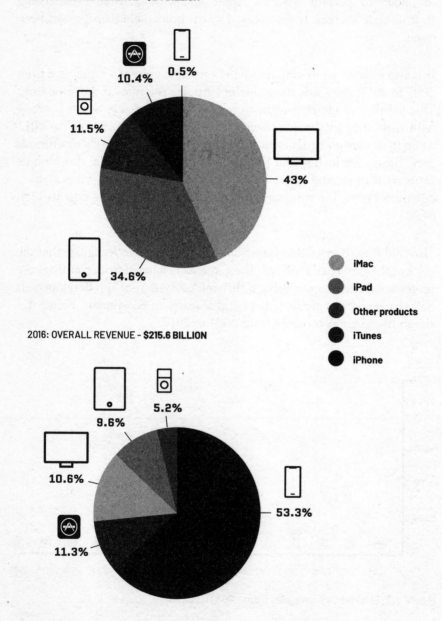

**Figure 1.3**   iPhone's phenomenal growth from the year 2007 to 2016
(Adapted from Statista)

# From Books to Ecommerce

*"Josefowicz shook hands with the devil and handed him the online business."*

**—Mike Edwards, the then-CEO, Borders**

Headquartered in Ann Arbor, Michigan, Borders was an international book and music retailer that dominated the big box retail format trailing just behind Barnes & Noble in its industry. In the 1990s, both these companies were on a growth spree and started consolidating the market, leaving very little room for independent book sellers to survive. With more than 600 stores and nearly 20,000 employees during its heyday, Borders was certainly a big player to reckon with in its space. While Borders was busy expanding aggressively in international markets and diversifying into DVDs and music in its retail outlets, a different kind of competitor was setting its sight on the industry.

## A Legend is Born

Jeff Bezos was a Wall Street professional working at DE Shaw & Co. In 1993, he witnessed something transformative happening around him: "The wakeup call was finding this startling statistic that web usage in the spring of 1994 was growing at 2,300 percent a year. You know, things just don't grow that fast. It's highly unusual, and that started me thinking, 'What kind of business plan might make sense in the context of that growth?'" says Bezos.[10]

He made a list of top 20 products that he could potentially sell to capitalize on the phenomenal growth of the Internet. He zeroed in on books because of their universal demand and low cost. He was quick to understand that books lend themselves to be distributed in digital form. Furthermore, the publishing industry does not really care about the channels where books are sold, as long as they are sold. In July 1994, at the age of 30, he quit his job and started what we today know as Amazon. He relentlessly focused on choice for customers, superior customer service and of course, great deals.

## The Fateful Decision

Unable to cope with the onslaught of digital books and intense competition with Barnes & Noble, Amazon and mass retailers such as Walmart and Costco, the then-CEO of Borders, Greg Josefowicz took the fateful decision to partner with Amazon to outsource its web-based sales. Border's annual report from the year 2000 explains the rationale for this baffling move. "Our online investment will be channeled to support our in-store platform, while Borders.com will continue to be utilized as a convenience retail channel," the report reads.[11]

Borders.com was relaunched as an Amazon partner. Under the terms of their agreement, Amazon handled inventory, shipping, site content, and customer service while Borders drove sales by leveraging its iconic brand name. "While our customers' needs are met online by the people who do it better than anyone else, we will provide them with what we do best: the books, music and movies they love to explore in an engaging shopping atmosphere," said Josefowicz.[12] Many analysts observed at the time that this was akin to handing over the keys to the competition. Years later, Mike Edwards, the CEO who succeeded Josefowicz, said "Josefowicz shook hands with the devil and handed him the online business".[13]

It was not until March 2007 that Borders finally decided to pull the plug on the fateful deal. But by then, the damage was done. Borders never recovered from their series of lost opportunities and missteps.

Barnes & Noble, interestingly, had a different approach. The company decided to disrupt itself with its online strategy braving the risks of cannibalization. Their annual report in 2000 notes that "Our position has always been that if we pay a visit to our customers at home through Barnes & Noble.com, they will return the favor at our stores."

The Amazon Kindle came out in November 2007. It took another 2 years for Barnes & Noble to launch its Nook reader. Borders' Kobo came out in May 2010, a month after Apple had launched its iconic product, iPad. It is a classic story of too little, too late.

Borders began racking up losses at an astronomical rate. They lost a combined USD 344 million in 2008 and 2009 and eventually filed for bankruptcy in February 2011. Interestingly, Amazon had struck a similar deal with Toys "R" Us in 2000, leading to an eerily similar outcome for the toys retailer. Toys "R" Us filed for bankruptcy in 2017. Figure 1.4 shows the growth of Amazon vis-à-vis traditional book sellers.

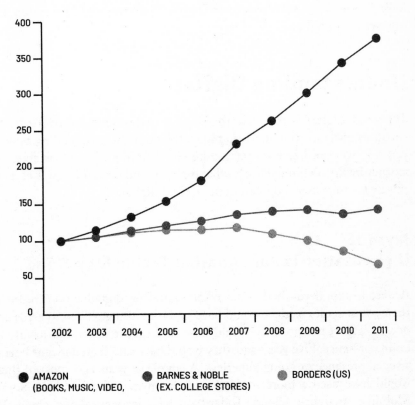

● AMAZON          ● BARNES & NOBLE          ● BORDERS (US)
(BOOKS, MUSIC, VIDEO,    (EX. COLLEGE STORES)

**Figure 1.4** Growth of Amazon vis-à-vis traditional book sellers

Blockbuster, RIM and Borders were all Fortune 500 companies. While Blockbuster and Borders were traditional companies in the movie rental and book retail businesses respectively, RIM was at one time, at the cutting edge of technology. All of them have slipped out of the Fortune 500 list in the last decade.

# Making Sense of Digital Disruption

In all these cases, the new breed of competitors started using superior playbooks powered by digital technologies. The winners in all the three cases disrupted industries and competitors by leveraging digital platforms. Before we understand the three types of disruptions in further detail, let us look at three important concepts: Digital, Platforms and Disruption. Let us start with Digital.

# Understanding Digital

The word 'digital' is probably the most tossed around buzzword in the corridors of the corporate world today. The problem is, depending on who you ask, you are likely to get a different definition. So, let us start our journey by first defining clearly what digital is and what it is not. Let us do this by busting some popular myths around digital.

## Myth 1.
## Digitalization Is Just Another Technology Trend

A decade ago, if you had asked what 'digital' or 'digitalization' meant to them, most senior leaders would have said something related to zeros and ones. Eight years ago, they would have said that it was about having an online presence. Five years ago, they would have said digital means having a social presence or going paperless. A couple of years ago, most of them would have used a more sophisticated acronym called SMAC—Social, Mobility, Analytics, Cloud. Today, you hear leaders talking about 3D printing, Internet of Things (IoT), robotics or some other advancement in digital technology. While it is true that these technology trends can potentially supercharge the trajectory of a company and in some cases, even industries, this is not the complete story.

Digitalization, in fact, is not just about the ones and zeroes, neither is it just about new technologies that are surfacing each day with the potential to disrupt old ways of doing things. In fact, it is not a destination. Neither is it a thing. Digital has become so interwoven into our lives today that it has become a natural way of working and living. In the context of business, it is an overarching transformation in the way businesses create, deliver and capture value.

## Myth 2.
## Digitalization Is the Same as Digitization

Digitization is the process of converting something that is physical and analog into something that is virtual and digital. Think about how in the last decade everything from movies, to books, to music, to business processes to even money has been made available in the digital format. That is digitization. Overall, digitalization is a new way of doing things by leveraging technology to create exceptional customer experience, become agile from a process standpoint and unlock new value by leveraging the power of data. In a nutshell, digitalization has more to do with business models than technology.

## Myth 3.
## In an Organizational Context, Digital Is Only for Senior Leadership or IT to Worry About

The playbook for business has changed in the digital world. Digital has become all-pervading and all-encompassing in an organization. Going beyond business and IT, everyone in the organization needs to know the rules of the new game. Digital brings a fundamental shift in the mindsets, skillset and toolsets of all employees. Hence, it is imperative that digital gets baked into the core DNA of an organization.

---

To sum up, Digital is a way of working that leverages technology to accomplish three main purposes:
  a.  Create stellar customer experience
  b.  Make processes agile
  c.  Unlock new, exponential value by leveraging data

---

# Understanding Platforms

Earlier we observed that Blockbuster, RIM and Borders lost to digital platforms. Now that we have understood the first part of that keyword, let us turn our attention to the second part, platforms.

The term 'platform' is used in a variety of contexts in the business world. The auto industry, for instance, uses this word to refer to common design and components on which a family of products can be built. For example, Fiat Panda, Fiat 500 and Fiat Uno use the Fiat Mini platform. This is an example of a product platform.

There are instances where products, services and technologies serve as the foundation not just for product lines inside an organization but for the industry ecosystem. Intel has served as the platform for the PC industry for a very long time. Manufacturers of PCs and other computer accessories base their design and development efforts on the core architecture used by Intel. This is an example of an industry platform.

The underlying infrastructure on which applications are built is referred to as the computing platform. The Windows Operating System is a great example of this type of platform. In today's context, this infrastructure is made available as an online service by a host of providers including Amazon, Google and Microsoft. This online service is referred to as Platform as a Service (PaaS).

Just about every company today seems to be building a platform to become an 'Uber for X' or 'Airbnb for Y'. While the core idea in these cases is the delivery of a product or service 'on demand', that is only the operational part of the business. In this book, the word platform refers to the business model as a whole, not just the delivery model.

> A platform is a plug-and-play business model that allows multiple parties—producers, consumers, service providers—to connect, interact, create and exchange value.

The idea of a platform business is not new by any stretch of imagination. Malls connect consumers and merchants; newspapers connect subscribers and advertisers. What has changed in the digital context is that the new-age platforms are powered by digital technologies that connect producers and consumers in an on-demand fashion often powered by data.

Digital platforms have the following unique characteristics:

• Digital platforms enable technology-enabled business models, facilitating exchanges between multiple groups. In this model, consumers can be producers and producers can be consumers. For example, YouTube is a platform on which video uploaders create value and viewers consume value. The same uploaders are also consumers of other videos. If you think of eBay, the sellers are the producers and the buyers are the consumers. However, nothing stops the buyers and sellers from switching their roles. On Twitter, every time you tweet, you are in a producer role, and when you start reading your tweet stream the next second, you have moved to consumer mode. Many platforms are also multi-sided—they have many types of producers and consumers. On LinkedIn, for instance, professionals using LinkedIn are producers and consumers of interactions and status updates, thought leaders on LinkedIn are curated producers and recruiters are producers of job listings and consumers of relevant user profiles.

Figure 1.5 shows LinkedIn as a multi-sided platform.

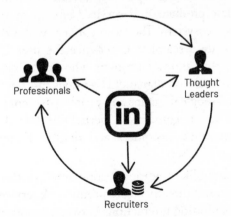

**Figure 1.5** LinkedIn as a multi-sided platform

- The value delivered by digital platforms is proportional to the size of the network. This is called the network effect. The more the contributing members in the network, the more the value one can get. Without the community, a digital platform is worth nothing. The first fax machine or the phone that was sold had practically no value, because there was no other device to communicate to. As the number of devices in the network increases, the value of the individual device and that of the network increases manifold. Figure 1.6 illustrates the concept of network effect.

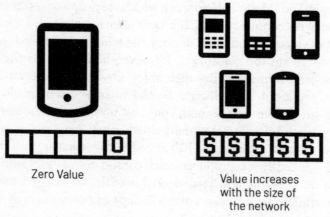

Zero Value

Value increases
with the size of
the network

**Figure 1.6** Network effect

- Digital platforms have an open architecture wherein other companies can create new products and services on top of the platform, thus extending the ecosystem. They also connect with other platforms and services to create a seamless experience the user. Uber, for instance, is a platform that allows customers who are looking for cabs to get connected with cabs on demand. Uber does this not all by itself but by tying up with Google for maps and various payment gateways to enable payments. When it comes to UberEATS, it facilitates interactions between restaurants, customers and drivers. Figure 1.7 shows the platform setup of Uber.

- In many cases, unlike traditional companies, platforms such as Uber and Airbnb do not directly create products or services. They are in the business of facilitating interactions between various parties that create and consume products or services on the platform.

**Figure 1.7** The Uber platform

- The platforms engender trust where producers and consumers can interact with each other without the fear of any economic or reputational risk. eBay was one of the earliest successful Internet companies to provide a trustworthy platform to transact with strangers online. Unlike many other players during the dot-com period, eBay did not invest in building inventory, warehouses and an elaborate supply chain. Instead, it provided the digital infrastructure for a marketplace to exist and built a community that is trustworthy. It made money by charging a nominal commission to the seller for the goods that were sold in the marketplace. The founder of eBay, Omidyar, in the early days of eBay said "What makes eBay successful—the real value and the real power at eBay—is the community. It's the buyers and sellers coming together and forming a marketplace".[14]

## Platform Business in a Traditional Industry

Many Years before Uber and Airbnb started using the platform business model, many traditional companies had been using the same model to great success, albeit in a non-digital manner.

Amul is an Indian dairy cooperative, based at Anand in the state of Gujarat, India. Formed in 1948, it is a brand managed by a cooperative body, the Gujarat Co-operative Milk Marketing Federation Ltd. (GCMMF), which today is jointly owned by 3.6 million milk producers in Gujarat. Amul spurred India's White Revolution, which made the country the world's largest producer of milk and milk products.[15] Today, Amul is a USD 5.9 billion company. Its products are exported to 60 countries around the world. What is unique about Amul's model? Much like Uber that does not own any cars, Amul does not own any cows. It aggregates milk from milk farmers from many villages. Most milk farmers were small-time farmers who could deliver, at most, 1–2 litres of milk per day. The idea was to setup a cooperative in each village to collect milk from the farmers and aggregate the supply centrally before processing could be done. In a nutshell, Amul operates using a platform business model sans digital technology.

## Software Platforms are Eating the World

In 2011, Marc Andreessen wrote a Wall Street Journal essay where he made an important assertion: "Software is eating the world".[17] Six years later, in 2017, it is notable that the five largest companies in the world by market capitalization—Apple, Alphabet, Microsoft, Amazon and Facebook—are all software companies and more importantly, they are all platform companies.[16] This phenomenon is not just limited to the US. Here are some eye-popping statistics from Chinese digital platforms: Baidu enjoys 70 percent of the revenue in the search business; in e-commerce, Alibaba has a whopping 80 percent of the online shopping revenue; and Tencent has 500 million active WeChat users and 815 million QQ users—about 60 per cent of the country's total population.[18] Considering this, it would be accurate to say that software platforms are eating the world.

Figure 1.8 shows how the oil barons have been replaced by digital platform companies from the year 2001 to 2016.

# Understanding Digital Disruption

So far, we have understood two terms: Digital and Platforms. Now let us delve deep into the third term, Digital Disruption.

Digital disruption refers to the fundamental impact that an organization experiences when new business models enabled by digital technologies affect its value proposition and core business model. Let us understand the three case studies we looked at earlier through the lens of digital disruption.

**Figure 1.8** The largest companies by market capitalization are all platform companies in 2016 (Adapted from an image from visualcapitalist.com)[19]

## Digital Disruption #1: Reach vs. Richness

### Blockbuster vs Netflix

In the case of Blockbuster vs Netflix, Netflix did not have the fixed costs associated with physical stores. It made renting movies convenient for customers through the online site and moved into an economic model that was easy on the customer's wallet. They risked cannibalization of their DVD-by-mail rental business when they moved into on-demand movies. By then, movies and entertainment shows, their core products, had become digital. What used to be available in a physical form was now being streamed online in the digital format. Netflix changed its business model accordingly to support a completely online subscription model. Blockbuster, on the other hand, could not simultaneously manage the economics of a declining brick-and-mortar business and a fledgling online business.

In the popular 1999 book *Blown to Bits*, authors Evans and Wurster noted that e-commerce blows up the richness versus reach trade-off. Richness refers to customization, comprehensiveness and interactivity between providers and consumers. Reach refers to simply the spread of the product or service to several consumers. Prior to the dot-com era, companies faced a challenge in making rich products and services reach a large community of users. Digital technologies allowed organizations to break that trade-off. Blockbuster had a reach limitation owing to its physical nature of business, whereas Netflix could cater to users far and wide and at the same time, create rich interactive experience online.

In the last decade, many products, such as music, movies, books and money, that used to exist purely in a physical form are now also available in digital form. Unlike in the physical world, in the digital world, the cost of copying an original and transmitting the copy is close to zero. This means that the cost of servicing an additional customer is near-zero. As the number of users grows, the cost of servicing the users does not go up proportionately and hence digital companies tend to make huge profits once they acquire many customers. Also, since the product is now digital, there is no question of stock-outs and opportunity loss.

In the industrial era, companies leveraged economies of scale extensively for driving growth. Companies tried to either beef up their production to reduce the unit costs and/or tried to scale up their distribution to be able to control the value chain of an industry. While to an extent, economies of scale can help an organization to drive down the average unit cost, after a certain point, the company enters the zone of diseconomies of scale. This happens because the organization now must spend significantly on overheads to keep the operation going.

To expand to different geographies, Blockbuster had to incur huge setup costs and over time, experienced diseconomies of scale. Netflix, however, has unlimited reach to customers worldwide and because of near-zero marginal cost, its business does not get impacted by diseconomies of scale.

Figure 1.9 shows the difference between the economics of running Blockbuster and Netflix. This demonstrates that once business crosses a certain threshold of users, physical businesses lose their competitive edge owing to escalating costs, whereas digital businesses will have the potential to experience increasing profitability with increase in the number of users.

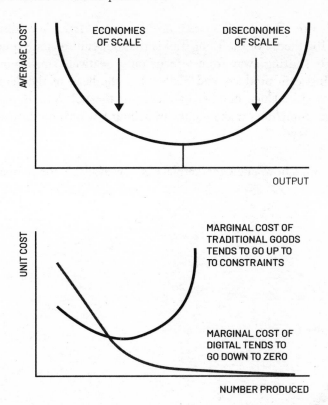

**Figure 1.9** Difference between the economics of running a digital business and a physical business

## Digital Disruption #2: Long Tail Phenomenon

### Borders vs. Amazon

In the case of Borders vs. Amazon, Borders saw web-based retailing as no more than a distribution channel whereas Amazon saw it as an all-encompassing business model that offered unprecedented cost efficiencies and hyper-personalization that delighted the customers.

This disruption was brought about by what is known as the 'Long Tail' phenomenon, a phrase coined by Chris Anderson, the author of *The*

*Long Tail: Why the Future of Business is Selling Less of More.* According to Anderson, "The theory of the Long Tail is that our culture and economy is increasingly shifting away from a focus on a relatively small number of 'hits' (mainstream products and markets) at the head of the demand curve and toward a huge number of niches in the tail. Simply put, in this paradigm, companies make money by selling few of more instead of selling more of few".

Figure 1.10 shows how a new marketplace is now available for companies to expand to.

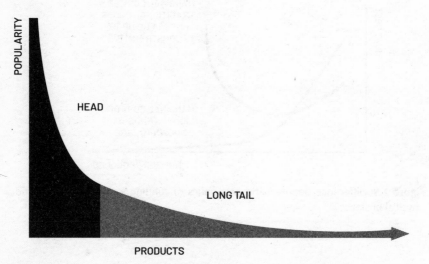

**Figure 1.10** New marketplace unlocked by the long tail phenomenon

While traditional businesses are limited by supply side constraints such as shelf space, digital businesses have the potential to scale infinitely. Borders could at any point in time carry a few thousand books in its big box format, whereas Amazon can keep adding millions of titles to its digital catalog without much incremental costs.

To address the long tail demand, small companies and individuals started participating in value creation at scale. They were now able to create value faster, cheaper and better by focusing on niche products and services. To leverage the value created by these small companies and individuals, larger organizations started building digital platforms that connect these small players to their customers. This presents a great win-win-win opportunity. Customers get unprecedented selection and choice at competitive prices, smaller players get access to the market and the larger players get an opportunity to earn revenues out of previously unaddressed demand and supply.

In other words, long tail increases the economic pie and gives the digital player a robust competitive edge. Brick-and-mortar players do not get a piece of this pie. The long tail phenomenon, along with zero marginal cost gives digital organizations an edge over traditional brick-and-mortar companies. Over time, brick-and-mortar companies typically get marginalized and commoditized by their digital counterparts.

The long tail phenomenon is seen in a host of industries ranging from the education industry to the music industry. In the education industry, Massively Open Online Courses (MOOCs) cater to the demand for niche courses and programs that may not be found in regular degree programs offered by established institutions. In the music industry, music streaming platforms such as Spotify make eclectic songs available to millions of listeners at their fingertips.

## Digital Disruption #3: Products vs Ecosystems

### RIM vs. Apple

In the case of RIM vs. Apple/Google, RIM remained by and large focused on what made it successful: the product. Their response to the new kind of competition was to go back to what they did well. They doubled down on product features and specs. Apple and Google, on the other hand, started focusing on building ecosystems that provided unprecedented choice to the customers and helped unlock new value from developers and partners from anywhere in the world.

It is now clear that platforms and ecosystems are at the pinnacle of business models in the digital age. In this paradigm, you are either leading an ecosystem or forming a significant part of one created by someone else.

Traditional companies try to defend their businesses by building a moat formed of product or service features and specs. In today's rapidly shrinking product and service development cycles, the product or service moat does not last long. It is easy for competitors to quickly neutralize any advantages a company may have from superior features. Digital platforms, however, build their moat using network effects. Put simply, as the number of users on the platform grows, the value that users get from the platform grows exponentially. With this, you are not just competing based on features and specs, you are also bringing to the table the exponential value that the community of producers and consumers are creating and consuming. The community is the new moat.

There are many open source social networks that are available on the Internet. One could download the source code and start operating a network like Facebook and Twitter. The challenge does not lie just with the technology. Getting billions of engaged users and a thriving network of partners and providers on the platform, a tremendous feat achieved by Facebook, is the key challenge that forms the barrier for entry to new competitors. After Apple and Google set up their app stores and enticed developers to develop apps on their platforms, it became difficult for RIM, Nokia and even Microsoft with all their money and marketing muscle to bridge the moat and overwhelm the incumbents. That is the power of community and networks.

The virtuous feedback cycle created by having many producers and consumers on the platform gives the platform owner tremendous opportunity to generate revenues from millions of transactions that take place on the platform. It also allows the platform owner to harness data at scale, produce insights and derive new value out of interactions that happen on the platform. Using Artificial Intelligence (AI) and algorithms, platform owners create hyper-personalization for customers and tremendous efficiencies for cost reduction.

Figure 1.11 shows the virtuous cycle that has made Apple into an economic tour-de-force. Using stellar product design and marketing, Apple delivers a fantastic value proposition to its customers. Customers flock to the product and pay a premium for the differentiated devices. App vendors develop apps to fulfil the needs of the Apple user community. Apple users enjoy the functionality provided by these apps and are willing to pay a premium for the apps. App vendors thrive, and more app developers join the Apple fold. Apple can then further increase the value it delivers to the customers and the cycle continues.

The three types of disruption reveal underlying shifts that have erased many lines that companies rooted in the industrial age take for granted. In the next chapter, we will delve into the four blurring lines that cause severe disorientation to large companies.

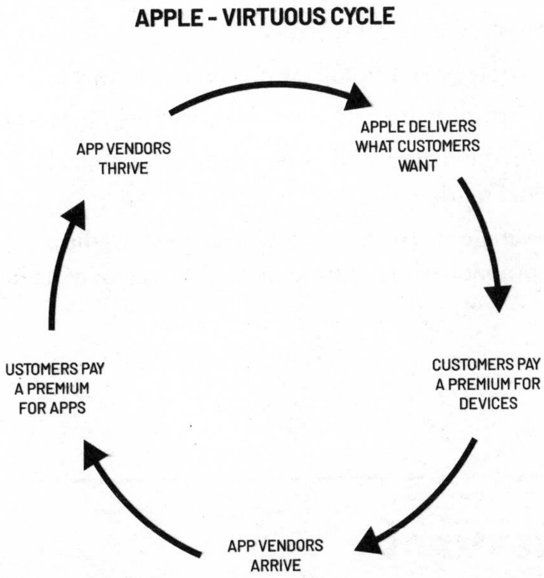

**APPLE - VIRTUOUS CYCLE**

APP VENDORS
THRIVE

APPLE DELIVERS
WHAT CUSTOMERS
WANT

USTOMERS PAY
A PREMIUM
FOR APPS

CUSTOMERS PAY
A PREMIUM FOR
DEVICES

APP VENDORS
ARRIVE

**Figure 1.11** The virtuous cycle that drives the growth of Apple

# Reflect and Share

1. Digital is a way of working that leverages technology to accomplish three main purposes:
   a. Create stellar customer experience
   b. Make processes agile
   c. Unlock new, exponential value by leveraging data
2. Top 3 myths of digitalization
   a. Digitalization is just another technology trend

    b.  Digitalization is the same as digitization

    c.  In an organizational context, digital is only for senior leadership or IT to worry about

3.  A platform is a plug-and-play business model that allows multiple parties—producers, consumers, service providers—to connect, interact, create and exchange value.

4.  Software platforms are eating the world.

5.  Community is the new competitive moat.

6.  What do Digital Born Organizations do differently?

    a.  They successfully break the reach vs. richness trade-offs

    b.  They use the Long Tail phenomenon to unlock new value in traditional markets

    c.  They leverage ecosystems to win against traditional companies. When products and ecosystems collide, ecosystems have a higher chance of winning.

## Key Questions

- Are you using digital to create exceptional customer experience, become agile and unlock new value?
- Are you driving awareness of digital across the organization beyond senior leadership?
- Are you taking advantage of digital economics in your business?
- Are you expanding your market to reach the long tail of demand?
- Are you building an ecosystem around your business?
- Are you building a virtuous cycle in your business?

# CHAPTER 2
# THE FOUR BLURRING LINES

"If the rate of change on the outside exceeds the rate of change on the inside, the end is near."

—Jack Welch , Executive Chairman, The Jack Welch Management Institute, ex-Chairman and CEO, GE

# Enter the Era of the Digital BLUR

Many successful organizations from the industrial age and early parts of the information age, such as Blockbuster, RIM, Borders, have failed to leverage the power of digital in their businesses and have become obsolete or are becoming increasingly irrelevant in the digital age.

What is worth analyzing is that these are the same organizations that were on the top of their game, till just a few years ago. Furthermore, this is not the first time that these companies are facing a transformational business situation. The same companies have overcome challenges such as industrial automation, globalization, tough mergers and acquisitions. They have some of the best leaders in the corporate world, titans who have weathered many a daunting storm. So, what has changed in the digital world?

The previous chapter focused on the different types of disruption. We will now delve deep into some of the tectonic changes that have been ushered in by these disruptions. It is interesting to note that these disruptions have altered the laws of physics behind businesses. Along the mass dimension, we are seeing a rapid dematerialization of products and services into bits and bytes. Speed of business is accelerating, thereby reducing time taken to serve the customer, and everything is getting connected to everything else. These disruptions have blurred away some important lines that were held sacred in the industrial age.

Many business leaders are increasingly talking about experiencing lack of visibility and heightened uncertainty in their businesses in the digital age. Put simply, they are experiencing a state of BLUR.

Consider the following examples:
1. What do Uber, Skype and Airbnb have in common? Their business models are all about facilitating interactions through their digital platform without owning the physical infrastructure.
2. Abbott, the American healthcare company, has launched Freestyle Libre, an easy-to-wear, painless sensor that continuously monitors a person's glucose levels and can show the results on a smart phone.[1]
3. A significant portion of a bank's revenue these days comes from selling movie tickets and other lifestyle products on their digital platform.

4. According to the World Economic Forum, the time taken by an average unicorn to reach a billion-dollar valuation is roughly 4.4 years. A typical Fortune 500 company took 20 years to achieve this status.[2]

These examples reveal an underlying shift that has happened in the last decade. We now live in the age of the Digital BLUR—an age where many of the crucial lines that governed businesses in the past have started blurring away. Essentially, these are lines that separate the organization from the outside world, lines that separate the physical and digital world, lines that separate industries and lines that separate the now from the new and the next.

Figure 2.1 shows the four crucial lines that are blurring away in the digital age.

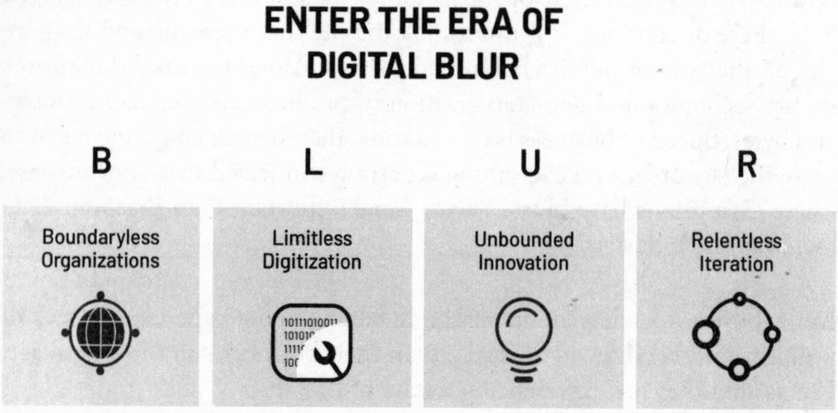

## ENTER THE ERA OF DIGITAL BLUR

**B**              **L**              **U**              **R**

Boundaryless Organizations    Limitless Digitization    Unbounded Innovation    Relentless Iteration

**Figure 2.1** Digital BLUR Framework

BLUR is an acronym that stands for:
- Boundaryless Organizations
- Limitless Digitization
- Unbounded Innovation
- Relentless Iteration

# Boundaryless Organizations

## Lines Defining an Organization are Blurring Away

Uber does not own any of the cars that operate in its network and the drivers are not on its payroll. Airbnb does not own any of the rooms in its network. Skype does not own any network towers. These companies operate their business by orchestrating fluid networks of people and assets that are external to the organization.

In the digital age, the lines separating internal and external sources of value creation for an organization are fast blurring away. The lines within the organization are also blurring away. Internal silos present severe challenges for organizations to respond fast in the digital age. Consequently, the lines separating different functions within the organization are coming under scrutiny. ANZ Bank made an announcement in September 2017 that they are blowing up their internal hierarchies to structure themselves as 150 start-up teams and adopting agile work practices embraced by technology companies such as Google, Amazon and Facebook.[3] In this way, this large, well-established Australian bank has not only acknowledged the need to disrupt its traditional structures but also is taking the bold step to act.

We will delve deeper into boundaryless organizations in chapter three.

# Limitless Digitization

## Lines Separating the Physical and the Digital World are Blurring Away

The world around us is getting limitlessly digitized. Practically every object we see in the physical space can potentially be digitized just by slapping a cloud enabled sensor on it. From movies to books to music to money, many things that used to exist purely in the physical form are now also available in the digital form. While there are about 7 billion people on the planet today, connected devices are estimated to be around 20.4 billion by 2020, outnumbering humans by a factor of three.[4]

Limitless digitization has a big impact on the future of work. While industrial automation has existed for a very long time now, automation of cognitive jobs is slowly but surely becoming mainstream. The world's first Robocop was launched in Dubai in 2017. Dubai Police says that 25 percent of its unarmed police force will be robotic by the year 2030.[5] The line between the human and the machine is also blurring.

We will go deeper into limitless digitization in chapter four.

# Unbounded Innovation

## Lines Defining Industries are Blurring Away

Many digital innovations such as automated cars, bitcoins and 3D printing do not just impact one industry. Such unbounded innovations simultaneously cause deep disruptions across multiple industries all at once. Companies in the logistics industry, for example, must worry about not just about competitors in their own industry, they must also think about the impact of 3-D printing on their industry. Many industry lines are likely to get blurred by emerging technologies.

Today, it is tough to say which industry a company belongs to. Is Airtel, a leading Indian player, a telecom company, a payments bank or a media streaming service?

We will look at unbounded innovation in more detail in chapter five.

# Relentless Iteration

## Lines between the Now, the New and the Next are Blurring

While in the industrial age, there was a concrete end-state for products and services, in the digital age, products and services undergo relentless iteration without a specific end-state. As a result, everything is becoming, everything is arriving. Consequently, products and services are blurring away along the time dimension.

Back in the day, software organizations launched a major version of their software once a year. Today, it is tough to keep up with the versions of software on the cloud and in the mobile app stores. Versions change overnight, and the consumer is blissfully unaware and does not care as long as the experience is stellar.

The same phenomenon is being seen in the world of physical products as well, thanks to 3D printing and rapid prototyping The Ford 3D Store is an official store that allows customers to purchase or download detailed 3D printable files of several of their top selling cars. We can certainly envision a future where not just miniature models, but a large variety of physical products can be made available in a 3D-printable form. These trends tremendously reduce the time it takes to prototype products, deliver product updates and achieve predictive maintenance.

We will gain deeper understanding of relentless iteration in chapter six.

# Factors Causing Digital BLUR

There are five main factors that are causing Digital BLUR:
- Connected customers
- Smart technologies
- VUCA environment
- The great unbundling
- A new breed of competition

## Connected Customers

Power has tilted squarely in favor of customers and it is safe to say that we are now living in the age of customer experience. Thanks to the wide availability of information on companies, products, services, prices and so on, customers now have a clear advantage in the buying process. Companies that used to make their margins by utilizing the opaqueness of their industry are now having to deal with radical transparency ushered in by digital marketplaces.

Customers are becoming rapidly networked. It took 30 years to connect the first two billion people to the Internet. It will take less than seven years to connect the next two billion. Acceleration of the connected customer phenomenon produces eye-opening effects. The idea of six degrees of separation drives home this point well. Six degrees of separation is the idea that everyone in this world is connected to another person in a maximum of six steps in a chain of 'friend of a friend' connections. What is interesting about this is that the number six is from the pre-social networking era and needs an update in the digital era.

Reza Bakhshandeh and other social network researchers have worked to determine the degree of separation between two users in social networks such as Twitter. Their optimal algorithm finds an average degree of separation of 3.43 between two random Twitter users.[6]

This finding has huge implications on our societies and the way we function. As social media is fast reaching the entire population, six degrees of separation will keep shrinking further, making the world a smaller and more connected place.

Hyper-connectedness informs customers of the latest trends and the best deals. Customers want the best experience that their network enjoys. Companies consequently must work hard to differentiate themselves based on customer experience. According to salesforce.com, 64 percent of consumers expect companies to respond and interact with them in real time.[7] This expectation forces businesses to operate in an 'n = 1' hyper-personalization model where an individual's needs are uniquely fulfilled in real-time. Customers today demand personalization of products and services and are also co-creating products with companies to fulfil their unique needs.

Companies are responding to the connected customer phenomenon by organizing themselves with the customer right at the center, taking care of end-to-end customer experience through boundaryless partnerships.

## Smart Technologies

What is enabling connected customers is the proliferation of affordable devices and technologies, largely thanks to falling hardware costs and broadband access. Smart technologies are enabling limitless digitization of everything that an organization does. These technologies also unleash the potential to innovate across industry boundaries in an unbounded fashion. There are five technologies that help companies create the experience that customers want.

### Mobile

Mobile phones are perhaps the biggest enablers of connections between people in the digital age. In 2016, an estimated 62.9 percent of the worldwide population owned a mobile phone. The number of mobile phone users in the world is expected to pass the 5 billion mark by 2019.[8] With access to mobile phones and broadband, consumers suddenly become not just passive consumers of information, they also become active producers of information and information goods.

### Cloud-enabled Services

Simply put, cloud computing is the delivery of on-demand computing, be it hardware resources or software applications, over the internet. Cloud enabled services offer unprecedented access to resources and capabilities to companies and individuals at dramatically economical rates.

Earlier, computing used to be sold as a product where companies made significant investments to own the infrastructure. That model has given way to infrastructure as a service model where companies consume resources in a pay-as-you-go model. This new economic shift from Capital Expenditure (Capex) to Operating Expense (Opex) has played a big role in the limitless digitization phenomenon because it is now economically viable to digitize everything at scale. This has also resulted in the lowering of entry barriers in many industries leading to a hyper competitive environment and reduction of prices for customers.

## Artificial Intelligence (AI)

AI promises unprecedented possibilities for organizations to anticipate, understand and react to customers' intentions much before these intentions become stated needs.

Sundar Pichai, the CEO of Google, says "Artificial intelligence (AI) is going to have a bigger impact on the world than some of the most ubiquitous innovations in history. AI is one of the most important things humanity is working on. It is more profound than electricity or fire."[9]

While the technologies and algorithms underlying AI have been in existence for a very long time, it is the availability of data and the advancements in computing power that are driving AI's prominence today. From driverless cars to Siri on the mobile phone, the application and the impact of AI are mind boggling.

## Internet of Things (IoT)

Internet of Things refers to the vast network of devices connected to the Internet, including smartphones and tablets and almost anything with a sensor on it—cars, production plants, machinery, meters, point-of-sale terminals, jet engines, wearable devices, and more. IoT promises to enhance real-time customer experience and unlock new value from data. Ericsson's 2017 Mobility Report says that by 2023, over 30 billion connected devices are forecast, of which around 20 billion will be related to the IoT. Between 2017 and 2023, connected IoT devices are expected to increase at a compound annual growth rate (CAGR) of 19 percent, driven by new use cases and affordability.[10]

## Big Data Analytics

Åse Dragland from SINTEF in his 2013 article, *Big Data—For Better or Worse*, says that 90 percent of world's information was produced in the last two years.[11] There appear to be two reasons behind this phenomenon. First, widespread access to broadband and mobile devices has led to an unprecedented growth in user generated content. Second, exponential growth of connected devices has led to relentless generation of data.

Big Data analytics examines large amounts of data coming out of these sources to uncover hidden patterns, correlations and other insights. From

TV shows to stock markets to agriculture, organizations and individuals are using Big Data analytics to derive value from data.

## VUCA Environment

Today's business environment is characterized as Volatile, Uncertain, Complex and Ambiguous (VUCA). VUCA was coined in the US Army College in the late 1990s as the cold war era drew to a close. Essentially, it signifies the transition from a predictable bipolar world to a chaotic multilateral world. Gradually, the term has made its way into the corporate world. The phenomenon is amplified by globalization, digital technologies and demographic shifts across the world.

The VUCA environment is one of the primary drivers behind the emergence of Digital BLUR. In his thought-provoking article, Marco Mancesti, Director of R&D at IMD, asks "Is VUCA the end of strategy and leadership?".[12] The business environment is changing so fast that in many cases two business leaders might argue whether they should spend their time discussing strategy or focus on organizing immediate action. The sense of constant action without clarity in direction disorients organizations and leaders and creates a BLUR in the minds of employees. This has resulted in the need for relentless iteration in the quest to achieve clarity.

## The Great Bundling and Unbundling of Industries

We are witnessing the great unbundling of many industries wherein large monolithic value chains are being carved up into many small niches that are served by nimble and agile start-ups. Without the overheads of the large organization, these smaller companies are now able to offer products and services to customers at a fraction of the cost and in an incredibly agile fashion. Banking is one industry that has gone through great unbundling in a fundamental way. The various product areas of traditional banks—lending, deposits, credit cards and payments and so on—have all become breeding grounds for Fintech start-ups.

What is interesting is that there is a great bundling happening at the same time. Customers are facing a problem of abundant supply and limited attention span. To help customers make choices, we are seeing the emergence of digital curators, who cut down the noise and clutter by becoming the primary interface for accessing the deluge of services. WeChat, the popular social messaging platform, is a great example of this phenomenon. WeChat users conduct pretty much all their transactions, from hailing a cab to booking flight tickets, from the same platform.

## A New Breed of Competitors

Back in the day, when industry lines were clear, the competitor set was also very clear. Coca-Cola had to think primarily about Pepsi. ABB had to think primarily about Honeywell. Toyota had to think about the competitive moves of other car manufacturers. But today, every industry leader is losing sleep over the emergence of a new set of competitors, fashionably called either 'GAFA' or 'FANG'. GAFA stands for 'Google, Amazon, Facebook, Alibaba' and FANG stands for 'Facebook, Amazon, Netflix, Google.' The new breed of competitors are masters at the art and science of driving unbounded innovation.

The industrial playbook is well understood by digital disruptors and they know well how the incumbents work. The digital playbook, however, is not well understood by incumbents, or if understood, they do not have the DNA to respond effectively. The result is a situation where the incumbents are found playing defense, protecting their turf, whereas the digital born companies are playing offense, gobbling up value wherever they find it. The blind pace of attack by the digital disruptors is causing a huge state of BLUR for incumbent leaders.

The problem is not that many organizations do not notice this phenomenon, rather those who do notice it do not acknowledge it and others who do acknowledge it fail to respond in a timely manner. This is the story of digital disruption in the last decade and a half.

Figure 2.2 reveals a telling story. According to the World Economic Forum, the time taken by an average unicorn to reach a billion-dollar valuation is roughly 4.4 years[13]. The typical Fortune 500 company took 20 years to achieve this status. Digital born organizations have shifted gears and are playing by vastly different rules that are currently poorly understood by incumbents, resulting in widespread disruption across the board. There are many that point out the business sustainability issue with digital born organizations. Irrespective of the fate of these individual companies, the reality is that the disruption they have caused is real.

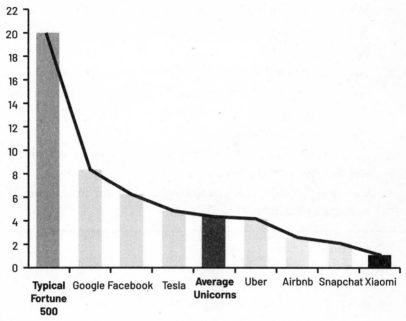

**Figure 2.2** Time taken by companies to reach billion dollars in valuation.[13]

# Reflect and Share

1. BLUR stands for Boundaryless Organizations, Limitless Digitization, Unbounded Innovation and Relentless Iteration.

2. Many lines from the industrial age are blurring away causing massive disorientation to leaders in traditional companies.

3. Essentially, these are lines that separate the organization from the outside world, lines that separate the physical and digital world, lines that separate industries and lines that separate the now, new and the next.

4. BLUR is caused by five major factors—connected customers, smart technologies, VUCA environment, great bundling and unbundling of industries and a new breed of competition.

## Key Questions

- What sort of lines are blurring away in your industry?
- Are you or your competitors in your industry operating in a boundaryless fashion?
- Are you digitizing your assets and your core processes?
- Are you witnessing the emergence of a new breed of competitors?
- Are you looking beyond your industry lines for discovering uncontested marketspaces?
- Are you operating in an agile manner both from an operational and strategic perspective?
- Can you list down the technologies that are fundamentally reshaping your industry?

# CHAPTER 3

# BOUNDARYLESS ORGANIZATIONS

"By 2020, your company will either lead a digital business ecosystem you have created or be part of one created by someone else…if you are still in business."

—Gartner

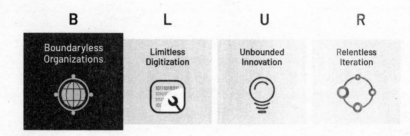

| B | L | U | R |
|---|---|---|---|
| Boundaryless Organizations | Limitless Digitization | Unbounded Innovation | Relentless Iteration |

# Boundaryless Agriculture

India's agriculture industry and allied sectors like forestry and fisheries account for roughly 13.7 percent of the GDP and about 50 percent of the workforce.[1] The industry is beset with numerous issues such as fragmented farms, weak rural infrastructure, lack of access to markets and the existence of numerous intermediaries. ITC Limited, an Indian conglomerate, kick-started an initiative called e-Choupal in the year 2000 across many villages in India to directly link with rural farmers for procurement of agricultural products. The company provides computers and internet access in 6,100 e-Choupal centers in over 35,000 villages in 10 states in India, touching the lives of around 4 million farmers.[2] e-Choupal has brought tremendous savings in transaction costs for the farmers and better yet, they get higher income levels due to better predictability of demand, removal of middlemen and greater efficiency in production. The company benefits by reducing procurement costs and gets access to many farmers directly across the country. Online access helps farmers stay up-to-date on best farming practices and to place orders for agricultural inputs such as seeds and farm equipment.

The company aspires to have 10 million farmers connected to e-Choupal by 2022. The company also has plans to become an aggregator of services for farmers. "This transformative fourth-generation model, e-Choupal 4.0, will be an aggregator of agricultural services," says S Sivakumar, Group Head, Agri and IT businesses, ITC. He further goes on to add that "Whatever has been done through various stages of e-Choupal over the years can be extended to a digital ecosystem. The primary objective is to create more value through a model that has products and services."[3]

e-Choupal is a great example of how a company builds infrastructure to extend the enterprise beyond conventional boundaries and using the same infrastructure, changes the business model to serve the needs of its ecosystem better.

Organizations, such as ITC, are great examples of boundaryless organizations. This approach is akin to what Amazon has done over the years. From starting as an online book seller to becoming a purveyor of anything under the sun on their digital platform, Amazon's presence is felt in many industries.

# Lean at the Core, Expanding at the Periphery

From a business model perspective, organizations are becoming lean in their core operations while expanding their influence in adjacent areas through an ecosystem play. Apple, for instance, has drastically reduced its own internal inputs in its hardware devices. In fact, Apple sources key hardware components from arch rival Samsung.[4] At the same time, Apple has unlocked terrific business potential through its widely successful Apps Store where it captures 30 percent of the revenues made by apps that it does not produce.

We can look at boundaryless organizations through three major lenses: internal, external, and geographic.

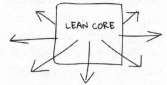

## Internal Lens: Boundaryless State Within an Organization

The concept of boundaryless organizations was originally pioneered by Jack Welch, the ex-CEO of GE, in the '90s.[5] While traditional organizations have hierarchical lines running horizontally and vertically inside the organization, boundaryless organizations are built on the premise of self-directed teams that eschew formal hierarchical structure.

The need for boundaryless organizations stems from business realities ranging from customer's needs for real-time instant gratification to agility and resilience in execution to balancing innovation and efficiency. Traditional organizations, saddled with silos and rigid structures, are ill-suited to meet these needs. There is another major incentive for an organization to become boundaryless internally: unlocking the diversity of knowledge, talents and ideas of its people. This is, perhaps, the biggest competitive edge that an organization can build in today's dynamic business environment.

Work-Out, GE's initiative of the early 1990s, turned GE into a boundaryless company. Boundarylessness was embraced in the organization both as a management philosophy and an execution model. Jack Welch aspired to create a work environment where people could react quickly to changes. He wanted GE to operate in self-directed units that allow decentralized decision-making and free flow of information and ideas. As a result, the organization can operate with great flexibility and adaptability to the ever-changing needs of its business.

Clearly, the structure of an organization plays a vital role in its ability to respond to rapid changes. From a top-down hierarchy to a matrixed organization structure to a more diffused networked organization model now, organizations have evolved to meet the needs of the business environment.

Holacracy is a model that has been proposed more recently to provide an approach to build customizable self-management practices for organizations. Here are some ways in which Holacracy tries to make an organization boundaryless internally.[6]

| In Traditional Companies | With Holacracy |
|---|---|
| **Job descriptions**<br>Each person has exactly one job. Job descriptions are inaccurate, rarely updated and often irrelevant. | **Roles**<br>Roles are defined around the work, not people, and are updated regularly. People fill several roles. |
| **Delegated Authority**<br>Managers loosely delegate authority. Ultimately, their decision always trumps others. | **Distributed Authority**<br>Authority is truly distributed to teams and roles. Decisions are made locally. |
| **Big Re-Orgs**<br>The org structure is rarely revisited, mandated from the top. | **Rapid Iterations**<br>The org structure is regularly updated via small iterations. Every team self-organizes. |
| **Office Politics**<br>Implicit rules slow down change and favor people "in the know". | **Transparent Rules**<br>Everyone is bound by the same rules, CEO included. Rules are visible to all. |

Boundaryless organizations often operate in a geographically dispersed fashion with independent 'pods' located in diverse countries and cultures. For this kind of a model to function well, these organizations need to have a massively transformational purpose, strong vision and values that bind its employees together.

## External Lens: Boundaryless State Between the Organization and the Outside World

The line that separates the organization from the outside world is becoming blurred. The digital arena is now filled with networks of firms or individuals not bound by formal employment-based relationships. Here are some prominent examples.

### Gig Economy aka 'Uberization of the Workforce'

As of May 2017, Uber had completed 5 billion rides operating out of 450 cities across the world.[7] Uber adds 50,000 drivers to its network every month, none of them on their payrolls.[8] The beauty of its business model is that Uber does not own the cars that are added to the network.

Uber drivers, and freelance employees of many other such ecosystems constitute a growing population, leading to a phenomenon called the Gig Economy, a labor market characterized by the prevalence of short-term contracts or freelance work ('gigs') as opposed to permanent jobs.

The freelance workforce grew from 53 million in 2014 to 55 million in 2016 and represents 35 percent of the U.S. workforce, according to a study commissioned by Upwork and the Freelancers Union.[9]

Wikipedia is another classic example of a platform that uses the services of many people, either paid or unpaid, to create massive repositories of human knowledge via a crowdsourcing model.

### Porous Organizational Boundaries

Today, data is operating in a boundaryless format. What was earlier considered as confidential internal HR information—employee satisfaction score for example—is now widely available on the Internet on sites such as Glassdoor.

Organizations are increasingly operating in a boundaryless fashion with their value chain partners. Complex systems are becoming connected through Application Programming Interfaces (APIs) and data flows from one organization to the other on a real-time basis. Supply Chain Management (SCM), for instance, in the manufacturing industry spans multiple organizations that participate in the value chain. In the financial industry, the concept of Straight Through Processing (STP) automates end-to-end processing of financial transactions without needing manual re-entry across different participating players.

### Geography Lens: Boundarylessness From a Global Perspective

Information is crossing country borders in ways that were unimaginable in the past, even with state-imposed restrictions on free information flow in many countries. According to a study by McKinsey, the amount of cross-border bandwidth has grown 45 times larger since 2005.[10]

Previously, global trade was an option only for advanced economies and large multinational companies. Today, small and medium enterprises, start-ups and millions of individuals can setup virtual storefronts and become global exporters of goods and services. These organizations and individuals are also gaining global reach through e-commerce marketplaces such as Alibaba, Amazon, eBay and Flipkart. In short, anyone can become 'born digital' and 'born global' in a few clicks today. This essentially means that any company can challenge an incumbent organization from anywhere in the world.

These organizations not only get access to global markets through large platforms but also receive the monetary support necessary for bringing their ideas to life. Peer-to-peer (P2P) lending platforms such as Prosper and Lending Club have generated over USD 6 billion in loans. Although this is just a drop in the ocean compared to the overall consumer debt market size of USD 3 trillion, these lending platforms have the potential to cut banks out of the lending market. Platforms such as Kickstarter help individuals and small businesses to find resources and support they need to make ideas come to life. Kickstarter describes itself as an enormous global community built around creativity and creative projects. Over 10 million people, from every continent on earth, have backed a Kickstarter project.[11]

# Reflect and Share

1. Lines separating the organization from the outside world are becoming blurred.
2. Organizations are moving away from the traditional hierarchical structure to a more amorphous structure.
3. Information flows are blurring away geographical boundaries.
4. Digital organizations believe in being lean at the core and expanding at the periphery, which naturally encourages them to be boundary less.

## Key Questions

- What is the right internal organizational structure that helps your organization become intensely customer-centric and agile in execution and innovative?
- What new competencies will you focus on for your employees across levels to operate in the boundaryless world?
- What enabling cultures should your organization build to thrive in the boundaryless world?
- How does your organization stay relevant in the competitive landscape where new entrants from across borders and sizes can threaten your survival?
- How do you manage the change associated with decentralization and dismantling of organization structures from the industrial era?

# CHAPTER 4
# LIMITLESS DIGITIZATION

> "It's no longer possible to think of the physical and digital as two different worlds."
>
> —Angela Ahrendts, Senior Vice President, Apple

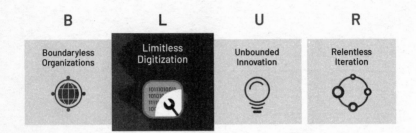

# Digital Twins

At the Minds + Machines 2016 Conference in San Francisco, the Vice President of Software Research of GE, Colin Parris, wore an augmented reality headset and used voice recognition to demonstrate how the concept of the 'digital twin' can be used to predict wear and tear in a steam turbine.[1] He went on to present several options to address the issue based on the turbine's properties and historical maintenance record.

A digital twin is essentially a concept that blurs the line between the physical and digital world. "For every physical asset in the world, we have a virtual copy running in the cloud that gets richer with every second of operational data," says Ganesh Bell, Chief Digital Officer and General Manager of Software & Analytics at GE Power & Water.[2] GE has 551,000 digital twins that were deployed as of 2016, with more created every day.[3]

Maserati, the luxury car manufacturer, reduced the production time of its Ghibli sports car from 30 months to just 16 months by experimenting on the digital twin in the virtual world without frequent costly and time-consuming changes in the physical world.[4]

Figure 4.1 shows the concept of Digital Twins.

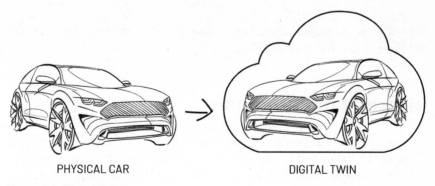

PHYSICAL CAR                                            DIGITAL TWIN

**Figure 4.1** Digital Twins

Digital twins are created by integrating smart sensors with physical items to gather data about their real-time status. The components are connected to a cloud-based system that receives and processes all the data the sensors monitor. Real-time inputs are analyzed against business and other contextual data to derive meaning and actionable insights.

The concept of digital twins was born in the research department of NASA, where they have the challenge of maintaining and repairing space systems that are physically present thousands of miles away. Interestingly, it was the innovation of digital twin systems that allowed engineers and astronauts to formulate ways to identify and fix issues on live missions. Today, NASA uses digital twins to develop new designs of aircrafts and maintain existing space shuttles. "The ultimate vision for the digital twin is to create, test, and build our equipment in a virtual environment," says John Vickers, NASA's leading manufacturing expert and manager of NASA's National Center for Advanced Manufacturing. "Only when we get it to where it performs to our requirements do we physically manufacture it. We then want that physical build to tie back to its digital twin through sensors so that the digital twin contains all the information that we could have by inspecting the physical build."[5]

It is quite evident that digital is becoming all-pervasive. In the last few decades, we have witnessed the evolution of this domain, from the Internet of Computers to Internet of Humans to the Internet of Things (IoT). In the future, everything will be 'plugged in'. The immediate impact is that we will be living in an era of exponentially exploding data, information, and algorithms.

We will look at limitless digitization through two primary lenses: Internet of Humans and Internet of Things.

# Internet of Humans

According to the International Telecommunication Union, as of June 2017, 51 percent of the world's population is on the Internet.[6] That is roughly 3.7 billion people connected to each other and the digital world around us. Owing to the widespread availability of broadband and smartphones, each person connected to the Internet has now become a producer of content. Every minute of the day on the internet, connected humans are producing a staggering 2.5 quintillion bytes of data.[7] Every year, the amount of content generated by Internet users is doubling.

Going beyond social connections, human beings are now becoming digitized in the physical sense. In July 2017, New York Times wrote an article about a company called Three Square Market in Wisconsin, USA, where employees volunteered to have microchip implants injected between their index finger and the thumb.[8] Once the implant is in place, any activity that involved reading an RFID tag—be it swiping into the office or paying in the cafeteria—could be done with a wave of a hand.

Nicholas Negroponte, the founder of the MIT Media Lab, says that biotech is going to govern the next decade of thought at major research institutions. At MIT's Being Material Symposium in April 2017, he proclaimed that "Biotech is the new digital."[9] Negroponte believes we have now reached a stage when the natural and the artificial have started blurring. Today, with the advancements in synthetic biology, living organisms are being increasingly used to develop new products— buildings powered by algae, plant starch material used for packaging, glow in the dark plants, and clothing created by bacteria are some examples. Going forward, it is going to be virtually impossible to differentiate what is natural and what is not.

# Internet of Things (IoT)

Internet of Things (IoT) is the network of physical devices, vehicles, and day-to-day objects that are embedded with software, sensors, and network connectivity which enable these objects to collect and exchange data.

It is evident that the IoT has made its way into a multitude of everyday applications.

## Smart Racquets and Bats

The game of tennis had remained unchanged over a long period of time until recently when Babolat, the tennis racquet manufacturing company, launched the connected racquet. The Babolat AeroPro Drive Play connected tennis racquet comes with a sensor embedded in the handle plus a matching app that syncs via Bluetooth, recording data relating to a player's performance. The Babolat Play detects stroke types (forehand, backhand, smash, first, and second serves). It measures the speed, power, spin, and rally times and maps where the ball strikes the racquet. These data points can give a player critical insights on the quality of game play.

Figure 4.2 shows how a mobile app helps tennis players improve their game.

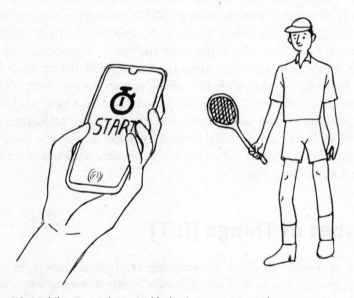

**Figure 4.2** Mobile app analyzes and helps improve game play

We are witnessing similar advancements in other sports such as cricket. The International Cricket Council organized the Champions Trophy in India in 2017.[10] It was touted as the first smart cricket tournament that introduced cricket bats with Intel Inside chips. The batsman could now see data on things like back-lift, bat speed and follow-through.

## Smart Homes

Several start-ups such as Nest (acquired by Google) or AlertMe (acquired by British Gas) as well as multinational corporations like Philips, Haier and Belkin, are pushing the boundaries on smart homes. Smart home technologies help control and automate lighting, heating, ventilation, air conditioning, and home security. Home appliances such as washer/dryers, ovens or refrigerators/freezers are also getting connected to coordinate household activities.

Google, Apple, and Amazon are vying for this space as well. Google Home, Apple HomeKit, and Amazon Echo are offerings from these tech giants in the home automation space. While Google Home and Amazon Echo are hardware hubs, Apple HomeKit allows household gadgets from Philips, Honeywell, and more to be controlled via the Home app in the iPhone, iPad and Apple TV.

## Wearables

Wearable technology is gaining momentum in both personal as well as business segments. Activity trackers, smart watches, smart glasses, and smart clothing are the four main product categories that are emerging.

Health is the primary reason why consumers are buying wearables. Even in the corporate segment, employee wellness is the top reason for wearable purchases. According to the 2016 PWC Wearable Future Report, 88 percent surveyed consumers believe that activity trackers help exercise smarter.[11] Activity trackers such as Fitbit Flex, Jawbone UP have caught the fancy of consumers across countries. It is reported that one out of every five American adult has a wearable device.

## Smart Cities

The quality of urban living across the globe is under scrutiny. With pressing issues such as waste management, traffic, security, and pollution rearing their ugly heads, we need urgent solutions to make our cities livable again. IoT solutions in the area of smart cities promise to solve some of these tough challenges through smart use of monitoring and real-time data-enabled decision making. Here are a few examples of global cities using IoT to enhance the quality of living.

Market research firm Juniper Research (Basingstoke, UK) has named Singapore as the smartest city on earth after sifting through factors including their adoption of smart grid technologies, intelligent lighting, use of information technology to improve traffic, Wi-Fi access points, smartphone penetration, and the app landscape.[12] The city has installed such massive numbers of sensors and cameras around the city that today, it can detect if people are smoking in unauthorized zones or if people are throwing litter out of high-rise buildings.

Amsterdam's smart city initiative has many public-private collaborative projects that aim to reduce traffic, save energy, and enhance public safety. The city of Amsterdam runs annual challenges accepting proposals from residents to meet its objectives. MobyPark is an example of a resident developed app that allows owners to rent out their parking spots. The data from the app helps the city administration gauge traffic and demand for parking spots across the city.[13]

Barcelona has been a pioneer when it comes to employing sensors to monitor and manage traffic. It has also been on the forefront when it comes to managing water supplies. After the city faced severe drought a few years ago, it developed a smart city sensors system to forecast rain to modify the city's sprinklers accordingly to conserve water.

## Industrial Internet

Industrial Internet is a term coined by GE and refers to the integration of complex physical machinery with networked sensors and software. The promise of the industrial internet is that it combines assets, data, analytics, and applications to transform the industrial world. Such systems connect and control the physical assets such as machines, vehicles and so on in real-time.[14]

Siemens, the industrial manufacturing giant, has created MindSphere, a cloud-based, open IoT operating system that connects products, plants, systems, and machines, enabling an organization to harness the wealth of data generated.[15]

## AI, Robotics, and Automation

The line between humans and machines is blurring. Robotic process automation (RPA) is one such application of technology that allows a company to configure computer software or a 'robot' to process transactions, manipulate data, trigger responses, and communicate with other digital systems. These software robots can perform high volume and highly transactional process jobs without errors and with high efficiencies.

Just as industrial robots are helping manufacturing industry boost productivity and eliminate quality issues, RPA robots are revolutionizing the way companies configure business processes, remote infrastructure management, IT support processes, and back-office work. RPA provides tremendous improvements in productivity, accuracy, and cycle time.

Here are some other striking examples of the use of robots in daily life:

- Robots are likely to be educational buddies for the younger generation. Robots can help in personalization of learning, helping students learn concepts at their own pace linking theoretical principles with relevant examples based on their learning curve. NAO, an interactive, fully programmed humanoid robot, is one such robot dedicated to educational purposes.[16]
- Moley, a robotics start-up, has created the world's first robotic kitchen.[17] The prototype was premiered in 2017 to widespread acclaim at Hanover Messe, the international robotics show. Moley says that the consumer version set for launch in 2018 will be supported by an iTunes' style library of recipes.

Increasingly, robots are starting to perform tasks that we thought were uniquely human. From driving a car to composing music to writing poetry, robots are starting to perform as well, if not better than humans in a variety of fields. These developments raise the important question of how humans will work alongside robots in the future. There are obviously concerns around job losses across industries through robotic automation. But then, newer kinds of jobs will emerge from these innovations as well. These are pertinent socio-economic issues that need to be addressed rather quickly.

# Expert Interview

## Ashok Krishnan, Head of Customer Experience and Data, AXA Insurance

Ashok Krishnan is the Chief Data Officer and Head of Customer Experience for AXA Hong Kong and Macau's Life, Health, and P&C businesses. His core focus is to ensure that customers have the best experience with AXA.

A UK qualified accountant with an MBA from Cranfield University, Krishnan's experience in the insurance industry includes senior roles ranging from Corporate Strategy, Distribution, Marketing, Operations, Finance and Risk Management. His career has taken him to live and work across various ASEAN and European countries.

## RJ: What according to you is digital? In the same breath, what is not digital?

**AK:** For me, digital is about the way we think and do things. In very concrete terms, what I am looking at is, 'how does a company create value in terms of either generating new business or servicing existing customers, or even working internally in terms of the different processes.' That, to me, is digital.

As for what digital is not:

1.  It is not an IT program.
2.  It is not a department.
3.  It is not a new thing to be done.

    Digital is like electricity for a company. About 20-30 years ago, computers were the new thing. Today, however, nobody goes into the market to say 'We have computers for all our employees'. It's not something that is advertised. Digital is like that. In the future, no company can go out to attract employees and customers and say, 'We're a digital company'. It is expected.

4.  Digital cannot replace all things.

Digital can complement and enhance the way we do things and ideally reimagine the way we do business—fit for purpose for the new age. But that does not necessarily mean that things are fundamentally going to be different in all aspects. For an insurance company, the core purpose of existence is to protect people's lives. People are the biggest asset for insurance companies. If, by using digital, the company can do that well, that's great. But, it cannot be that 'I am a digital company, so I am a great insurance company'.

**RJ: There is this common perception that every company is becoming a technology company—technology company first, bank next; technology company first, insurance company next. What is your take on this?**

**AK:** It is true that a lot of companies are reframing their value proposition or their positioning. However, from a value generation standpoint, there is a reason why conglomerates do not necessarily get the same value in the stock market compared to organizations which focus on their core competence. Over economic cycles, it has been proved that core competence and staying with your core competence is valuable. From that standpoint, I would echo the sentiment of technology-led or technology-first organization. But, to me, it's about being a technology-led or technology-first insurance company. This is very different from saying, "I am a technology company who also happens to be selling groceries".

I understand that in a lot of ways Amazon and Google are becoming modern oligopolies. They are redefining business models. However, what we forget is that Amazon and Google are first and foremost technology companies. Technology is their core competence. You do not see people comparing Amazon with Walmart or Tesco. They compare Amazon with Microsoft and Google. There is a reason for it. Amazon uses its expertise in technology to do retail better or differently. Tomorrow, if Amazon can redefine insurance or utilities, I am sure there will be market value for it. In some ways, I see this as a welcome change, because we achieve progress by redefining the boundaries of industries and a lot of times an outsider can be a good catalyst to change industries and move them forward as whole—similar to what Tesla is doing for the (electric) car industry.

What I find fascinating is the change in industries with strict regulatory constraints, such as insurance, banking, utilities. For example, utilities have some regulatory constraints in terms of how many utilities can be out in the market, the price they can charge, etc. Can a technology company fundamentally redefine those industries which have specific regulatory constraints? I do not know. I am eager to see how it evolves.

**RJ: What are some of the exciting things that are happening in the insurance space?**

**AK:** Some of the exciting things within the insurance space, I would say for example, are:

1. **Focus on enabling healthy living**
   Insurance companies are using a nudge principle by giving customers a wearable device that tracks how many steps they take or simply an app which links to health data recorded in your smartphones. If you walk long enough, we would probably give you a premium discount or even free insurance cover. I think that is an excellent way of using technology to arrive at an outcome that is beneficial for everyone—if you are healthy, you will fall sick less and that means I will have to pay you less claims. I think that is a great example of how industry can use digital for the benefit of all parties involved.

2. **The Internet of Things combined with AI and Big Data/analytics**
   Big Data is going to have a huge impact in how the insurance industry currently operates. Take home insurance as an example. Today, you have home insurance, which allows you to claim insurance to fix damage caused by gas leaks and water leaks. What if the insurance company already gives you some kind of fire alarm monitor or water leakage monitor in the house? The moment there is a fire or water leakage, I am not thinking about paying claims. Instead, I would directly call the service provider who can rush to

the place and fix it. So, it is good for you as the customer because your priority is not claiming insurance, your priority is protecting your home.

**RJ: How are large organizations responding to digital transformation and what are the challenges you foresee for large organizations?**

**AK:** I think most of the industry is now very much on the digital journey, some going faster than others, of course. The challenge I see is in managing the distribution system. A lot of insurance companies, traditionally, have been very intermediated businesses, that is, the distribution system has been through bank partners or agents. As much as digital is valuable, the intermediary partners will have a significant role to play. It is more a question of how insurance companies or financial services companies will enable and support their intermediary partners without necessarily thinking about digital only. That is going to be critical.

Another challenge or fault line I see is that of data privacy. Data privacy is a huge topic of importance. I have had the fortune of living a working in different countries and cultures. Therefore, I know that some countries are more open to sharing their data compared with other cultures. This could be a cultural difference, or it could also be a result of lack of awareness in the value. That is an emerging area of interest which can make or break digital transformation, because without data, true digital transformation cannot happen. So, for me, it is going to be interesting to see how it emerges in different markets of the world.

**RJ: Many companies are trying to embrace the platform business model. Why do you think companies are trying to do this? Secondly, what is your advice for companies that are trying to position themselves as platforms?**

**AK:** Just to ensure that we are on the same page, my understanding of a platform is an Uber or an Airbnb, wherein the value is in facilitating interactions between multiple entities, not so much about manufacturing—production of things in itself.

A platform business on paper sounds great, because we are essentially asset light. Having a platform business puts you in the shoes of a broker, and you get a cut of the fees from both sides; it sounds great. It is awesome if you can create THE go-to platform for a particular market/industry. It's a winner takes all sort of game pretty much, in any platform kind of industry. That's one part of it.

The other part of it is that for any platform, you need to have enough consumers and you need to have enough producers. If everyone wants to be a platform, who is the producer? That's the question to be dealt with. For example, in insurance, you need to have enough insurance manufacturers because if you do not have a manufacturer, what are you distributing on the platform?

Platform businesses are great. But as an organization, we must really ask ourselves if that is the way we want to go. It should not be that we are doing it just because everyone else is doing it. Is it our core competence? Is that how we are best placed to add value to our customers? The customer must be at the center of the decision-making process.

**RJ: We hear a lot these days that 'data is the new oil'. How do you interpret this? What is your data strategy?**

**AK:** If that is a metaphor for saying it is very important, I could not agree more. Not because I hold the title of Chief Data Officer, but because, for example, in the field of insurance, what we do is, we price risk, and how we price risk is by using different data points. The more data points we have, the more accurate we can price a risk.

So, it goes to the very heart of what we do as a company and an industry. That is why I think data is so fundamentally important. It has always been important. The only difference now is that we have more data than we did before. We have far better technology to harness that data, make meaning out of it, and extract value out of it.

As for a data strategy, I would say, first and foremost, we need to be very clear about what we want the data for and how do we use it to create real value. Once we have that clarity on the goal and outcome, that means we have clarity on what we am trying to achieve. That also means that the data is not going to be abused.

If I were to summarize a data strategy, it would be four points:

1. What goal do I want to achieve?
2. What data do I need to achieve my goal?
3. Where do I source the data from?
4. How do I use the data obtained optimally?

In large organizations, typically, there are a lot of islands of data. As a result, there is less of an availability problem and more of an access problem. So, when large companies think about data strategies, what are some key challenges that they will have to overcome?

While data availability and access are important issues, I would say that something which is underrated but extremely important is data quality. You probably have data but, (a) it is in different islands, so one part of the company does not know that another part of the company has this data; (b) poor quality of data.

The other piece I would say is data privacy, or the ethical use of data, which, to me, is extremely important. Now, we have access to different types of data, but how do we use it in the right way? That is extremely important.

**RJ: I have heard that for many companies, their data strategy is all about compliance. They are gathering and storing data mainly for compliance and they are not looking at it from an innovation or value-creation lens. What is your take on this?**

**AK:** For AXA, compliance is a non-negotiable thing. Without question, it is a fundamental thing. Now, with that established as a base, we have started to go beyond compliance, for:

1. Doing what is right for customers and AXA
2. In the process, how do we create value for both sides?

We have made good progress with this. The wearable space is one way in which we are doing this. In some of the markets, we have launched usage-based car insurance, wherein you pay for how much you drive, or how well you drive.

**RJ: How do you link data and customer experience? What I find interesting in your title is that you are heading both.**

**AK**: I cannot speak for other organizations or other situations where two different people have these two jobs. Personally, I find there is an incredible pleasure handling both together, because you can make a lot of difference combining these two components. For example, when a customer calls a call center, who should respond to that call? With data, we can pin pointedly say that for this type of customer or this type of query, this is the best person to answer that. And an allocation of the right resource can be made to talk to the customer.

It immediately improves your customer experience, and the internal metrics in terms of the call center's performance: which salesperson should talk to which corporate or customer, depending on the sale's person's capabilities, and what the customer expects. This has a direct impact on your sales: when a customer is thinking of leaving us, we can use data to predict which customer is likely to leave and take some corrective action; or which customer will buy more. All of these are scenarios where you can use data to improve the customer's experience with us, at the same time generate more business and reap higher profits.

## Reflect and Share

1. Practically, every object in the physical world can have an existence in the digital world as well in form of a digital twin.
2. In the future, everything can be 'plugged in'.
3. We are witnessing massive explosion in data—primarily driven by the Internet of Humans and Internet of Things.

4. Connected devices are growing at an exponential pace resulting in massive amounts of data production.

5. Limitless digitization is the base on top of which new business models and customer experiences are developed by digital born organizations.

## Key Questions

- What is your game plan to deal with the explosion of data in your business?

- How do you plan to derive value from your existing data?

- What kind of leadership traits are required to drive data-enabled decision-making in your organization?

- What cultural enablers will you need for your employees to embrace data-driven decision-making?

- Are there areas in your business where robotic automation can yield great results?

- How will you manage the human-machine confluence?

# CHAPTER 5
# UNBOUNDED INNOVATION

"Really we compete with everything you do to relax. We compete with video games. We compete with drinking a bottle of wine. That's a particularly tough one! We compete with other video networks. Playing board games."

—Reed Hastings, CEO, Netflix

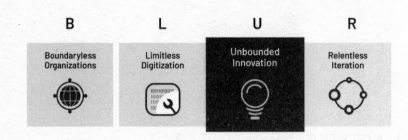

B      L      U      R

Boundaryless Organizations

Limitless Digitization

Unbounded Innovation

Relentless Iteration

# Boundaryless Innovation

Imagine you are hungry and all you had to do was to press a large red button in your shoes to order your favorite pizza. Does that sound like a ridiculous idea? Well, that is exactly what Pizza Hut has pulled off with its Pie Top series of shoes.[1] Figure 5.1 shows how the shoe works as a pizza ordering system. Whether this will end up just being a marketing gimmick or turn into mainstream success remains to be seen, but if Amazon can introduce Amazon Dash, the button-based ordering system[2], who is to say that Pizza Hut cannot do the same?

**Figure 5.1** Pie Top series of shoes launched by Pizza Hut

Beam is a new-age dental insurance company that is built around a smart toothbrush. The company gets data based on the oral hygiene of the customer and brushing habits and can reward customers on good habits.[3]

Go-Jek, Indonesia's first billion-dollar tech start-up, offers various services to the people of Indonesia, including transportation, delivery, lifestyle, and payment services. Go-Jek's approach echoes what Travis Kalanick, ex-CEO of Uber, famously said in an interview: "If we can get a cab to you in 5 minutes, we can get anything to you in 5 minutes".[4]

What these examples tell us is that companies are going beyond conventional boundaries of their industries and producing breakthrough innovations in uncontested spaces with the objective of delighting the customer.

There are quite a few lines that are blurring away when we speak about unbounded innovation. Disruptive innovations such as automated cars or the blockchain are likely to erase the boundaries of many industries at the same time. These innovations are, in other words, truly unbounded. Another important aspect is that innovation is no longer just done in secret labs inside an organization. In many cases, customers, experts, freelancers, and value chain partners outside the organization are important co-creators of innovative solutions for the organization.

# Open Sourcing and Open Innovation

Innovation knows no boundaries today. Companies use open source software, tools, methodology, and media to cut down on development time and focus on value added activities. They are also open sourcing their intellectual property. ExxonMobil, for instance, has released an open source developer toolkit to help oil and gas companies adopt standard data formats.[5]

R&D used to be a closed activity within an organization. But now, companies are embracing open innovation to bring innovation from their ecosystems into the organization. "We believe openness leads to inventiveness and usefulness". says the GE Open Innovation Manifesto. One of GE's projects is First Build, a collaboration platform, which connects designers, engineers, and thinkers to share ideas with other members.[6] The ideas presented at First Build focus on solving problems and creating new home appliances.

# Blurring Industry Lines

Digital native organizations do not box themselves within traditional definitions and boundaries of an industry. Amazon, for instance, started as an online book retailer and today, is competing against Walmart on physical retail, with Google and Microsoft on cloud computing, and with television production studios and broadcasters through their original streaming content. In 2018, Netflix broke HBO's 17-year streak as the most nominated network at the Emmy Awards.[7]

This may not seem like a new phenomenon. Conglomerates of the past have always operated in diversified businesses. The difference now is that the core value proposition is offered from a unified digital business platform.

This phenomenon is most visibly observed in the Financial Technologies (FinTech) space where start-ups are disrupting large banks by unbundling the products and services of a traditional bank (loans, savings accounts, and payments among others). While large banks are busy protecting their end-to-end value chain, the nimbler Fintech companies are attacking the revenue and profit growth of the industry by unbundling products, offering scale and convenience to the end user. All this, while avoiding the burden of regulations associated with full-service banks.

Incumbents also face the challenge of the so-called 'Innovator's dilemma'. As Clayton Christensen of Harvard Business School says, "The reason that it is so difficult for existing firms to capitalize on disruptive innovations is that their processes and their business model, which make them good at their existing business, actually make them bad at competing for the disruption."[8]

Disruptors, however, have the luxury of imagining their business models from the ground-up. While most senior leaders believe that the disruptors in their space will be both incumbents and start-ups from their own industry, there is an ever-growing threat of 'outsiders' springing out of nowhere to deliver a lethal blow. Apple, an outsider to the music industry, disrupted the way music was consumed by millions. Education technology (EdTech) companies such as Coursera and Udacity are disrupting online university-level education through their low-cost, scalable model where an expert is connected to a community of learners across the globe.

Many disruptive digital innovations have the capacity to disrupt multiple industries all at once. Let us look at a few examples.

## Autonomous Cars and Rocket Propelled Travel

Recent studies show that there will be 10 million self-driving cars by 2020, and by 2030, up to 25 percent of the new cars sold will be autonomous.[9] Let us do a quick scan of various industries that will get disrupted when autonomous cars go mainstream.

Already, Uber has introduced self-driving cars in the US, piloting in Pittsburgh.[10] All drivers and driving professionals will get adversely affected when driverless cars go mainstream.

Horse riding is a hobby today, but it was a necessary life skill in the last century. Car driving may achieve a similar status. Driving schools and large Government departments issuing licenses for millions of people will become obsolete. We will still need a few of us to know how to operate cars in future, just in case.

Expensive parking garages in city centers can be done away with. Automated cars can be programmed for scheduled pick-up and drop-off. Law enforcement agencies will spend lesser time dealing with road violations.

It is estimated that 90 percent of automobile accidents could be avoided if we had autonomous cars.[11] The auto repair industry will therefore experience its own major dent as accidents become scarce. Fewer road accidents will mean less patients for healthcare companies. Insurance companies will be forced to change their business model completely from individuals buying policies to vehicle providers footing the bill in case of accidents.

With the tedium of long-distance driving removed, self-driving cars will most likely pose a threat to alternative forms of travel such as trains and flights, and rest stops will no longer be required, impacting motels, hotels, road side restaurants and so on.

Imagine traveling from New York to New Delhi in 30 minutes. Elon Musk has unveiled a futuristic vision of doing exactly that: intercity rocket-propelled travel where transit to anywhere in the world would take minutes and cost no more than the price of an economy airline ticket. "Fly to most places on Earth in under 30 minutes and anywhere in under 60. Cost per seat should be about the same as full fare economy in an aircraft," says Elon Musk.[12] Clearly, a lot of industries will get fundamentally altered if and when this vision becomes reality.

Elon Musk's Tesla has ambitions that expand beyond that of a car company. Tesla's digital strategies span across multiple existing industries. The company is leveraging their energy storage research into home products that have the potential to disrupt the traditional utility model. Tesla

Network will create a fleet of personally owned Tesla vehicles that can be used for self-driving ride-sharing. This creates a radically new model for urban transport, car ownership, and carpooling.

Tesla, and many other digital born organizations, are employing a diverse digital strategy that not only helps them compete with incumbents from a variety of industries but also helps them shape new industries. The under-attack incumbents, however, lack the maturity of a digital ecosystem to compete in their own industry, let alone to influence the shaping of new industries.

## Unbounded Impact of the Blockchain

Trust is the lubricant that makes commerce work. Can something that is as intangible as trust be codified? Yes! Blockchain is a great example of codifying trust.

Blockchain is a distributed ledger technology that underlies cryptocurrencies such as bitcoin and platforms such as Ethereum. It provides a way to record and transfer data in a manner that is transparent, safe, auditable, and resistant to outages. This technology can make the organizations that use it transparent, democratic, decentralized, efficient, and secure.

Blockchain obviates the need for intermediaries like banks and law firms to establish trust in transactions. By distributing the verification process across nodes on the internet, it brings a completely new model for establishing trust through decentralization.

Hypertext Markup Language (HTML) is the protocol for communication for the Worldwide Web. Similarly, blockchain is slated to become the protocol for trusted transactions.

Blockchain is likely to disrupt many industries in the coming decade. The following are some of the industries that are undergoing disruption:

### Banking and Payments

Joi Ito, the director of the MIT Media lab says, "My hunch is that blockchain will be to banking, law, and accountancy as the internet was to media, commerce, and advertising. It will lower costs, disintermediate many layers of business and reduce friction. As we know, one person's friction is another person's revenue."[13]

Many banks like Barclays are also working on adopting blockchain technology to make their business operations faster, more efficient, and secure.[14] Banks are also increasingly investing in blockchain start-ups and projects in the areas of fraud protection, smart contracts, and payments.

## Insurance

Blockchain is a new way of managing trust and can be used to verify many types of data in insurance contracts such as the insured person's identity. With the possibility to integrate real-world, real-time data with blockchain smart contracts, it is now possible to trigger transactions based on the occurrence of certain events, for example, floods, fire, and status of crops.

## Supply Chain Management

As noted earlier, with blockchain technology, transactions can be documented in a permanent decentralized record, and monitored securely and transparently. This can also be used to monitor costs, labor, waste, and environmental impact at every point of the supply chain.

Provenance is a blockchain company that says "Every product has a story. We enable great businesses to build trust in their goods and supply chain. Provenance powered data helps shoppers choose your product."[15] Provenance solves the challenge of lack of transparency in the supply chain process. The company provides a digital stamp for each product that helps customers know the authenticity and the origin of a product.

## Government

Dubai is aiming to put all its government documents on blockchain by 2020.[16] Blockchain-based systems can significantly increase responsiveness, security, efficiency, and transparency of government operations.

## Real Estate

The real estate industry faces some serious issues relating to bureaucracy, fraud, human errors, lack of transparency, and trust. Customers deal with at least six intermediaries while transacting real estate leading to a cumbersome, error prone experience. Blockchain is likely to disintermediate these six intermediaries: brokers, government property databases, title companies, insurance and property databases, escrow companies, inspectors and appraisers, and notary publics.

## Reflect and Share

1. Unbounded innovations are blurring away industry boundaries.
2. Incumbents face the 'innovators dilemma', whereas digital born organizations imagine their business models from the ground up.
3. Incumbents are busy protecting their traditional value chains, whereas digital born organizations are busy bundling and unbundling industries, and attacking pockets of value.
4. Incumbents are largely looking inwards, playing defense while disruptors are expanding at the periphery, playing offense.
5. Organizations are increasingly embracing open innovation to spur growth beyond their traditional domains.

## Key Questions

- What competencies will you develop in your teams to encourage innovation that goes beyond the current landscape of business?
- How will your organization drive innovation by becoming customer-centric and not get bogged down by internal ways of looking at the customer?
- How will you manage uncertainties involved in the innovation process?
- How do you build a culture that permits failures as part of the innovation process?
- Do you leverage open source technologies in your business? Are you contributing open source technologies to the community?

# CHAPTER 6
# RELENTLESS ITERATION

"Whatever is flexible and flowing will tend to grow; Whatever is rigid and blocked will wither and die"

—Lao Tsu, Ancient Chinese Philosopher

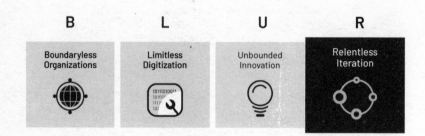

B     L     U     R

Boundaryless Organizations

Limitless Digitization

Unbounded Innovation

Relentless Iteration

# Relentless Iteration in Formula One

Formula One (F1) ranks ninth in the world of professional sports in terms of annual revenues. The Euro 1.8 billion franchise owned by the Formula One group is considered one of the greatest examples of technological prowess used in sports. F1 cars accelerate from 0 to 190 mph in 10 seconds and decelerate by 60 mph in just 0.7 seconds.[1] These cars negotiate turns around corners at such high speeds that the drivers experience a G-force like Apollo astronauts do during re-entry to earth. The most astonishing thing about all this is that these machines are designed, manufactured, and tested from scratch every year.

Racing teams constantly seek to push the boundaries on innovation to find a unique edge that will help them outperform their competitors. Each team is allowed a maximum of 25 teraflops of computing power to simulate the aerodynamics of the car in a virtual setup.[2] Using these simulations, teams test out their designs in rapid iterations. To make the exercise more challenging, no track is the same. Whilst Monaco has a lot of tight corners, Monza is known for its long straights. In fact, between races, a new vehicle design is rolled out within two weeks to meet the needs of each track.

F1 racing is a fine example of relentless iteration using digital technologies. Modern enterprises can take great inspiration from F1 teams to build agile and innovative organizations.

There is a quip doing rounds in conference circuits these days. "In today's context, it is not the big fish that eats the small fish. It is the fast fish that eats the slow fish". Agility is the name of the game in the digital age. From project management to new product development to business models, companies are constantly tweaking the status quo to iteratively up their game.

Through a relentless process of building, measuring, learning, and rebuilding, digital savvy organizations are changing the pace of the game and pushing the laggards off the track.

In the physical world, a product or a service can be labeled as 'done' once the production is complete and the consumer has consumed the offering. In the digital world, products and services have become real time and are constantly improved in short bursts. In the digital world, everything is in a constant state of becoming. As Kevin Kelly, the founding executive editor of the Wired magazine succinctly puts it, "In this era of 'becoming,' everyone becomes a perpetual newbie."[3] Consequently, in the digital world, there is no concrete state of 'doneness'. Products and services are constantly living and breathing data and are continuously creating new opportunities for improvement. Companies must embrace agility to make the most of these opportunities that emerge on a continuous basis.

# The Agile Manifesto

The Agile Manifesto, also called the Manifesto for Agile Software Development, is a formal proclamation of four key values and twelve principles to guide an iterative and people-centric approach to software development.[4] Agile Manifesto states "The highest priority is to satisfy the customer." The manifesto lays down four major values that guide the world of work for software organizations:

- Individuals and interactions over processes and tools
- Working software over comprehensive documentation
- Customer collaboration over contract negotiation
- Responding to change over following a plan

There are many variants of Agile that are used by organizations based on what fits their needs.

Agile is transforming the world of work in fundamental ways and has become a massive global movement with hundreds and thousands of Agile practitioners around the world. Agile took shape in software development in the early 2000s and is now embraced by organizations of all sizes across industries.

In an HBR article titled *Embracing Agile*, Darell K. Rigby, Jeff Sutherland and Hirotaka Takeuchi say that "Agile methodologies involve new values, principles, practices, and benefits and present a radical alternative to command-and-control-style management and are spreading across a broad range of industries and functions and even into the C-suite."[5]

The following are the well-recognized lenses one can use to understand agility in an organization:
- Agile Teams
- Agile Functions
- Agile Organizations
- Agile Strategy

Figure 6.1 shows the four lenses of agility. While the first two lenses represent 'Operational Agility', the remaining two are key for 'Strategic Agility'.

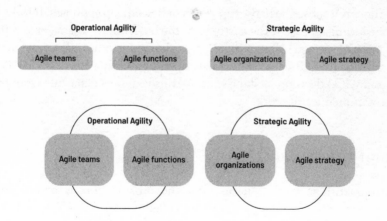

**Figure 6.1** The four lenses of agility

Author Stephen Denning talks about three key principles that bring to sharp focus the essence of agile.

## Law of Small Numbers

While setting up Agile Teams, Amazon uses the two-pizza rule as a guideline for limiting the number of attendees at a meeting. Agile teams typically have seven to ten members, just enough that can be fed with two-pizzas. The two-pizza rule is supposed to be the brain child of Jeff Bezos, founder and CEO of Amazon, who believes that more people only create bureaucracy and get in the way of quick decision-making.

## Law of the Customer

The role of a manager in a traditional team is to identify what tasks need to be accomplished, instruct the team members what to do, and get things done according to a set plan. The role of the employee is to follow the directions as given, trusting the judgment of the manager to ensure that the right work is being done in the right way.

Agile does not subscribe to the top-down or bottom-up approach. It follows the outside-in approach. The customer is the boss, not the manager and the only focus of tne agile team is delivering value to customers. The agile team is a self-directed group of individuals operating with a lot of ownership, autonomy, and decision-making powers. This is quite a departure from the way traditional teams work.

## Law of the Network

"Agile practitioners at all levels view the organization as a fluid and transparent network of players that are collaborating towards a common goal of delighting customers,", says Stephen Denning.[6]

It is now well understood that traditional top-down hierarchies and matrix organizations are ill-suited for an organization to execute agile practices. This is not to say that agile organizations do not have hierarchies at all. The senior management still provides the vision, mission, and values of the organization. One crucial point of difference, notes Stephen Denning, is that the hierarchy in an agile organization is a hierarchy of competence, not a hierarchy of authority.[7]

As a network, the organization then starts to behave like a living, breathing organism, constantly growing, learning, and adapting to changes happening internally and externally. An agile organization is perhaps the best bet for survival in VUCA times.

More and more organizations, big and small, are embracing the lean start-up model. The lean start-up model, developed by Eric Ries, applies lean methodology to create and manage start-ups and enable them to deliver desired products in the hands of the customers faster. At the core of it, the lean start-up model starts off with the assumption that the future is unknown and that organizations must develop multiple hypothesis on what might be the right strategy. Inherently, the model espouses the values of testing hypothesis, validated learning, and an accelerated feedback loop using the build-measure-learn cycle.[8]

Relentless iteration presents a lot of challenges to organizations. Relentless iteration at a team or functional level does not automatically mean that the organization can be agile and iterative as well.

- The organization may be relentlessly iterative from an operations standpoint but rigid from a strategic perspective. When business model disruptions happen, such organizations face severe existential consequences.
- The organization is optimized for maximizing shareholder value whereas the agile iterative teams are obsessing about customer delight. While it may seem intuitive that customer delight will drive shareholder value in the long run, many organizations have issues embracing this mindset.
- The role of management in an organization must be redefined in the light of self-organizing teams. In most agile setups, there is no one playing the role of a conventional manager. Instead, you would find product owners, agile coaches, and team members.
- More horizontal conversations promoting collaboration are needed rather than top down communication.
- Organizations need to give more autonomy for teams to ensure success for their work using iterative cycles and direct customer feedback, instead of 'state of doneness' defined by senior management and bureaucratic rules.

- Transparent feedback loops and continuous improvement, driven by data are to be embraced.

Figure 6.2 shows the different agile structures one can find in organizations.

Building agile teams, functions and organizations can help an organization deliver incremental innovation to customers. Building an agile strategy, however, may call for breakthrough innovation.

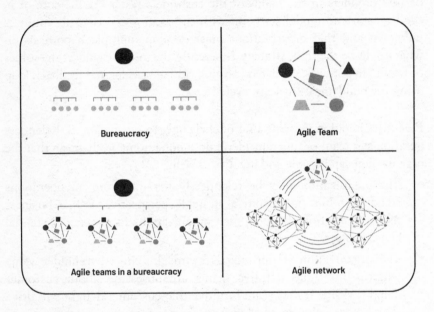

**Figure 6.2** Different agile organizational structures

# The Blue Ocean Strategy

Blue Ocean Strategy, the framework developed by INSEAD Professors Chan Kim and Rénee Mauborgne, provides a structured approach for devising breakthrough innovations to get into uncontested market spaces. Blue Ocean Strategy provides a systematic approach to achieving strategic agility. It highlights the six principles that every company can use to successfully formulate and execute blue ocean strategies. The six principles show how to reconstruct market boundaries, focus on the big picture, reach beyond existing demand, get the strategic sequence right, overcome organizational hurdles, and build execution into strategy.[9]

# Moore's Law for Business Model Agility

Moore's law was coined by Intel co-founder Gordon Moore in 1965. He observed that the number of transistors per square inch on integrated circuits had doubled every year since their invention.[10] Moore's law predicts that this trend will continue into the foreseeable future. Thanks to Moore's law, we have seen a refresh to chips, computer hardware, software and peripherals every 18 months. Now the same phenomenon is starting to happen in the context of strategy. Senior leaders are developing a strategy game plan for 18 months instead of five years. It may be a good idea to question underlying assumptions, leverage new technologies and upgrade the digital business model every 18 months.

# Reflect and Share

1. In the digital age, there is no state of doneness. Everything is constantly arriving and constantly becoming.
2. Agility can be achieved at four levels—Agile teams, Agile functions, Agile organizations and Agile strategy.
3. According to Stephen Deming, Agile uses three core principles:
   a. Law of small numbers
   b. Law of the customer
   c. Law of the network
4. Agile teams, agile functions and agile organizations help in pursuing incremental innovation. Agile strategy happens when there is a constant pursuit of breakthrough innovation in business models.
5. Moore's law is now applicable to business models. Companies need to revisit their business models every 18 months.

## Key Questions

- Does your organization try to maximize customer value over anything else?
- Do your teams use structured approaches to validate new ideas?
- What percentage of your organizational teams is operating in an agile fashion?
- Does your leadership team work closely with management and product builders to make your organization agile as a whole?
- What roles do your managers play when your teams are operating in an agile fashion?
- Have employees been trained on agile methodologies in your organization?

SECTION 2

# IMPACT OF DIGITAL BLUR

# CHAPTER 7

# DIGITAL BLUR IN THE RETAIL INDUSTRY

"It's no longer B2B or B2C; it is B2Me."

—Karen Walker, Chief Marketing Officer, Cisco

*"Are the delivery drones not working today?"*

# INDUSTRY IMPACT

The way that Digital BLUR impacts different industries varies. Whilst some industries and companies are already operating in a boundaryless fashion, others are still rigid and defined by tight boundaries. Some industries employ data for real-time decision making, while many traditional industries still rely on rudimentary heuristics in their decision-making process. Some industries have a heavy tilt towards design and customer experience, whereas others are still driven primarily by internal efficiencies at the cost of customer experience. Some industries iterate rapidly and have turbocharged their product and service development cycles, whereas others still follow scheduled annual release cycles.

Figure 7.1 shows the current state of various industries when it comes to experiencing the Digital BLUR.

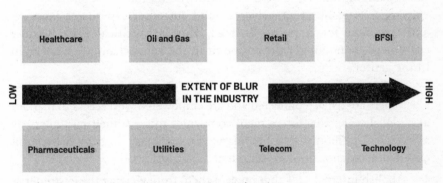

**Figure 7.1** Extent of Digital BLUR in various industries

While the Banking and Financial Services (BFS) and Technology industries are exposed to a high degree of Digital BLUR, lines in industries such as healthcare and pharmaceuticals are blurring away relatively slowly.

Let us first understand Digital BLUR in the context of the retail industry.

# Boundaryless Retail

Boundaryless retail is an evolution of omni-channel retail. In this format, retailers focus on meeting the consumers' needs on an anytime, anywhere, anything basis. The customer has the freedom to choose the way he/she wishes to interact and engage with brands. With AI and voice driven devices such as Amazon Echo and Google Home inside our homes, we are starting to have an Aladdin-like experience by ordering our digital genies to fetch products from our favorite stores. Taco Bell has made purchasing easier by partnering with enterprise social network, Slack, to launch 'TacoBot', where customers can order directly through the instant messaging app.[1]

In the industrial age, companies were organized around products and services. The series of activities around products and services where value is added at each step, also called the value chain, was the organizing principle of that era. In the digital age, companies are starting to organize themselves around customer experience journeys and customer touch points instead. This is a critical shift because customers are no longer the endpoint in the value chain, they are right in the center.

Customers are hyper-connected and are empowered with access to markets at a global scale. This forces retail companies to serve their customers on a 365×24×7 fashion with a boundaryless experience. To truly deliver this experience, organizations must do two things well:

1.  Abolish internal silos that prevent them from viewing the customer as a single entity, which is to say, become boundaryless internally.
2.  Build partnerships with other platforms that give access and reach to the customers, which is to say, become boundaryless externally.

# Limitless Digitization for an End-to-End Customer Experience

Digitalization is also compelling global retail suppliers to re-engineer their internal processes. Manufacturers need to manage their network of suppliers to practice just-in-time delivery of products and to ensure minimal wastage.

Retailers and e-retailers must now tread a fine line, ensuring that they operate in a lean manner, yet their product is always in stock for the 2:00 am shopper. The 'IoT in retail' revolution plays a significant role in achieving a leaner supply chain management. Leveraging IoT capabilities, products are now tracked in real time across different geographical locations. Stock records can be maintained with great precision to the extent that as soon as a product is picked up from the shelf, a signal is sent back to the back-end server that the retailer or the supplier needs to replenish the stock.

# Unbounded Innovation Driving Deeper Understanding of Customers

Digital disruptions are clearly challenging the industrial definition of marketing. The well-defined framework of the marketing four Ps: Product, Price, Place, and Promotion is being replaced by anytime, anyplace customers hunting for the best deals in a connected world. Organizations are now capturing latent needs through social media activity and data analytics. Often, an interesting product catches the eye of a customer online and a few minutes later, remarketing algorithms ensure that the same product flashes on the users' social media page. To the users' surprise, in a matter of hours, promotion for the same product pops up with an additional discount. It is this virtual supply and demand for a product which is propelling retailers to adopt dynamic pricing. The 4Ps of marketing are not static anymore.

The industrial age definitions of segmentation, targeting, and positioning are now getting turbocharged by data and becoming hyper-personal. One-to-many broadcasts have given way to broadcast to the size of one (n = 1) model.

While the digital retail revolution is at its peak, there are also a lot of customers who prefer to touch and feel the product in a physical store. Endless aisle, a new-age augmented reality experience in a physical store, perfectly merges digitization into the physical store by allowing customers to browse through the catalog in an immersive manner in the physical retail space.

The lines between a brick-and-mortar store and virtual stores are blurring. On January 22, 2018, Amazon opened its first no checkout Amazon Go store to the public in Seattle.[2] The Amazon Go offers the perfect mélange from an in-app to store experience for the customer. Multiple in-app clicks and delivery delays make way for a single swipe at the turnstile. Smart cameras and sensors map purchases made in a physical store to the customer's virtual cart on the Amazon app.

# Relentless Iteration to Meet Real-time Demand and Supply

Until recently, fashion houses planned a year in advance for their seasonal collection but due to digital marketplaces and connected customers, product life cycles are shrinking. Retail players need to practice relentless iteration to meet this real-time cycle of demand and supply.

Going beyond just reacting to real-time customer demand, companies are using data to create new demand. It is estimated that Amazon makes 35 percent of its revenues through its recommendation engine.[3] Using predictive analytics, Amazon deciphers customer preferences and buying patterns to aid the customer in the purchase process. Reacting to needs is passé. This is an era of creating and anticipating needs in an iterative and agile manner.

Authors Travis Wright and Chris J. Snook reinforce this point in their book, *Digital Sense*. "There is no online/offline world in which we exist. It is now an always on world."[4]

# CHAPTER 8

# DIGITAL BLUR IN THE BANKING INDUSTRY

"Silicon Valley is coming and if banks don't up their game, then tech companies will take over the industry's business. There are hundreds of start-ups with a lot of brains and money working on various alternatives to traditional banking."

—Jamie Dimon, CEO, J.P. Morgan

L ines in the banking industry have become blurred to a great extent. Let us understand how Digital BLUR plays out in the banking industry.

# Boundaryless Banks

Globally, the banking industry is experiencing the great unbundling. Figure 8.1 shows how Amazon is eating into the different products and services offered by the bank. There is a whole industry of Financial Technology (Fintech) companies that are unbundling the banking industry in a similar fashion. These companies chip away at the profitable layers of the industry without incurring huge overheads of running a full-service bank. LendingClub, for instance, focuses tightly on lending products as opposed to providing an end-to-end banking service. Credit Karma focuses

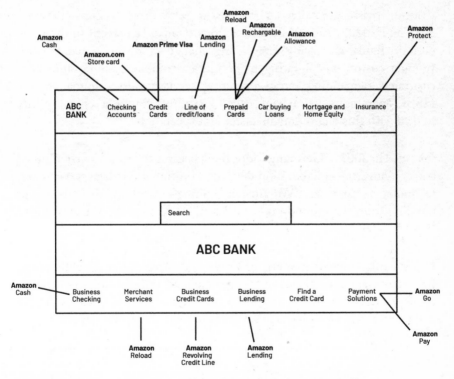

**Figure 8.1** Amazon unbundling the bank (Adapted from CB Insights)[1]

on borrowing and credit. LendingHome focuses on home lending. As a response, many large, traditional banks are now integrating themselves with Fintech companies on an integrated platform to provide the best of both worlds: security and trust associated with large banks and the innovation and convenience offered by Fintechs.

# Limitlessly Digitized Banks

Digitization has completely altered the concept of money and matters related to finance. Banks around the world are aggressively driving customer interactions to digital channels to lower the cost of doing business. Many banks experience a higher Net Promoter Score (NPS), a critical customer satisfaction metric, on digital channels as opposed to all other channels. It is a critical insight that digital not only reduces transaction and operating costs for the bank, but also increases customers' willingness to engage, and eventually pay.

Consumer visits to retail bank branches are set to drop 36 percent between 2017 and 2022, with mobile transactions rising 121 percent in the same period.[2] Banks are facing a sweeping change in customer habits, with younger customers migrating to online and mobile banking and older customers demanding more consulting services with a human touch. HSBC operates its digital bank, called Firstdirect.com, as a separate entity to deal with this dichotomy in customer expectations.[3]

Founded in 2009 in Germany, Fidor Bank became the world's first 'Fintech bank,' pioneering collaboration between traditional financial services and technology businesses. "We are reimagining everything about banking, building from the ground up," said Matthias Kröner, the CEO of Fidor Bank.[4]

Fidor Bank provides modern products and services like crowdfunding, trading of virtual currencies and 60-second bank transfers. Fidor's banking concept offers consumers an online community in which they can give and receive financial advice, offering them rewards for the same.

# Unbounded Innovation in Banking

Limitless Digitization is complemented by unbounded innovation in the banking industry. Digital innovations like Robo-advisory, which have almost zero to negligible registration fees, use algorithms to manage funds and are turning out to be a boon to millions of people who do not have access to personalized financial advice.

Conventionally, banks have been focusing on product selling—be it loans, insurance, or fund management—it has been a static product selling model. Most modern banks are now transforming themselves into a multifaceted platform which is not only a virtual bank but also a lifestyle kiosk selling movie tickets and other lifestyle products. Traditionally the gatekeepers of customers' money, banks are now also their lifestyle partner. In the digital age, banks are crossing industry boundaries and becoming ubiquitous.

# Relentless Iteration to Enhance Customer Experience

A bank's digital footprint needs to be constantly worked upon to enhance customer experience. A mobile banking app for example cannot remain static for a long time; it needs to continue building a unique user experience every day. In fact, one of the challenges faced by most banks is that when a customer walks into a bank branch, employees at the branch often have no idea what the customer has experienced in the digital world. Herein lies the challenge of most modern banks: How to enable employees to provide a seamless customer experience across channels?

# CHAPTER 9

# DIGITAL BLUR IN THE AIRLINE INDUSTRY

"The most important part of Air Asia is the engagement. You must engage customers to be relevant. If you lose the engagement, you're just a commodity."

—Tony Fernandes, Group CEO, Air Asia Group

# Interview with Tan Sri Tony Fernandes

Tony Fernandes is the Group CEO of Malaysian born low-fare airline AirAsia Group, which has associates in Thailand, Indonesia, Philippines, India, and Japan. Known as a flamboyant, cool, and ruthless businessman, Fernandes' focus is to build AirAsia as a global travel partner. Tony's biggest achievement has been to open up countries within the South-East Asian region to new budget carriers, which previously did not have open-skies agreements, and making air travel affordable to the masses.

Tony started his career as an auditor with Virgin Records, quickly moving to Virgin Communications as Financial Controller, and subsequently joining Warner Music as Senior Financial Analyst. An alumnus of the London School of Accounting as well as a member of the Institute of Chartered Accountants in England and Wales, Tony is also the founder of no-frills hotel chain Tune Hotels and Caterham Formula One team, and formerly Chairman of the Queen's Park Rangers Holdings Ltd.

Tony attributes his unique, pioneering business outlook to his experience and interest in a wide range of industries, allowing him to reimagine the value that his organizations provide their customers.

**RJ: What is digital, according to you?**

**TF:** Digital comprises three pillars:

1. Using digital technology to give our customers a better physical experience. This includes the consumption experience as well as the IT experience:

    a.  The consumption experience—giving customers what they want rather than what I think they need. Using data to enhance the customer transaction experience is a selling point.

    b.  The IT experience—Using technology for predictive decision making.

2.  Using data to run a better organization to make processes easier and more quantifiable, to analyze people more efficiently, and hire and train in the right way.

3.  Using digital to explore new businesses and disrupt existing ones—digital has given me the ability to enter areas that I wasn't able to as a traditional airline and position myself as a travel partner rather than just a transport carrier.

To me, digital is about reducing the human guesswork, and using data to make more informed decisions. It is important to remember, however, that data will never be able to tell certain things. Decision-making is ultimately a function of human minds. Data and digital help make that process more efficient.

**RJ: In the same breath, what is not digital?**

**TF:** Digital is not about taking over human decision-making. I think too many companies are now using quantitative analysis to decide everything. There is no human intervention. Digital provides quantitative data, which doesn't know the human character, and the human ability to change one person. The quantitative analysis may say that someone is an underperformer. I may feel that I can change the underperformer to a performer. He may be in the wrong field.

In other words, digital doesn't replace everything. It is a very strong, useful tool, and I encourage making the most of what digital has to offer. At the same time, one needs to remember that digital doesn't replace everything.

**RJ: What do you think are the new capabilities needed for an organization to become boundaryless?**

**TF:** Let's take airlines first. We are not a conventional airline, in the sense that we are not bound by the old rules. I believe that there are no boundaries to what we can sell, where we can fly and how many times we can fly.

I believe that I can sell a lot of things to my customer—I can take the whole travel ecosystem from the moment we book the ticket, to duty free to travel, to the activities customers want to do during their travel (like getting a massage), to where my customer wants to eat; I can provide my customers all of this. In other words, we can provide an end-to-end travel experience solution.

I am on a journey to radicalize the way we work and remove any bureaucracy that may be there. We place boundaries around ourselves. Boundaries don't exist. I believe that one must be aggressive if we want to change. That may sound cruel, but if we don't do that, we are in trouble. This is true for any organization in any industry across the globe. Amazon and Alibaba are examples of what happens when you push the proverbial boundaries.

**RJ: If you want to make digital the core DNA of the organization, where do you think it operates—Is it at a group level? Is it embedded inside each business?**

**TF:** Digital must operate throughout the organization. It starts with the leadership, but it cannot be pushed down. That becomes a little bit like 'brain-washing' where everyone is chanting that we're digital, but what does that really mean?

What is important for me is to know what digital means to my 20,000+ employees. That's a cultural thing, and that comes from the top. I like to consider this as 'Internal Branding'—before we go out and tell the world that we're a digital company, everyone within the organization needs to not just believe that, but also understand what that entails. I can't be telling the world that we're a digital-first company if my group CFO is saying that we're an airline company. That's the journey we're on right now, and that's where culture plays a big role. Ultimately, however, the organization is very concentrated on self. That is the reality. Therefore, there will be resistance. It is important to get the resistance out. That means either getting rid of the feeling of resistance or getting rid of the resistors.

**RJ: Banks today are calling themselves 'lifestyle partners'. What do you think will be the new positioning for airlines?**

**TF:** We are travel partners. I'm trying to form a travel infrastructure that can deal with moving. Some of the pieces may be outside the travel infrastructure. Amazon is basically an e-commerce provider. It is a marketplace for e-commerce, but also has multiple subsidiary businesses, which make you question why they are together. One day, Amazon may grow to be a travel company. Therefore, that's the question for us as well—will we remain an airline that raises exponential capital or will AirAsia take another life of its own? Those are the decisions we have to make, in terms of where we want to take the company.

Every business that we now run is in the travel ecospace. Where I see our focus is on enhancing your travel experience. Some of my businesses may morph into more. That means if bitpay and bitcoin become a bank, they will still provide services to our travelers, but they will provide services outside as a lifestyle partner. I think to rename a bank as a lifestyle partner is stretching their imagination. But, this is a world of evolution and change. So, you never know.

**RJ: The industrial age was about thinking within a box. Canon thought only about cameras, and they knew who their competition was. So, leaders knew where to focus. In the boundaryless world where competition stretches beyond the confines of a single industry, what does it do to the leadership within an organization? What is the capability that leaders inside the organizations need to have when there is no clarity?**

**TF:** If you think about Air Asia, it is still a 'boundaried' company, and my job is to make it boundaryless. We just about have processes set for our functions. I still think that some of my senior management does not react quick enough, which is a problem, because the things we have today may not be relevant tomorrow. Therefore, we need radical change. If you are cautious of change, someone else is going to step up and enable the change:

1. Traveloka has a better website than us—quicker, leaner, and meaner than Air Asia. We're still dilly-dallying on whether to hire someone or not, whether they are good enough or not. I'm really stuck here.

2. You see how quickly Amazon processes and changes. When I tell my team that the mobile web check-in is bad, rather than saying 'let's check, let's get empirical evident, let's fix it', there are thousands of reasons for it.

Airlines may not exist in the form that they are right now. My competition is against every other company out there. Am I as good as Amazon? Is my HR process as good as the best company in the world? We need to be quick in our evolution, and not get stuck in the confines of what we consider to be absolute:

1. Blackberry was king. We all walked into this room 8 years ago with a blackberry. It's not there anymore.

2. I thought that Apple was a horrible phone; I've got it now.

3. I thought I could never get away from the keyboard. I don't even have a computer anymore. I run my company on a portable tablet and my phone.

My message to my people is that the war has started. I'm not worried about the companies that exist. It's the new companies that I am worried about. Airlines may just become providers of seats, in another world. To survive, you must redo your model.

**RJ: How will the airline industry look in 2025?**

**TF:** The most important part of Air Asia is the engagement. You must engage customers to be relevant. If you lose the engagement, you're just a commodity. Air Asia has 80% of its customers on the internet. I am fighting against platforms like Kayak and SkyScanner to keep our customer data because a travel agent or a travel platform doesn't care if it is AirAsia, or Qantas, or someone else's tickets they're selling. I can't sell to that because I don't know the customer. I may have his phone number, but he hasn't transacted with me. So, engagement is the most important, because we engage at all levels—whether it is workplace, or salesforce, or social media, etc. The transaction must be frictionless.

If we don't sort ourselves out and change people and the culture within this organization, Amazon and Kayak will do it 100-times better, Then you lose the engagement battle. Moreover, engagement and transaction are interlinked.

Ultimately, we're an engagement company, and engaging our own staff is equally important. Everything that we have said about digital—you engage your staff, you tell them what digital is, you tell them why it is important, why you have it, is all extremely important to build the engagement layer.

**RJ: How will the world look in 2030?**

**TF:** I think it will be a boundaryless world. You have a lot of industries merging. You won't have a banking sector. You could have a lifestyle company becoming a bank, a taxi company could become a bank. Amazon has become a hardware company, it has become the IBM of 40 years ago. Unisys was selling big mainframes, and now it's controlled by the bookseller. I think that:

a.  A lot of industries will crossover

b.  Silos will break

c.  There will be frictionless movement

d.  Quality of life will be much better

e.  You will see a more self-service, on-demand world

# SECTION 3

# DIGITAL LEAPFROG FRAMEWORK

CHAPTER 10

# LEAPING FROM A LINEAR BUSINESS TO NETWORKED BUSINESS

"Ecosystems are the new bedrock of digital. The top 15 public platform companies already represent USD 2.6 trillion in market capitalization worldwide."

—Accenture Technology Vision, 2016

*"Let's see who can jump higher"*

# Leaping Into The Networked Business Model

Until just half a decade ago, business playing fields were well defined. Companies chose to stay within these neatly defined industry lines, rarely venturing outside. In the last few years, however, the situation has dramatically changed. Digital technology has brought to the fore new ways of unlocking value and has lowered entry and exit barriers in virtually every digitally contestable market space. This has prompted digital savvy organizations to persistently attack related and sometimes unrelated spaces in search of new value while fiercely protecting their core.

In the industrial age, companies focused on products and services that were delivered to the customer through a predominantly linear value chain. The recipe for market domination largely rested on the companies' ability to harness supply side economies of scale. The company that had large production capability with the ability to control the value chain called the shots and walked away with the lion's share of the industry profits. Owning physical assets was considered a crucial lever for success, and leaders in these organizations obsessed over Return on Assets (ROA) and asset utilization. Many decisions were optimized for increasing asset utilization. Any conversation around corporate growth would naturally be anchored towards organic and inorganic growth models.

In the digital age, however, companies are focused on building platforms that connect many ecosystem players. The recipe for market domination in this model depends on the companies' ability to delight customers by orchestrating and delivering value offered by ecosystem partners. The company that does well in this model is the one that is able to harness the demand-side economies of scale, which translates to the ability to acquire and meet the needs of millions of customers. Ownership is over-rated in the new model. Instead, just-in-time access to resources is considered more important. Leaders in digital organizations obsess over customer engagement, adoption, and stickiness. Conversations around corporate growth typically revolve around virality and exploiting network effects in the ecosystem.

In effect, as shown in Figure 10.1, we are witnessing a transformation from linear business models to networked business models.

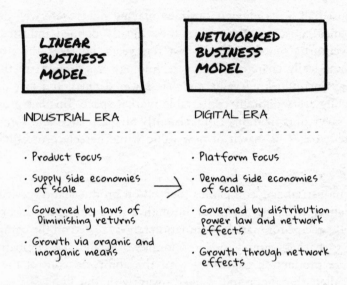

**Figure 10.1** Linear to Networked Business Models

Companies such as Alibaba, Alphabet, Amazon, Apple, Facebook, LinkedIn, Salesforce, Tencent, and Twitter are leading the charge when it comes to networked business models. Not to be left behind, many companies from non-tech sectors are also rapidly building digital networks that leverage ecosystem partners. Examples include those of Bosch, Disney, GE, Merck and Schneider, to name just a few. The basic principle that guides thinking in these companies is that networks consistently win against standalone companies.

## Business Models: The New Battleground

Back in the day, the term innovation was mainly used in the context of products, later it described the introduction of new product categories and then, it became more about processes that enabled an organization to consistently churn out breakthrough products and services. While all these dimensions are still relevant, the innovation battleground today has shifted to a new arena called business models.

Earlier, we understood the difference between a linear business model and a networked business model. It is important to note that networked business models can come in two forms: Hybrid business models and Ecosystem-based models.

Figure 10.2 shows the three business models that we need to pay attention to.

Alex Osterwalder, in his book "Business Model Generation", defines business models as the rationale for how an organization creates, delivers, and captures value.[1] The book introduces a tool called the Business Model Canvas. The canvas, shown in Figure 10.3, allows organizations to articulate clearly what their value proposition to the customer is and how this value is created, delivered, and captured.

While the business model canvas does a great job creating a structure to visualize complex businesses, the key insight is that this framework has an inherent bias towards the linear business model. The business model canvas implicitly assumes customers to be the end-point of a company's value chain. It does not account for new possibilities such as co-creation of products and solutions with customers. As noted earlier, digital business models are increasingly networked and nonlinear. There are many stakeholders in the ecosystem that come together to create, deliver, and capture value. The nuances of digital business models are not captured well in the traditional business model canvas.

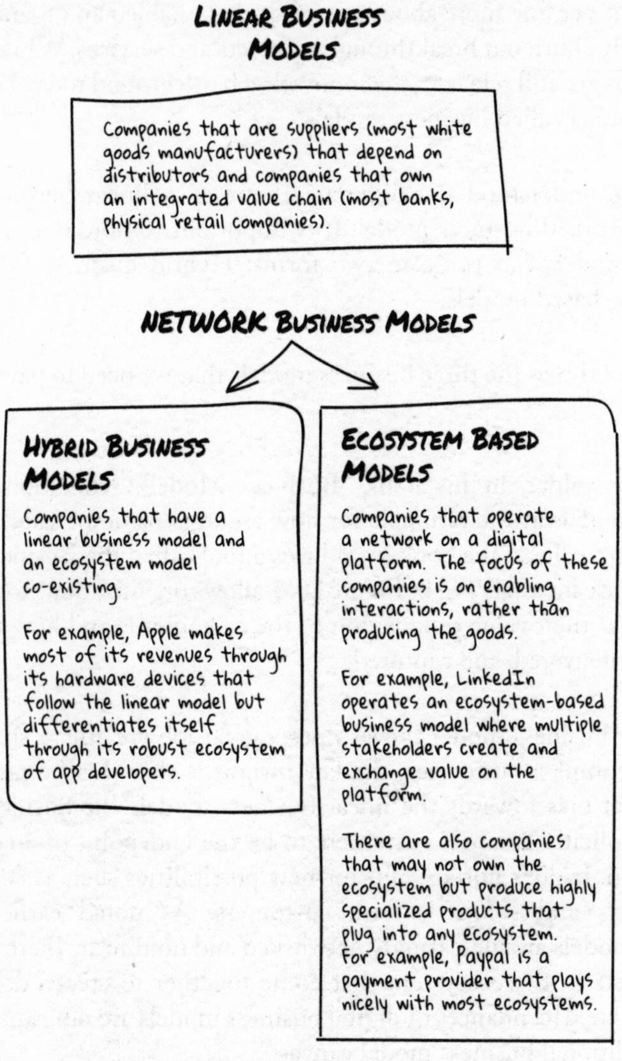

## LINEAR BUSINESS MODELS

Companies that are suppliers (most white goods manufacturers) that depend on distributors and companies that own an integrated value chain (most banks, physical retail companies).

## NETWORK BUSINESS MODELS

### HYBRID BUSINESS MODELS

Companies that have a linear business model and an ecosystem model co-existing.

For example, Apple makes most of its revenues through its hardware devices that follow the linear model but differentiates itself through its robust ecosystem of app developers.

### ECOSYSTEM BASED MODELS

Companies that operate a network on a digital platform. The focus of these companies is on enabling interactions, rather than producing the goods.

For example, LinkedIn operates an ecosystem-based business model where multiple stakeholders create and exchange value on the platform.

There are also companies that may not own the ecosystem but produce highly specialized products that plug into any ecosystem. For example, Paypal is a payment provider that plays nicely with most ecosystems.

**Figure 10.2** Three types of business models

We need a different framework to capture the essence of networked businesses (hybrid and ecosystem based). In the next chapter, we will understand and apply a breakthrough framework called the Digital LEAPFROG Framework (DLF). This framework provides a pathway for any organization that has a linear business model to evolve into a networked business model.

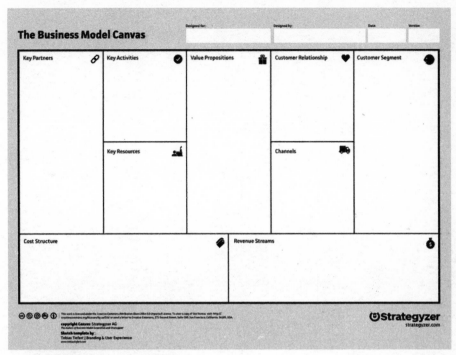

**Figure 10.3** Business Model Canvas
(Strategyzer.com)

# CHAPTER 11
# THE DIGITAL LEAPFROG FRAMEWORK

> "Most of the executives I talk to are still very much focused on digital largely as a way to do "more of the same," just more efficiently, quickly, cost effectively. But I don't see a lot of evidence of fundamentally stepping back and rethinking, at a basic level, "What business are we really in?"
>
> —John Hagel III | Co-Chairman at Deloitte LLP Center for the Edge leaders

# Essence of the Digital LEAPFROG Framework

The digital LEAPFROG framework allows an organization to evolve from an industrial, linear business model to a networked, digital business model using a series of structured steps. The framework also enables organizations to formulate specific strategies to clear the Digital BLUR.

This framework is applicable to just about any business across industry verticals—from agriculture to manufacturing to biopharma to e-commerce.

The framework allows an organization to identify opportunities to:
1. Unlock exponential growth using the ecosystem
2. Build competitive advantage and a competitive moat for the business
3. Create a thriving ecosystem that adds tremendous value to customers

The framework relies on the following basic tenets to achieve these outcomes:

- Every business, either in parts or in whole, can be a digital business. As long as there is information flow in the business (which is the case in all businesses), it is possible to introduce digital elements in the business model.
- Every business operates in an ecosystem of producers, suppliers, partners, and consumers. It is, therefore, possible to create a networked business model, either in parts of the ecosystem (hybrid model) or in totality (ecosystem-based business model).
- Business ecosystems have an in-built mechanism for realizing the power of network effects. Ecosystems are built on the principle of increasing interconnections, making it easy and quick to connect everything.
- Business ecosystems offer unprecedented access to dynamic capabilities, resources, and talent on a global scale.
- Shifting to business ecosystems calls for a mindset that is open to radical changes in the way businesses are configured, in terms of the people, processes, and technologies that power the organization.

There are two key questions that need attention in this context:

1.  Is it possible to build networked business models for any business?
2.  Should all companies embrace networked business models?

# Is It Possible to Build Networked Business Models for Any Business?

The answer is yes. A typical organization relies on a network of resources, people, partners, and channels to create and deliver value to customers. These networks can be designed in the form of digital ecosystems. Even when the core product is physical, an organization can create a hybrid model around the physical product to leapfrog into exponential growth.

For example:

*   A medical device manufacturer can create a social network for its users to maintain a healthy lifestyle. By doing so, the company not only opens new revenue possibilities on the social network, it also reinforces growth of its core physical product by building a community around it.

*   An agriculture equipment manufacturer can become a one-stop shop for farmers to get access to farming insights, agricultural loans, and raw materials from multiple providers.

*   A retail bank can create a platform to provide lifestyle products, such as movie and flight tickets, to its customers going beyond traditional banking products.

Increasingly, in the digital age companies are going beyond the immediate needs that their products and services satisfy to something holistic that the customer is looking for.

# Should All Companies Embrace Networked Business Models?

It depends. There are quite a few successful digital born organizations that use the linear business model. Netflix is a prominent example of a digital-first company that uses the linear business model. Although Netflix is well known for its digital platform that serves on-demand movies and shows to its audience, its business model is linear. Netflix has an integrated value chain wherein it licenses shows from other producers, and produces its own shows, and delivers them directly to its subscribers.

Compared to a company operating in a networked business model, Netflix's unit economics operate in a traditional fashion. Netflix needs to keep investing massive amounts of money to procure and produce quality programming in hopes that more and more subscribers will flock to them. They will, however, face imminent competition from the likes of Disney. It remains to be seen how strong Netflix's competitive moat really is. In contrast, ecosystem driven companies like Google and Facebook enjoy a formidable competitive moat and a near monopoly status in their respective segments, thanks largely to network effects.

As noted earlier, even if a company is in the business of physical goods, it is prudent to envisage a networked model around the information component of the business. While the physical businesses grow linearly, ecosystems can propel the company into an exponential growth path. Apple, as noted earlier, makes most of its revenues through its hardware devices that follow the linear business model but differentiates itself through its robust ecosystem of app developers.

# Linking Digital LEAPFROG to the Digital BLUR Framework

LEAPFROG stands for:
- Liquid structures
- Economy of platforms
- Algorithms and analytics
- Programmable interfaces
- Formulate experience journeys

- Reach unchartered territories
- Obsessive customer centricity
- Game-changing adaptation

The digital LEAPFROG framework builds on top of the digital BLUR framework. Each of the four dimensions of BLUR is mapped to two elements of LEAPFROG. Figure 11.1 shows the link between the two frameworks.

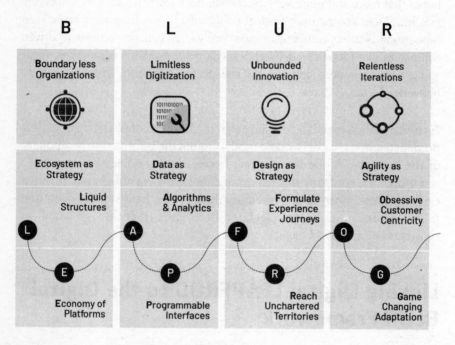

**Figure 11.1** Digital LEAPFROG framework

We will delve deep into the digital LEAPFROG framework in subsequent chapters.

The process of leaping from a linear business model to a networked business model involves a seven-step process as described in Figure 11.2.

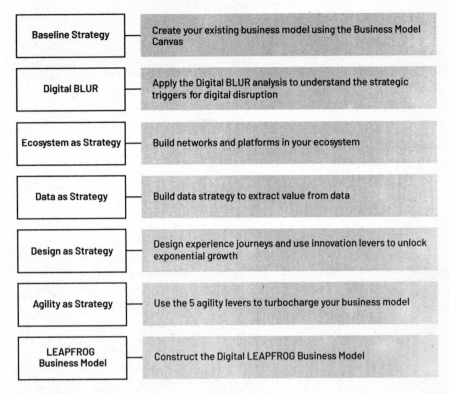

**Figure 11.2** The 7-step Digital LEAPFROG Process

# CHAPTER 12
# BASELINE STRATEGY

"The biggest impediment to a company's future success is its past success."

—Dan Schulman, CEO, PayPal

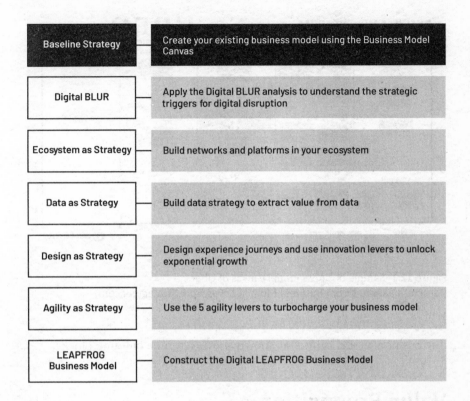

| | |
|---|---|
| **Baseline Strategy** | Create your existing business model using the Business Model Canvas |
| **Digital BLUR** | Apply the Digital BLUR analysis to understand the strategic triggers for digital disruption |
| **Ecosystem as Strategy** | Build networks and platforms in your ecosystem |
| **Data as Strategy** | Build data strategy to extract value from data |
| **Design as Strategy** | Design experience journeys and use innovation levers to unlock exponential growth |
| **Agility as Strategy** | Use the 5 agility levers to turbocharge your business model |
| **LEAPFROG Business Model** | Construct the Digital LEAPFROG Business Model |

Before we can create the digital LEAPFROG business model, we need to first create the 'as-is' linear business model on the business model canvas. To do this, organizations must gain clarity on the value proposition delivered to the customer and the rationale used by the organization to create, deliver, and capture value.

Figure 12.1 shows a sample business model canvas of Uber.

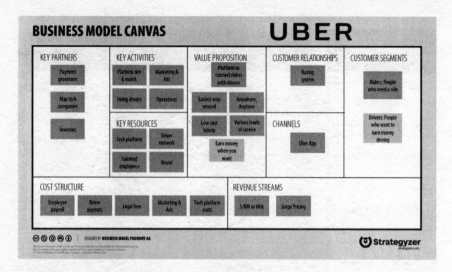

**Figure 12.1** Sample business model canvas of Uber
(Structure adapted from Business Model Canvas from Strategyzer.com)

The business model canvas, as shown above, has nine building blocks.

# Value Proposition

Value proposition is essentially the reason why a customer buys a product or service from one company instead of going to a competitor or settling for the status quo. For Apple, one of the key value propositions is product design. In the case of Uber, the canvas captures the value proposition for the driver, which is earn money when you want, and for the rider, it is the easiest way around.

# Key Activities

Key activities are the most important activities in creating a company's value proposition. For example, for Walmart, global procurement can be considered as a key activity since that forms the basis for the 'Everyday low price' value proposition of the company. For Uber, platform development and hiring drivers are key activities.

# Key Resources

Key resources are assets that an organization uses to create value for the customer. These resources could be human, financial, physical, and intellectual. For Uber, the network of drivers is a key resource.

# Key Partners

Partners are entities that collaborate with an organization to create the value proposition for customers. Partnerships can take the form of vendors, joint ventures, strategic alliances between competitors or noncompetitors. For Microsoft, Intel is a key partner when it comes to its personal computer products. For Uber, mapping companies are key partners.

# Relationships

To ensure customer delight, companies must identify their relationship strategy. Customer relationship strategies may take various forms including personal assistance, self-service, automated service and so on. Many banks, for instance, deploy relationship managers to cater to the needs of high net worth clients, whereas for retail customers, the bank may choose to use a low touch relationship strategy by leveraging mobile apps or ATMs. For Uber, customer service is by and large automated. The rating system is a way for Uber to regulate behaviors on the platform.

# Channels

A company can deliver its value proposition to its customer segments through different channels. There exist numerous types of channels, such as in-person, mobile, online, kiosks, and partners. Uber relies on its app to deliver value to its customers.

# Customer Segments

Customer segments refer to the sets of customers that the company is trying to cater to. Customers are typically segmented based on various needs and attributes. Tesla, the California based electric car manufacturer, caters to eco-friendly, tech-savvy, and entry-level luxury buyers. For Uber as a platform, there are two primary stakeholders: drivers and riders.

# Revenue Streams

Revenue streams refer to the model a company uses to make income from each customer segment. LinkedIn charges a subscription fee to users who want to use advanced features of the platform. It also charges a subscription fee to HR professionals who are looking to hire candidates from the LinkedIn network. In case of Uber, pricing based on distance and surge pricing are the primary revenue models.

# Cost Structure

Cost structure refer to the major cost drivers in the operations of an organization. Low cost airlines such as Ryan Air or Air Asia focus on minimizing their costs and operating on a 'no frills' basis. For Uber, driver payouts, and employee and platform costs are the major cost drivers.

Once the business model canvas is filled out, the linear business model is available in front of us as the baseline. We are now ready to leap from the linear model into the networked model.

# CHAPTER 13
# DIGITAL BLUR ANALYSIS

"When digital transformation is done right, it's like a caterpillar turning into a butterfly, but when done wrong, all you have is a really fast caterpillar."

—George Westerman, Principal Research Scientist with the MIT Sloan Initiative on the Digital Economy

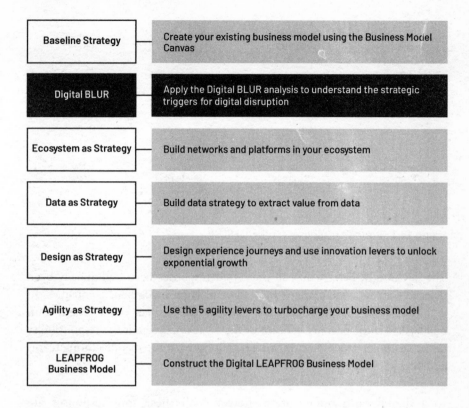

# Apply the Digital BLUR Analysis

Once the linear business model is constructed in step 1, it is time to apply the Digital BLUR analysis to understand the strategic triggers for digital disruption.

There are four strategic responses that organizations must consider:

1. Operating in a boundaryless world calls for an ecosystem play.
2. In the limitlessly digitized world, organizations need to learn to derive new value from data.
3. To survive and thrive in an unbounded innovation-driven world, organizations need to embrace design as a core strategy.
4. To be relevant in the rapidly iterating world, organizations must bring agility as a strategy to sharp focus.

Figure 13.1 shows the strategic responses for each of the dimensions of BLUR.

**Figure 13.1** Strategic responses for Digital BLUR

The key insight here is that all these four responses have traditionally been delegated to functional teams by leaders of large incumbent companies. In an industrial organization, ecosystem is what the business development team builds, data is the primary concern of the IT team, design is the responsibility of the customer experience team, and agility is what the manufacturing teams and engineers take care of.

In a digital born organization, however, all these four responses are squarely dealt with by the senior leadership teams and in most cases, these are themes for board level discussions. In fact, digital companies use precisely these four strategic approaches—ecosystems, data, design, and agility—to disrupt industries with legacy companies and incumbents that are typically ill-equipped to respond fast.

Here are some key questions that need to be addressed:

## Ecosystem as Strategy

1. Is your company leveraging resources that are not necessarily owned by your organization?
2. Is your company leveraging talent that exists outside the organization?
3. Are companies in your industry operating as an ecosystem with a platform business model?

## Data as Strategy

1. Is your company deriving value from the data that you acquire?
2. Are you or your competitors using AI algorithms to digitize core processes?
3. Are you using open APIs to allow others to connect with your products and services?
4. Are you leveraging APIs provided by other services to acquire new capabilities faster?

## Design as Strategy

1. Is your company focusing on customer experience and embracing design as a focus area in the organization?
2. Is your company using technology trends and business model innovation to enter unchartered territories?
3. Are you or your competitors executing an exponential growth model with accelerated timelines?

## Agility as Strategy

1. Is your company displaying agility in new product launches and innovation roll-outs?
2. Is your company continuously changing the industry play book through strategic agility?

Figure 13.2 (a worksheet) shows a structured process to apply Digital BLUR analysis.

It is also important to identify potential disruptors from within and outside the industry.

| BLUR | Strategic Response | Questions | Examples | Are you doing this? | Are companies in your industry doing this? |
|---|---|---|---|---|---|
| Boundaryless Organizations & Industries | Ecosystem as Strategy | 1. Leveraging resources that may not be owned by your organization?<br>2. Leveraging talent that exists outside the organization?<br>3. Using platforms to deliver superior value to ecosystem players in a consistent manner? | AirBnB<br><br>Uber<br><br>Salesforce.com | | |
| Limitless Digitization | Data as Strategy | 1. Digitizing your processes and work #ows?<br>2. Automating processes through algorithms?<br>3. Deriving value from the data that you acquire? | Google<br><br>Net#ix | | |
| Unbounded Innovation | Design as Strategy | 1. Using technology trends to disrupt multiple industries?<br>2. Using openness to acquire and distribute new innovations? | UberEats<br><br>PayTM Bank | | |
| Relentless Iteration | Agility as Strategy | 1. Displaying unprecedented agility in new product launches and innovation roll-outs?<br>2. Continuously changing industry play book? | Android OS<br><br>Apple | | |

| POTENTIAL DISRUPTORS |
|---|
| |

**Figure 13.2** Apply Digital BLUR analysis to understand the strategic triggers for digital disruption

It is imperative for organizations to understand the impact of underlying triggers for digital BLUR. You may recall that digital BLUR is caused by five key drivers: connected customers, smart technologies, VUCA environment, great industry bundling and unbundling, and new breed of competitors.

| Digital BLUR driver | Insights from your environment | Impact on your organization |
|---|---|---|
| Connected Customers | | |
| Smart Technologies | | |
| VUCA environment | | |
| Great Industry unbundling | | |
| New Breed of Competitors | | |

**Figure 13.3**  Drivers for Digital BLUR in your industry and organization

Figure 13.3 (a worksheet) shows a template for you to plot your insights on each of these components and the corresponding impact on your organization.

- Observe how the connected customers' trend is playing out in your industry and identify how it is impacting your organization.
- Track the key technologies that are shaping your industry and identify the impact on your organization.
- Identify the impact of VUCA on your industry and on your organization.
- Observe if your industry is undergoing digital bundling and

unbundling, and identify the impact on your organization.

- Track the new breed of competitors that are entering your industry and identify the potential threat for your organization.

This step allows the organization to understand the level of blurring that is happening in the industry and to appreciate the most important dimensions of BLUR that need to be addressed to thwart disruptors.

Let us now delve deeper into the four strategic response areas.

# CHAPTER 14
# ECOSYSTEM AS STRATEGY

"Alibaba is an ecosystem that helps small business to grow."

—Jack Ma, Founder, Alibaba

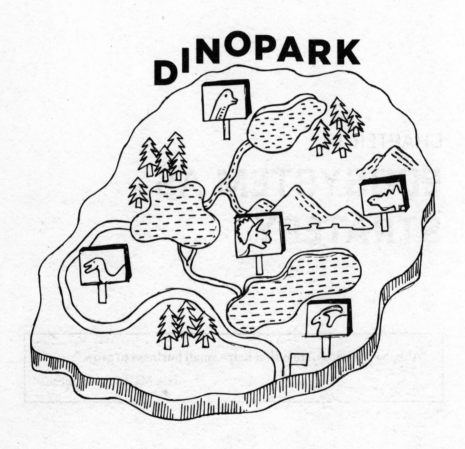

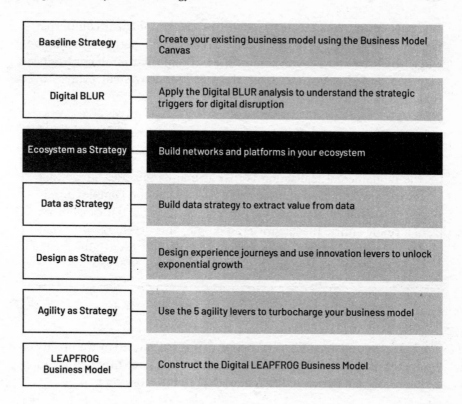

| Baseline Strategy | Create your existing business model using the Business Model Canvas |
| Digital BLUR | Apply the Digital BLUR analysis to understand the strategic triggers for digital disruption |
| Ecosystem as Strategy | Build networks and platforms in your ecosystem |
| Data as Strategy | Build data strategy to extract value from data |
| Design as Strategy | Design experience journeys and use innovation levers to unlock exponential growth |
| Agility as Strategy | Use the 5 agility levers to turbocharge your business model |
| LEAPFROG Business Model | Construct the Digital LEAPFROG Business Model |

# ECOSYSTEMS

In the industrial age, organizations were thought of as machines. In the digital age, organizations operate more like organisms.

Ecosystems are dynamic communities of diverse players who create, deliver, and capture value through collaboration, competition, and co-creation. The word 'Ecosystem', coined by the British botanist Arthur Tansley, first came into being in the 1930s.[1] The term was used to describe a community of living organisms that co-evolved by interacting and exchanging things with each other and with the environment around them. These organisms influenced each other's lives in intricate ways because they competed, collaborated, and co-created to ensure their survival. The environment frequently threw curve balls at the organisms by presenting external disruptions such as earthquakes, droughts, and floods. This shaped the behavior and dynamics of the organisms in the ecosystem in a deep fashion.

Business ecosystems are very much like their biological counterparts. Organizations engage, interact, and exchange value between themselves and with the business environment. The external environment introduces surprises and shocks that shape the way the ecosystem evolves over time.

> The fundamental realization is that as many industries are getting commoditized, creating new value that serves the complex needs of the customer is increasingly stretching beyond the capabilities of a single entity. The adaptive response to this development is that diverse set of organizations, big and small, and even individuals, come together to orchestrate new value for the customer.

The longevity and durability of ecosystems are determined by the quality of co-opetition (collaboration and competition at the same time), co-creation and co-evolution between different players in the ecosystem.

By building ecosystems, organizations start to operate like boundaryless entities with their reach expanding far and wide. By gaining access to the complex networks of resources, capabilities, products, and solutions in their ecosystem, organizations can satisfy the complex needs of customers without having to produce everything.

Companies can use the first two levers of Digital LEAPFROG to become boundaryless.

a. **Liquid Structures**: This lever is all about how an organization orchestrates a fluid network of resources and people to achieve a goal.

b. **Economy of Platforms**: This lever focuses on how an organization moves from a linear business model to an ecosystem-based model to serve the needs of many stakeholders at the same time.

Figures 14.1 and 14.2 show the levers for ecosystem as strategy.

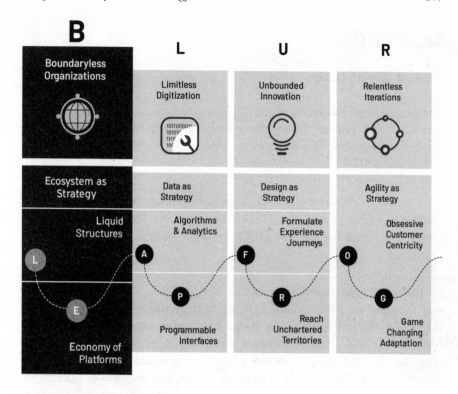

**Figure 14.1** Levers for ecosystem as strategy

| Boundaryless Organizations | | |
|---|---|---|
| ECOSYSTEM AS STRATEGY | Definition | Examples |
| **L** — Liquid Structures (Setting up a resource pool or network of staff on demand and autonomous self-directed teams) | Traditional linear value chains are giving way to a network of skills, resources and teams that are dynamically orchestrated to create value | Uber's workforce Skype |
| **E** — Economy of Platforms (Leverage external assets, Third-party apps, Communities and Crowds) | Moving from a linear product based business model to a platform based networked model that serves multiple stakeholders at the sametime | Apple Wikipedia AirBnB |

**Figure 14.2** Understanding the levers for ecosystem as strategy

# LEAPFROG

## Liquid Structures

The valuation of Nokia, the Finnish phone manufacturer, in the year 2006 was USD 140 billion[2]. It was the undisputed king of the mobile phone market at that time. Big disruption came in the form of Apple's iPhone in January 2007.

In a move to dominate mobile search and mapping, Nokia acquired Navteq in October 2007 for USD 8.1 billion. Navteq was a provider of digital map data for car navigation systems, mobile phones, and other platforms.

In the same year, another company called Waze, an Israeli company, was founded by Ehud Shabtai, Amir Shinar, and Uri Levine. Waze is the world's largest community-based traffic and navigation app. Unlike Navteq that depended on physical sensors installed on the roads, Waze relied on the GPS systems on the phones of the community of drivers. In just about a year, Waze had ten times the number of sensors on its network compared to Navteq.

In June 2013, Google acquired Waze for USD 1.1 billion and Microsoft acquired Nokia in April 2014 for USD 7.2 billion, valued lower than the amount it paid for the Navteq acquisition.[3] This is an example of how an organization, Waze in this case, unlocked exponential value by leveraging liquid resources of its users instead of investing on owning the resources needed to deliver the service. This model is also referred to as crowdsourcing.

Daren C. Brabham, the author of the 2013 book, *Crowdsourcing*, defined crowdsourcing as an "online, distributed problem-solving, and production model." It is a model where a function once performed by an organization is outsourced to many external networks of people. Wikipedia is a classic example of a crowdsourced online service that produces enormous impact on the internet. As of October 2017, Wikipedia is the world's fifth most popular website in terms of overall visitor traffic. Wikipedia is available in 299 languages and its worldwide monthly readership is approximately 495 million with annual revenues of more than USD 75 million. All of this has been achieved with a total employee count of just over 280 people.[4]

Creating liquid structures entails identifying skills, resources (monetary and technology), and teams that a business can access and utilize on-demand internally and externally without the need to have permanent structures that are associated with fixed costs.

Usage of liquid structures from a staffing perspective is not a new concept. This has been the default modus operandi for many industries for a long time now. We can take a leaf out of the Hollywood movie business here. A typical Hollywood movie is made on a budget of roughly USD 50 million and takes anywhere from 12 to 36 months and a team of 500 specialists. For this complex operation, a combination of freelancers, studio employees, diverse skillsets, and technology must be drawn upon. Liquid resources have been prevalent in the world of business consulting as well, where consultants come together for a specific client engagement and disband once the project is complete.

One of the crucial factors that necessitates setting up of liquid structures is the rapid change in role definitions and technologies in an organization. To keep up, companies are roping in freelancers who bring in specific skillsets to augment the capabilities of the organization.

Managing liquid teams requires an organization to develop a strong core that is built around the following principles:

**Rich Talent Analytics**: Deep understanding of the organization's needs and the current talent capabilities and identification of talent gaps in the rapidly evolving business environment.

**Rapid Talent Fulfilment**: Real-time matching of demand and supply of talent.

**Integrated talent platforms**: Managing a global, distributed workforce calls for an integrated talent platform that enables seamless operations and employee experience.

Figure 14.3 (a worksheet) shows a template where key activities and key resources are analyzed to see which of the fixed elements in these categories can be converted to liquid structures. For example, if manufacturing facilities are part of key resources of a company, there is an opportunity to develop a network of providers to supply on-demand instead of investing heavily in owning resources.

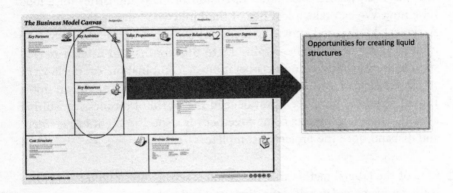

**Figure 14.3** Use the Key Activities and Key Resources sections of the business model canvas to identify opportunities for creating liquid structures (Strategyzer.com)

In a classic case of strategic outsourcing, Indian telecom major Airtel outsourced the contact center operations to Nortel in 2006. On the infrastructure and application services front, IBM was picked as the strategic outsourcing partner. All partners work on a revenue sharing basis, alleviating the need for fixed expenses for Airtel.[5]

# LEAPFROG

## Economy of Platforms

William El Kaim, in his book "Platform Thinking", defines platforms as a powerful type of ecosystem, typically created and owned by a single business or entity but designed to attract many other partners.

As noted earlier, the idea of a platform business is not new. Newspapers play the role of bringing readers and advertisers together. Television channels do the same for content producers, viewers, and advertisers. What is different now is that the current architecture is built on a digital backbone that can be deployed globally, in most cases in an open format where providers, partners and consumers can join the platform and start co-evolving, leveraging network effects.

In the article, "Pipelines, Platforms and the New Rules for Strategy", authors Marshall W. Van Alstyne, Geoffrey G. Parker and Sangeet Paul Choudary,[5] make a compelling point: When a platform enters a pipeline firm's market, the platform almost always wins.

The reason is that platforms leverage network effects, use data for orchestrating seamless interactions, and provide unbeatable convenience and choice for the customers. Pipeline companies, however, deliver value to their customers in a linear value chain, without any advantages of the network effect.

Many companies are now trying to transform into platforms. To achieve this, the authors say that organizations must undergo three crucial transitions:

## 1. From Resource Control to Resource Orchestration

This transition is a journey from the current model that revolves around building competitive advantage through access to scarce resources to orchestrating these resources from the community. The new journey is all about managing a network of producers, partners, and consumers. The key principle to remember is that while products have features, platforms have communities.

## 2. From Internal Optimization to External Interaction

Pipeline firms structure themselves in a linear value chain format around the product. Platforms, however, structure themselves around networks of external producers and consumers. The focus, then, is not internal optimization of fixed and variable costs of production. It is all about governing the interactions within the ecosystem.

## 3. From a Focus on Customer Value to a Focus on Ecosystem Value

Pipeline businesses view customers as the end-point of their value chain with customer lifetime value being the governing metric. But platforms seek to maximize the total value created in the ecosystem in an iterative, inclusive, and co-evolving process.

A platform is a foundational product that moves beyond product status by encouraging others to build, play, and iterate on top of it. The value and utility of the system is continually being discovered and expanded not just by the organization, but by its users and customers. So how does an organization know that it is ready to become a platform? The following list provides some guidance.

1. Can you identify at least two ecosystem players that may benefit through an interaction facilitated by you? In the case of Google search, millions of users use the search engine to search for things online. Advertisers also flock to the platform to get access to the users who use Google search.

2. Are there market segments that are unattractive to you but can benefit other players in the market? Apple's App Store has proprietary apps from Apple but also a plethora of apps adding

value to users in areas ranging from health to language learning to karaoke. By allowing external app producers, Apple effectively taps into the demand from the long tail without expending actual effort producing these apps.

3. Do you have a great product with loyal customers who want more? Google's Gmail allows other developers to develop utilities and plug-ins on top of its platform.

4. Can you increase the value of your products or services by augmenting the offering with products from third-party providers? Facebook opened its platform to many app developers to extend the functionality of the platform and provide a great experience to its users.

5. Companies that deal with physical products can build layers of ecosystems on top of their existing physical business model. These ecosystems can be customer focused (a user community for instance that delivers value beyond the company's own products) or supplier focused (creating a digital platform for suppliers to interact with the company and interact with others in the supply ecosystem).

Organizations typically choose to play one of three roles in the platform economy: the Matchmaker, the Architect, the Curator.

## 1. The Matchmaker

In this model, the platform owner aggregates different kinds of providers on one side and consumers on the other. Matchmakers create transactional marketplaces that seamlessly connect supply and demand. The 'What's in it for me' (WIIFM) for the supplier is a single window access to a large customer base and WIIFM for the consumer is the availability of large selection under one roof.

Success of the matchmaker model depends on the volume of buyers and sellers on the platform, frictionless transactions, and a robust mechanism for building trust in the ecosystem. Some of the key challenges for matchmakers in the early days are to identify the starting point for the virtuous cycle and then governing the pace of growth in the ecosystem once the tipping point is reached.

Examples: eBay, Uber

## 2. The Architect

Architects create platforms that allow third party developers to use the underlying toolkit to create innovative services and solutions that customers want. These platforms establish and enforce governance processes to make sure that the apps follow the guidelines of the ecosystem. The bulk of their focus goes towards making the development process easy for third-party developers. This model benefits the platform owner because the innovation risk lies with the external developers and there is limitless choice for the consumer. For the app developer, the platform provides route to market.

Success of the app ecosystem model depends on many factors: how open/closed the ecosystem is, the number of third-party developers, incentives for the developers to stay invested in the ecosystem and so on.

Example: Apple, Amazon Web Services

## 3. The Curator

Curator platforms provide exceptional customer experiences by defining the reference architecture for ecosystem partners and by orchestrating and personalizing the customer experience. Curation is done mainly through tightly governed APIs, social relevance, machine learning, and data analytics to serve the needs of the consumer in a personalized fashion.

Success of the curator platform depends on the effectiveness of the curation process and the motivational drivers of the end users.

Example: Facebook, Twitter, LinkedIn, Philips HealthSuite

To build ecosystems, an organization that aspires to be a platform owner must first identify the role it wants to play in its space and the different ecosystem entities that will participate in the ecosystem. There are typically four types of ecosystem entities: producers, consumers, partners and platform owners. Figure 14.4 shows how an organization needs to build the platform ecosystem.

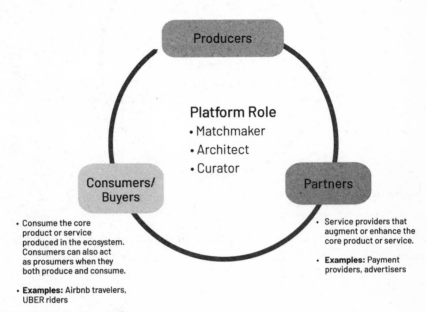

**Figure 14.4** Build a platform

Use Figure 14.5 (a worksheet) to identify the players in your ecosystem and the role your platform is going to play.

To build a platform, an organization must carefully craft the value proposition that attracts, retains, and grows the ecosystem partners and 'thereby' drive network effects. While doing so, the organization must identify the key activities needed to operate the ecosystem, the revenue streams and costs associated with each ecosystem partner. Sometimes, one ecosystem partner subsidizes the growth of the other partners. Google search, for instance, is free for the end users but advertisers pay for access to the users.

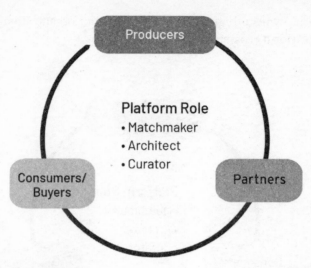

**Figure 14.5** Build a platform

Figure 14.6 shows the value proposition of entities in the Airbnb ecosystem.

## ENTITIES IN THE AIRBNB ECOSYSTEM

| | |
|---|---|
| PRODUCERS (ROOM OWNERS) | Utilize spare capacity |
| CONSUMERS | Choice, convenience and better price points |
| PARTNERS (HOUSEKEEPING PROVIDERS) | Steady revenue stream |

**Figure 14.6** Value proposition of entities in the Airbnb ecosystem

Figure 14.7 (a worksheet) provides a template to summarize the value proposition for each of your ecosystem entity.

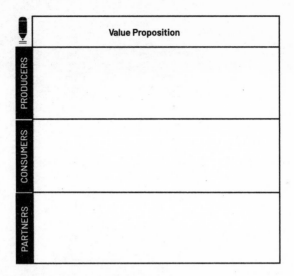

**Figure 14.7** Identify Value Proposition

We will use the inputs from this worksheet in the final step while putting together the Digital LEAPFROG business model.

# CHAPTER 15

# DATA AS STRATEGY

"The difference between oil and data is that the product of oil does not generate more oil, whereas the product of data will generate more (data)."

—Piero Scaruffi, Founding Director, Artificial Intelligence Center, California

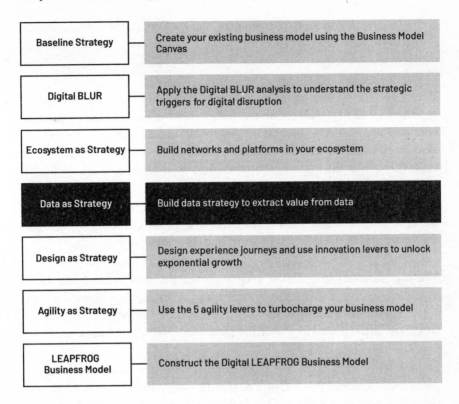

In the industrial age, consumerization and free trade generated enormous demand for goods and services. The core resources that enabled organizations to serve these needs were coal, oil, and electricity. Using these resources, organizations introduced automated machines to dramatically improve their productivity and achieve unprecedented scale.

In the digital age, however, connected customers generate enormous demand for new types of goods and services. The core resource that organizations use to serve these needs is data. Using this resource, organizations are introducing algorithms, programmable interfaces, AI, and machine learning to personalize their offerings and build hyper-scaled platforms. It is no surprise, therefore, that many experts call data the new oil.

We are producing unimaginable amounts of data every day on the internet and the pace of data generation just keeps growing exponentially year after year. The availability of broadband, the proliferation of smart devices, the amount of user generated content, and the falling costs of storage are the main drivers for the unprecedented explosion in data.

According to Deloitte's Center for the Edge, from the year 1992 to 2012, the cost of data storage fell from USD 569 to USD 0.03 per gigabyte[1], amounting to nearly a 19,000X drop in data storage costs.

Many companies struggle to keep up with the four 'V's of Big Data: Volume, Velocity, Variety and Veracity. As a result, studies show that only a small fraction of companies can harness data available with them to create the fifth 'V' and arguably the most important one, Value.

Digital born companies are built around data and analytics from the ground-up whereas incumbents deal with issues such as data silos, poor historical data, incomplete data, lack of data handling skills, to name a few. These are exactly the weaknesses of incumbents that digital born companies exploit when they attack traditional industries.

In this step of the Digital LEAPFROG process, companies can learn to navigate the limitlessly digitized world by deriving value from data. Following are the two LEAPFROG levers that can be used to achieve this outcome:

1. **Algorithms and Analytics:** This is a lever that is used to drive efficiencies and produce breakthrough insights for new product development, understanding customer needs, and governing the platform.

2. **Programmable Interfaces:** This is a lever that allows the organization to create loosely coupled connections with other players in the ecosystem to acquire new capabilities and drive network effects. This is what experts refer to as the 'API economy'.

Figures 15.1 and 15.2 describe the levers for limitless digitization.

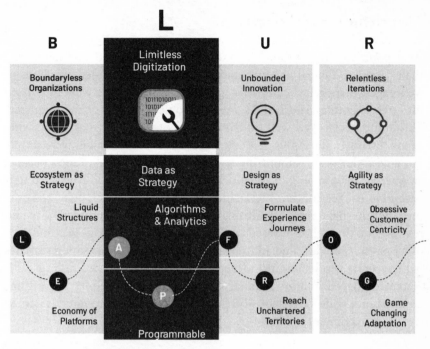

**Figure 15.1** Levers for limitless digitization

| | Definition | Examples |
|---|---|---|
| **Limitless Digitization** | | |
| **DATA AS STRATEGY** | | |
| **A** — Algorithms & Analytics (Driving eficiencies and producing breakthrough insights) | Use algorithms and analytics to derive value from data through efficiencies and insights | Netflix Facebook |
| **P** — Programmable Interfaces (Loosely coupled connections with other systems to acquire new capabilities and drive network effects) | Use APIs to offer capabilities to the external world and acquire new capabilities from ecosystem players | Apple Wikipedia AirBnB |

**Figure 15.2** Understanding Data as Strategy

# LEAPFROG

## Algorithms and Analytics

At a point in time, Yahoo was far more popular as an internet portal than Google. Yahoo was essentially a human maintained database of web pages, mapped to categories and subcategories that were organized into tree structures, much the same way books in a library are organized. This approach worked well till the number of webpages started growing exponentially in the 2000s. The employee organized databases were simply not able to keep up. Submitting webpages to be listed by Yahoo became an onerous task, arising in the mocking nickname Yahoo's frustrated user base gave it, 'Yet another hierarchical officious oracle'. Google, however, invented the page rank algorithm, which determines the popularity and relevance of the webpage based on the extent to which a page was linked to other pages. Google's algorithm became pretty good at matching searches with accurate results and it indexed pages in an automated fashion. This system outpaced Yahoo's manual system in no time. Today, algorithms are used in a wide variety of situations ranging from autonomous cars to wealth management.

Figure 15.3 shows the three disruption archetypes based on algorithms, data, and analytics.

Beside disruptions, companies are using big data and analytics to achieve many crucial business outcomes.

## Netflix Aces the New Product Development Challenge with Data

Media production is an industry where producing a winning product can be just a matter of sheer luck. Having great directors, A-list actors and big promotion budgets are no guarantee for success. In such an industry, the iconic success of 'House of Cards' produced by Netflix comes across as a revelation. The producers used big data analytics to foretell the success of the program. As of 2018, House of Cards is one of the most streamed content online with more than 40 million viewers.

| DISRUPTION ARCHETYPE | | UNDER ATTACK |
|---|---|---|
| BIG DATA ANALYTICS | Companies that can draw insights from massive amounts of data are able to unlock new value. | · Insurance<br>· Healthcare<br>· Infrastructure |
| HYPERSCALE REAL-TIME MATCHMAKERS | Companies use real-time information to enhance customer experience. | · Transportation & Logistics<br>· E-Commerce |
| PERSONALIZATION USING DATA | Companies tailor their platforms to match the unique needs of customers using recommendation engines and algorithms. | · Education<br>· Media<br>· Healthcare |

**Figure 15.3** Three disruption archetypes based on algorithms, data and analytics

Analyzing the director's track record, the popularity of the lead actor, Kevin Spacey (pre #metoo) and the audience reaction to the British version of the show, Netflix made the decision to purchase the rights for the show. With Netflix spending a reported USD 100 million to produce two 13-episode seasons of House of Cards, they needed 520,834 people to sign up for a USD 7.99 subscription for two years to break even. They brought in more than 17 million new members.[2] Going forward, Netflix intends to significantly increase its share of original content in its content catalogue.

## Google uses AI for Cost Optimization

In 2014, Google acquired DeepMind Technologies, a company with 75 employees at the time of acquisition, at an estimated price of USD 500 million[3]. DeepMind went on to develop AlphaGo, which became the first AI program to defeat a human professional player in the game of Go. DeepMind also reportedly enabled Google to reduce the cooling costs for its data centers by 40 percent, saving several hundred million dollars per year. Just this one application alone has the potential of paying off the steep acquisition price paid by Google. At the core of DeepMind is algorithms, machine learning and analytics.

## Deriving Value from Data

While these developments in data and algorithms are spectacular, ultimately what matters is the quality of analytics being done on the data. Figure 15.4 shows the five types of analytics that companies can use to derive value from data.

| TYPE | DESCRIPTION |
|------|-------------|
| DESCRIPTIVE ANALYTICS | What happened? |
| DIAGNOSTIC ANALYTICS | Why it happened? |
| DISCOVERY ANALYTICS | What is going on? |
| PREDICTIVE ANALYTICS | What will happen? |
| PRESCRIPTIVE ANALYTICS | What should you do? |

**Figure 15.4**  Types of analytics

To use analytics and derive value from data, we need to look at three types of data: core data, transaction data, and engagement data.

Let us use the example of a bank to understand the data types better. In the case of a bank, core data is the customer information, account status, and product information. Transaction data refers to the interactions that the customer has had with the bank and the insights that can be generated from the interactions. Engagement data refers to metadata on how the customer is engaging with the bank—through ATMs, mobile apps, branch banking; how long is the interaction; what does the customer look for; when does the interaction happen. Figure 15.5 shows the data layers in an organization.

ENGAGEMENT DATA

TRANSACTION DATA

CORE DATA

**Figure 15.5** Data layers in an organization

How can a bank derive value from data? Using core data, the bank can derive insights to develop new products or aggregate products to serve the needs of the customer. Using transaction data, the bank can start recommending new products and solutions. For example, if the bank knows that a customer is spending USD 100 every month eating Mexican food, it can start serving relevant deals to the customer. Using the engagement data, the bank can target its sales and marketing campaigns to attract prospective customers and retain existing ones.

A critical insight here is that the digital battle is shifting squarely to the engagement layer. Technology companies try to own the customer through the engagement layer and tend to commoditize the product and service providers. This explains why companies, both technology firms as well as incumbents, are making a mad rush towards becoming a platform to own customer engagement.

As mentioned earlier, Netflix used users' profiles, likes, and dislikes to produce its hit show 'House of Cards'. Amazon makes more than 35 percent of its revenues from the recommendation engine on its website.[4] Facebook obsesses over its users' engagement data. It continuously tweaks its news feed algorithm to make sure users are enticed to stay active on the network.

Figure 15.6 shows the various data layers and value drivers.

| DATA LAYER | VALUE DRIVERS | EXAMPLES |
|---|---|---|
| DATA | • Ad / Content Targeting<br>• Sentiment Analysis<br>• Customer Churn | Facebook tracks user engagement data to tweak its news feed algorithm |
| TRANSACTION DATA | • Price Optimization<br>• Cross-Selling / Up-selling<br>• Personalization<br>• Fraud Prevention | Amazon makes 35% of its revenues from the recommendation engine |
| CORE DATA | • Customer Lifetime Value New Product<br>• Development using Analytics | Netflix created the hit TV series 'House of Cards' based on its big data analysis |

**Figure 15.6** The three data layers and the value drivers

Use Figure 15.7 (a worksheet) to list down value drivers for different data layers in the organization and to create a compelling value proposition for different ecosystem players—producers, consumers, and partners.

| | List down the data types | Value Proposition |
|---|---|---|
| PRODUCERS | Engagement Data | |
| CONSUMERS | Transaction Data | |
| PARTNERS | Core Data | |

**Figure 15.7** Building Data Strategy

# LEAPFROG

## Programmable Interfaces

"We are building a digital society in which the virtual world and the physical world merge, and in which everyone and everything is connected."
—Paolo Malinverno, Gartner

In the networked business model, organizations create business ecosystems within and outside the organization to facilitate multiple ecosystem partners to co-evolve and create value for each other. Application Programming interfaces (APIs) are at the heart of such exchanges happening in the ecosystem.

APIs are the components that enable diverse platforms, apps, and systems to connect and share data with each other.

We live in an API economy today, where a set of business models and channels have been unlocked based on secure access of functionality and exchange of data between organizations. Today, digital businesses use APIs to connect with people, places, systems, and things as well.

A key insight here is that successful organizations in the digital world will view APIs as not just technology tools, but as sources of strategic value. APIs provide the following benefits to an organization:

# Building an Ecosystem

By allowing others to integrate with its platforms, a company can scale rapidly in terms of customer acquisition and offering innovation while keeping costs low. Walgreens offers an API, called the Photo Prints API,[5] that enables others to offer photo apps on its in-store photo printing platform. Walgreens' API gives developers a way to monetize their apps by earning commissions on each photo printed at a local Walgreens store location.

One of the key reasons behind Amazon's dominance over Walmart in the retail space is its open and modular architecture. As of 2015, Amazon had 33 open APIs and almost 300 variants of these APIs that enable e-commerce, payments, messaging, and search engine optimization. Walmart, however, had one, for the e-commerce tool.[6]

# Creating Differentiated Customer Experience

By integrating with features offered by a variety of providers, a company can offer choice, availability, and empowerment to its customers. Slack, the new-age collaboration platform, is enabling a thriving ecosystem of chatbots and integrated chat applications on top of the platform using the Slack API. This enhances the end-user experience, at the same time providing an opportunity for developers to monetize their innovations.

# Speed to Market

APIs allow an organization to use the data and functionality offered by other organizations to build new capabilities overnight. Uber leverages Google Maps through an API to enable its entire business model of matching drivers who have a vehicle with passengers who need a ride.

For payment apps, giving customers an easier way to send money to each other is a no-brainer and is easily enabled using APIs. Paypal, for instance, lets its users send and request money via a voice command with Siri. Simply say, "Hey Siri, send Bill $50 using PayPal." In 2017, the payment provider's annual payment volume amounted to 451 billion U.S. dollars.[7]

Reliance Jio is a fast-growing mobile operator in India. The company commercially launched its services on September 5, 2016 amid great fanfare. It is astonishing that within the first month, Jio acquired 16 million subscribers. This is supposedly the fastest growth witnessed by a mobile network operator anywhere in the world. Jio crossed the 50 million subscriber mark in 83 days since launch, subsequently crossing 100 million subscribers within 6 months.[8] While there are many reasons behind Jio achieving this level of success, one of the crucial success factors is the use of the Aadhaar platform. Aadhaar, setup by the Government of India, is the world's largest biometric system. It is a 12-digit unique identity number that can be obtained by residents of India, based on their biometric and demographic data. Jio used Aadhaar e-sign for digital signatures and Aadhaar eKYC for know your customer (KYC) processes. The entire process gets completed using Aadhaar APIs via biometric authentication. This enabled Jio to on-board customers in less than 3 minutes in a completely paperless fashion where the customer can walk into the store empty handed.

What is driving the rapid growth of the API economy is the availability of tools that promote programming ease, exponential growth of data, and the developer's mindset to focus on core features whilst using available APIs to rapidly build new capabilities without reinventing the wheel.

# API Based Business Models

Salesforce generates over 50 percent  of its revenues through APIs, eBay pulls in nearly 60 percent  and Expedia, over 90 percent.[9] John Musser of ProgrammableWeb, a leading source of information and news on APIs, says that to derive value through APIs, it is important for companies to answer the following questions:

1.  Why?
    What is the primary reason why a company would want to develop an API?
    Here are some top motivations for companies to develop APIs:
    a.  Offer APIs as a product
    b.  Acquire users
    c.  Enhance product capabilities
    d.  Drive innovation
    e.  Provide upsell opportunities

2.  Who?
    Who is the intended audience for the API?
    The audience could be internal to the organization, a close set of private partners or the public.

3.  What?
    What's the value being offered to the audience?
    Here are some examples of companies offering extraordinary value.

Figure 15.8 shows the value offered by companies based on the API based business model.

| VALUE | DESCRIPTION | EXAMPLE |
|---|---|---|
| SERVICE | Company offers a focused service through an API | Twilio offers a Cloud communications platform for building SMS, Voice & Messaging applications on an API built for global scale. |
| DATA | Company offers data for third party developers through APIs | Accuweather.com offers real-time accurate weather data |
| NETWORKS | Company offers access to its audience through APIs | Facebook offers app developers its network of users to develop apps for |
| FUNCTIONALITY | Company offers access to the marketplace that it controls | Salesforce offers its internal functionality to third party developers to develop innovative features |
| MARKET ACCESS | Company offers access to its internal functionality through APIs | EBay allows third party developers to access the market place through its APIs |
| TECHNOLOGY INFRASTRUCTURE | Company offers access to the technology infrastructure through its APIs | AWS offers cloud technology to millions of individuals and enterprises through its APIs. |

**Figure 15.8** Value delivered by API-based business models

## Pricing Models

Companies use various pricing models to monetize their API strategy.

1. **Free:** Company offers its APIs to ecosystem partners for free. Facebook is a popular example in this category.

2. **Developer Pays:** Company charges the developer for API access. Figure 15.9 shows the pricing models used by companies to monetize their API strategy.

| MODEL | EXAMPLE |
|---|---|
| PAY-AS-YOU-GO MODEL | Amazon Web Services offers its APIs in a pay as you go model without any minimum fee |
| TIERED MODEL | MailChimp offers multiple packages for their mail sending APIs |
| FREEMIUM MODEL | The Business version of the Google Maps API is charged whereas the individual version is free |
| UNIT BASED | Different APIs are charged differently based on units. Sprint uses this model for monetizing its APIs. |
| TRANSACTION BASED | Stripe and Paypal charge a transaction fee for their APIs |

Figure 15.9 Pricing models used by companies to monetize their API strategy

3. **Developer gets paid**: Company pays the affiliate for generating traffic using its APIs. Amazon Associates Program lets developers earn a cut out of the sales that they drive to Amazon.

4. **Internal Usage:** The most powerful use case for APIs is within the organization. Amazon, for example, requires businesses inside the company to interact with each other using APIs.

# Formulate API Strategy

The following questions need to be answered for formulating an API strategy:

1. What are the strategic reasons for embarking on the API strategy?
2. Who will be the primary beneficiaries of the APIs?
3. What is the value that you will offer to the ecosystem?
4. What is the revenue model for the API strategy?

Use Figure 15.10 (a worksheet) to identify areas for exposing APIs to ecosystem partners and consuming APIs from other partners.

| Identify 3 areas where you can expose APIs for your ecosystem partners |
| 1. |
| 2. |
| 3. |

| Identify 3 areas where you can consume APIs |
| 1. |
| 2. |
| 3. |

**Figure 15.10** Identify three areas where APIs can be exposed and consumed

Figure 15.11 shows the value proposition of entities in the Uber ecosystem coming out of data as strategy.

Use Figure 15.12 (a worksheet) to fill in the value proposition arising out of data as strategy for all the entities in your ecosystem.

| ENTITIES IN THE UBER ECOSYSTEM | VALUE PROPOSITION |
|---|---|
| PRODUCERS (CAB DRIVERS) | Use ride demand data to help drivers plan routes |
| CONSUMERS | Use cab location data to make cabs available on demand for customers |
| PARTNERS (GOOGLE MAPS) | Revenue stream based on real-time mapping data |

Figure 15.11  Value proposition arising from data for entities in the Uber ecosystem

| | List down the data types | Value Proposition |
|---|---|---|
| PRODUCERS | Engagement Data | |
| CONSUMERS | Transaction Data | |
| PARTNERS | Core Data | |

Figure 15.12  Building Data Strategy

# CHAPTER 16

# DESIGN AS STRATEGY

"Most people make the mistake of thinking design is what it looks like. People think it's this veneer—that the designers are handed this box and told, 'Make it look good!' That's not what we think design is. It's not just what it looks like and feels like. Design is how it works."

—Steve Jobs, Founder, Apple

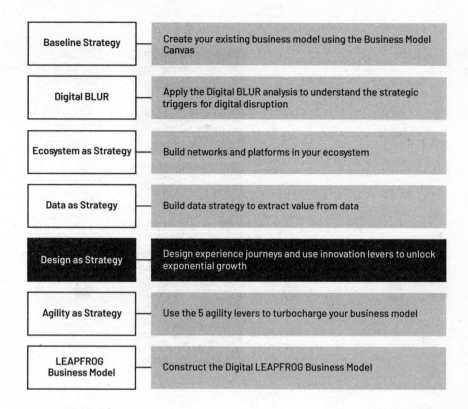

In this step of the Digital LEAPFROG process, companies must focus on formulating experience journeys and reaching unchartered territories to tap into exponential growth. Design is the center piece of this step.

Figures 16.1 and 16.2 show the two levers for Design as Strategy:

1. **Formulate experience journeys:** Using this lever, companies can create experience journeys for all ecosystem partners to identify opportunities for creating new value

2. **Reaching unchartered territories:** Using this lever, companies can embrace exponential growth by utilizing the 12 innovation levers

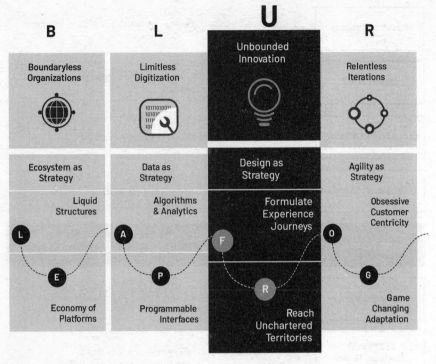

**Figure 16.1** Design as Strategy

| | Definition | Examples |
|---|---|---|
| **Unbounded Innovation** | | |
| **DESIGN AS STRATEGY** | | |
| **F** Formulate Experience Journeys (Focus on creating stellar experience for ecosystem stakeholders) | Identify the steps in the journey for your ecosystem partners and create an exceptional experience for them | AirBnB embraces Design Thinking |
| **R** Reach uncharted territories (Achieve exponential growth by using innovations that unlock 10x potential) | Embrace exponential growth by driving economic value, experience value and ecosystem value | Uber has many exponential levers in its business model |

**Figure 16.2** Levers for Design as Strategy

# LEAPFROG

## Formulate Experience Journeys

### Home Buying Experience

Buying a home is one of the most important decisions people make. It is also one of the most harrowing experiences we go through. We visit many properties with a realtor, pick something we like, and then knock on the doors of many banks to get a valuation and submit a mortgage application, hoping for the home loan to get approved. The whole process is laborious and leaves buyers stressed and often overwhelmed.

Recognizing this pain point, DBS Bank (Hong Kong) announced the launch of DBS Home 360 in September 2017. DBS Home 360 is the first banking mortgage app in Hong Kong to leverage the power of virtual reality (VR) in a mobile format to revolutionize the way people buy homes.[1] The 'Properties for me' feature of the app helps users shortlist suitable properties based on their price points and preferences. The Virtual tour feature lets users virtually tour properties from the comfort of their home. The app leverages professional valuation firm Cushman & Wakefield's database to provide preliminary indications of property market values. It also provides real-time updates and notifications on properties that the user is interested in. The budget calculator feature allows users to immediately obtain an estimate of how much they can expect to pay, including stamp duty, commissions and related fees. Users can then instantly find out if they qualify for a mortgage based on their finances and have a bank representative follow up and assist with the formal application. This is a great example of how an organization has understood the end-to-end experience journey of a customer and has made the entire process hassle-free and efficient whilst adding a fun experiential dimension too, clearly standing out from the crowd.

In the Digital BLUR world where innovation has overarching impact on multiple industries all at once, it is important for companies to understand the customers' view point. Innovation is of limited consequence if ultimately the customers' unmet, and in most cases, unstated needs are not satisfied. The trick is in discovering those needs as early as possible.

Furthermore, customer experience is turning out to be a crucial differentiator for companies. While products and features can be replicated in no time, customer experience is harder to replicate. According to a 2014 assessment by Design Management Institute, design-led companies such as Apple, Coca-Cola, Nike, and others have outperformed S&P 500 over the past 10 years by an extraordinary 219 percent.[2] Design-led firms produce these results through exceptional focus on customer experience journeys by embracing design thinking.

## Understanding Design Thinking

Great design produces great desire. Great design introduces a 'wow' factor that makes products more attractive and services more desirable for customers. Going beyond products and services, the design way of thinking can be applied to systems, processes, employee experience, and partner ecosystems. In fact, organizations these days encourage leaders and managers to think like designers and apply design principles to the discipline of work itself.

> In a nutshell, design thinking is a human-centered, prototype-driven innovation process.

It offers a structured framework for understanding the needs of customers and pursuing an iterative process to create real value. The design thinking process involves the use of empathy for discovering the needs of the customer, framing the opportunity, generating creative ideas, prototyping, testing, refining, and then ultimately scaling the solution.

Design thinking uses a classic blend of right brain and left brain thinking to create desired outcomes that benefit the customer. According to Tim Brown, the CEO of the hallowed design firm IDEO, "Design thinking can be described as a discipline that uses the designer's sensibility and methods to match people's needs with what is technically feasible and what a viable business strategy can convert into customer value and market opportunity".[3]

Figure 16.3 shows the three crucial dimensions of design thinking: desirability, viability and feasibility.

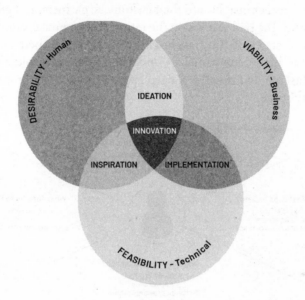

**Figure 16.3** Three crucial dimensions of design thinking: Desirability-Viability-Feasibility

Design thinking facilitates a business to use the desirability-viability-feasibility lens to arrive at an innovative solution. While desirability nudges the designer to think about human needs, viability and feasibility are about business and technical considerations, respectively. Getting this mix right holds the key for breaking the classic trade-off between innovation and efficiency.

By using the three lenses, design thinking minimizes the uncertainty and risk of innovation by engaging customers or users through a series of prototypes to learn, test, and refine concepts. Design thinkers rely on customer insights gained from real-world experiments, not just historical data or market research.

# Empathy Map for Understanding Human Needs

An empathy map, shown in Figure 16.4, is a collaborative tool that teams can use to gain a deeper insight into their customers, partners, and producers in the ecosystem. The tool focuses on the rational, economical, emotional, and psychological states of the stakeholder to understand their motivational triggers. This allows companies to understand the stakeholder's world in a holistic fashion and develop a deep appreciation of the problem or the opportunity space.

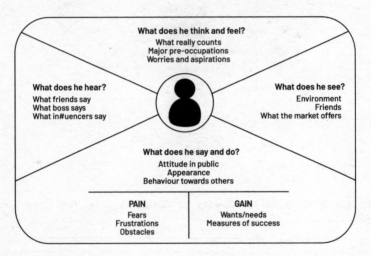

**Figure 16.4** Empathy map

# Customer Experience and Journey Maps

While the empathy map is a great tool to understand the problem and opportunity space associated with customer needs, it is important to bear in mind that it is only the first step in the process.

The customer typically goes through a long journey with the organization. At each of the touch points, from discovery to on-boarding to demand–supply matching to service fulfilment to on-going engagement, the customer goes through a host of experiences. It is important for an organization to map these experiences on to the empathy map to visualize what the end-to-end customer experience looks like and what can be done to create wow experience in every step of the way. Figure 16.5 shows a sample customer experience journey.

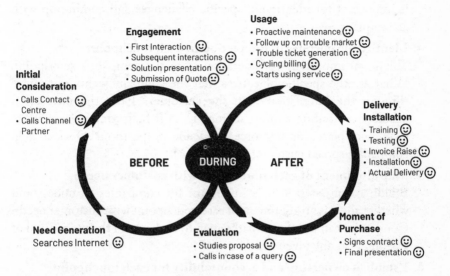

**Figure 16.5** Sample customer experience journey

# Creating Customer Experience Maps

Here is a checklist that companies need to work with to be able to create customer experience maps.

1. **Identify major customer segments**
   Customer experience is directly a function of the needs and behavior of a customer segment. These attributes could vary widely from one segment to the next. It is, therefore, important to start with a clear understanding of who the customer is. Developing a buyer persona is very helpful as a start.

2. **Create an exhaustive inventory of all customer touchpoints**
   The touchpoint inventory should include touchpoints across channels, both physical and virtual. These touchpoints are the moments of truth for the organization where experience is primarily created. It is important that the customer experience is standardized across channels.

3. **Categorize touchpoints based on the lifecycle stage of the customer**
   Companies need to categorize touchpoints based on the various stages in the customer journey: Discovery/On-boarding Demand–Supply Matching/Service Fulfilment On-going Engagement. This is important for identifying specific challenges and coming up with action plans.

4. **Identify the purpose of interaction in each touchpoint**
   This is an important consideration from the company's standpoint. What are the specific objectives that the company wants to achieve through the interaction with the customer? Does the interaction enable cross-selling and up-selling? Does it help companies educate customers better or reinforce the value proposition? Does it help companies spread customer advocacy?

5. **Map alignment of each touchpoint with customer needs**
   Building onto step 4, it is important for companies to understand whether there is an alignment of each touchpoint with customer needs. Companies can use the empathy map to understand the motivation of customers at any given touchpoint.

6. **Establish ownership and accountability for each touchpoint**
   Many companies make the mistake of assigning accountabilities based on channels. This leads to fragmentation of customer experience and lack of ownership within the company. It is important to assign a team to each touchpoint rather than a channel.

7. **Gather data**
   Companies can use a host of tools and methodologies to gather data from across different touchpoints in the customer experience process. Surveys, interviews, blog comments, testimonials, web analytics, social media activity, customer support interactions, and sales team interactions are popular sources for customer interaction data.

8. **Analyze customer data**
   Once the data is in place, it is time to analyze the data to extract patterns and meaning. Where are the high points in the interaction with customers? Where are the pain points? What's causing the variability in experience? What are the unstated and unmet needs of the customers at each touchpoint?

9. **Set new customer experience targets**
   Post the analysis phase, companies need to identify customer journeys where improvements can be made. Thorough investigation of specific

customer journeys can be initiated. It is important to set revised targets for teams owning different touchpoints based on findings. Targets can be in terms of Net Promoter Scores (NPS) or Cross-selling/Upselling numbers.

10. **Create an action plan**

    A company's success in this process primarily revolves around the ability to rally cross-functional teams to work on specific touchpoints that produce a wow experience for customers. An integrated experience can be produced for the customers when responsibilities for customer delight are mapped to functional teams for each customer touchpoint.

Figure 16.6 shows the five phases of the journey—discovery, onboarding, demand–supply matching, service fulfilment and engagement—in Uber's ecosystem.

| | DISCOVERY | ONBOARDING | DEMAND–SUPPLY MATCHING | SERVICE FULFILLMENT | ENGAGEMENT |
|---|---|---|---|---|---|
| PRODUCERS (DRIVERS) | • Communication to earn more money | • Registration process, account setup | • Getting enough rides to meet financial objective | • Getting paid fairly and on time | • Rewards based on number of trips and customer feedback |
| CONSUMERS (RIDERS) | • Easy discovery of cabs on the Uber app | • Easy booking process | • Availability of cabs as shown in the app | • Safe ride to destination, Hassle-free billing | • Upgrades on cars, deals. |
| PARTNERS (PAYMENT PROVIDERS) | • Agreement on commercial terms between Uber and payment provider | • Integration through APIs | • Ability to scale transaction volumes | • Smooth functioning of APIs as promised | • Discounts based on volumes of transactions |

**Figure 16.6** Experience journey for ecosystem entities in the case of Uber

Use Figure 16.7 (a worksheet) to identify the needs of each of the ecosystem stakeholders, producers, consumers, and partners, at various points in their experience journey, starting from discovery to on-boarding to demand-supply matching to service fulfilment to on-going engagement.

| | Discovery | Onboarding | Demand - Supply Matching | Service Fulfilment | Engagement |
|---|---|---|---|---|---|
| PRODUCERS | | | | | |
| CONSUMERS | | | | | |
| PARTNERS | | | | | |

**Figure 16.7**  Design Experience journey for ecosystem entities

# LEAPFROG

## Reach Unchartered Territories

It is clear by now that digital disruption is not just a technology phenomenon. It is a business model phenomenon enabled by technology. There are three main types of customer value that digital disruptors are focusing on at the core of their business models. These are the three Es: economic value, experience value and ecosystem value. The innovation grid in Figure 16.8 builds on the three Es and highlights 12 innovation levers that an organization can use to explore unchartered territories and unlock new value.

| INNOVATIVE PRICING MODELS | CO-CREATION | SHARING ECONOMY |
|---|---|---|
| Use of disruptive pricing models like Freemium, Free, Pay as you Go, Quick Delivery pricing etc  Linkedin: Freemium model | Involving a 3rd-party in the processes and ideation segment of product/ service development  Threadless: freelance designers design UBER: Liquid workforce of drivers | Economic system in which assets or services are shared between private individuals, either free or for a fee  Lending Club: peer to peer lending Filecoin: hard disk space sharing via blockchain |
| COST REDUCTION VIA EFFICIENCY | HYPER PERSONALIZATION | AUGMENTED CAPABILITIES |
| Reducing cost by leveraging data and APIs  Uber: Matching of riders with drivers | The use of data to provide more personalized and targeted products, services, and content  Youtube: Playlist creation | Leveraging the capabilities of another organization through the usage of APIs  GE-Predix: PAAS industrial IOT platform |
| DISINTERMEDIATION | DIY EMPOWERMENT | NETWORK EFFECT |
| Enabling a direct path from producer to consumer, removing middlemen  Zenefits: SAAS for managing HR, removing insurance brokers from middle | Empowering customers by giving them Do-it-yourself solutions  Redbus: Selecting seats Moto Maker/Moto Mods: customize your phone | A phenomenon whereby a product or service gains additional value as more people use it  Instagram: network created around user generated content |
| REAL-TIME PRICING OPTIMIZATION | INSTANT GRATIFICATION | DATA ORCHESTRATION |
| Using real-time retail insights to determine the price at which your products are sold  UBER: pricing optimization based on traffic and availability | Providing instant satisfaction to customers using agile methods  Amazon: Amazon Return Policy | Leveraging real time data to provide exponential value to customers, partners  AXA: use of drones to analyze real time data and disburse insurance |
| ECONOMIC VALUE | EXPERIENCE VALUE | ECOSYSTEM VALUE |

**Figure 16.8** 12 Innovation Levers

# Economic Value Experience Value Ecosystem Value

## Economic Value

Digital disruptors deliver extraordinary value to the customer by systematically lowering the cost of a product or service.

Kevin Kelley, in his thought-provoking book, "The Inevitable", points out how dematerialization is a major trend that allows companies to produce products with much less amount of physical matter leading naturally to lower costs.[4] He quotes the example of a product from the physical world to illustrate this phenomenon. Beer cans are pretty much the same shape and size that they have always been, but their weight has been reduced by almost a third by using better design and material. The difference is even more dramatic when we look at digital objects. Instead of saving rows of books on a shelf, we have one device that stores all of them—Amazon Kindle. Instead of racks of CDs, we now stream music online when we need it.

Furthermore, profit pools in various industries are partly a function of information asymmetries between the provider and the consumer. Today, digital disintermediates are introducing unprecedented transparency in the purchasing process for customers. Travel sites, such as Expedia.com and lending sites, such as BankBazaar.com, exert immense pricing pressure on incumbent companies by providing radical pricing transparency to the users.

Transportation apps such as Uber and accommodation services such as Airbnb do not own the assets in their respective industries, but they also exert immense pricing pressure on incumbent providers such as the airline companies, car rental companies, and hotels.

The connected customer phenomenon that we discussed earlier is giving the customer a view of the best deals available in the market at a click of a button. Companies have no choice but to respond to competitor moves in an aggressive fashion to gain customer attention. Ultimately, the customer wins.

The following are some key innovation levers that deliver economic value to the customer.

## 1. Innovative Pricing Models

In his book, "Free: The Future of Radical Price", Chris Anderson states that giving away stuff for free has been a long-standing attention-grabbing stunt. In today's business environment, companies can build sustainable business models by giving things away for free instead of charging for them. This is not just applicable to digital businesses. As it turns out, companies across domains are taking the 'Free' business model seriously. Internet based business models are, in fact, a race towards free.[5]

In addition to the free business model, we are also witnessing a growth in the pay-as-you-go model that promises to keep the up-front costs low for the customers and the payment to the provider is based on the usage of the products or service. Most of the software as a service (SaaS) companies such as Salesforce, HubSpot, and so on, operate on this model. Rolls-Royce Holdings, the world's second largest manufacturer of aircraft engines, sells business outcomes, namely engine uptime, rather than equipment as a capital expense.[6] This is enabled by real-time analytics that is available on product usage.

## 2. Cost Reduction Via Efficiencies

Digital disruptors use liquid networks, extended workforce, and physical resources to keep their costs low and are happy to pass on their cost savings to their end customers.

According to Juniper research, chatbots could help trim costs for businesses by more than USD 8 billion per year by 2022.[7] Industries which manage large volumes of human interactions such as banking, healthcare, and retail, can benefit enormously from this new technology. Juniper predicts that between 75 percent and 90 percent of queries in these industries will be dealt by chatbots within the next five years resulting in tremendous cost savings. In the wealth management space, robo-advisors are starting to revolutionize the business. Instead of paying high salaries for experts, companies are now starting to rely on robo-advisors that do the job at a fraction of the cost. This development not only helps drive down costs but also helps customers get faster and more accurate answers for the problems they face.

## 3. Disintermediation

Companies are using digital platforms to enable a direct path from the producer to the consumer, removing middlemen. This is not a new phenomenon. Dell effectively used this playbook in the '90s, first using telephones for enabling direct orders from customers and later through the internet.[8] Today, with the proliferation of the platform model and access to connected customers, companies can do this very efficiently and effectively.

## 4. Real-time Pricing Optimization

Thanks to advancements in real-time data capabilities, companies can provide real-time pricing updates and benefits to customers.

The most familiar example of real-time pricing is the surge pricing model used by transportation apps such as Uber to balance demand, and supply during peak hours. The airline industry has been using this model for quite some time now. This is now being used in a variety of other industries. Electricity prices change from hour to hour, but currently, customers are forced to pay the same price no matter when they use electricity. Real-time pricing lets consumers adjust their electricity usage accordingly.

In modern retail, shoppers are armed with real-time information from price comparison sites. In such a situation, real-time pricing (RTP) becomes a crucial strategy for companies. RTP is used to respond to external factors such as competitor pricing, conversion rates, traffic, and demand. The pricing is also guided by internal factors such as supply, sales goals, brand image, and more. Amazon is a poster child for dynamic pricing. It dynamically reprices products every 10 minutes to consistently be the lowest price in the market.[9] This helps the company expand its market share at a furious pace.

# Economic Value Experience Value Ecosystem Value

## Experience Value

Today's customers no longer differentiate between physical and digital when it comes to the experience they expect. The expectations have risen significantly because they are well-informed on the best practices across industries. Today's customers value convenience, control, real-time delivery, and hyper-personalization. The great unbundling phenomenon has led to a situation where customers can pick what they really want and pay for only what they use. This presents significant challenges for companies that straddle the physical and the digital world to focus on customer touchpoints and provide consistent experience across channels.

The following are the innovation levers that heighten experience value for customers:

### 5. Co-creation

Going beyond the traditional model where they are the end-point of the value chain, customers are today actively involved in co-creating the product along with the producers. Facebook's richness as a platform comes from the daily posts from its 1.5 billion+ users. We contribute to the richness of the platform and the platform further curates what we experience based on our participation. This is the virtuous cycle in customer experience that causes great stickiness on online platforms.

Threadless.com is a great example of co-creation where freelance designers and amateurs can contribute to the design of apparel and monetize their creation in the process. The opportunity to co-create is giving rise to prosumers—a new breed of consumers who produce as well.[10] Threadless holds weekly design contests to crowdsource popular designs from the community. The company prints only T-shirts with the most popular designs and sells them to their large customer base. By doing so, Threadless obviates the need to hire artists to create T-shirt designs. It does not need to do extensive marketing because the designers themselves spread the word in their network to solicit votes. Furthermore, by outsourcing production, Threadless minimizes its inventory costs. This asset light model allows Threadless to scale rapidly without a corresponding increase in its cost structure.

## 6. Hyper-Personalization

Market segmentation is an industrial-age concept that has long served us well. The concept is coming under tight scrutiny for relevance and usefulness in the digital age. Today, with access to not just demographic data but also access to highly personal behavioral data, companies are now transitioning from a 'one to many' model to a 'one to one' model. Be it marketing communication or product configuration, one size fits none in the digital age.

Generali, an insurance provider, launched a new death and disability insurance plan, called Vitality, in the German market in July 2016.[11] The uniqueness of this plan is that it ties in the behavioral data of the customer—gym visits, diet preferences, smoking habits—with the insurance premium that they pay. The company is convinced that this will promote a healthy lifestyle with their customers and help build a strong bond between the company and the customers.

Hyper-personalization is fast entering the field of medicine. Creating a complete human genome sequence has gone from a price of USD 20 million in 2006 to less than USD 1000 in 2016, and the cost keeps dropping thanks to the falling prices for computational resources.[12] With the price point now within the grasp of the masses, soon, we will get personalized medicines for different ailments.

## 7. DIY Empowerment

Be it selecting seats on a plane or a bus or making devices and spare parts through 3D printing, digital technologies empower customers to follow the 'Do It Yourself' (DIY) model to create experiences and things that they really want.

Until 2009, 3D printers were mostly limited to industrial uses, but post the expiration of the patents around the technology, the annual sale of 3D printers is growing rapidly. 3D printing is predominantly used by car manufacturers, doctors, dentists, architects, among others. 3D printing is spawning off-design hubs that allow individuals and businesses to rapidly prototype new designs before the production can be scaled up.

Moto Maker is an excellent example for DIY empowerment. Motorola's online studio gives customers the control to custom design their MotoX smartphone.[13]

### 8. Instant Gratification

Digital has unleashed a slew of products that allow customers to herald a product or service at the touch of a button. From cabs to plumbers to food, everything is just a touch away on the mobile. From communication to coordination to commerce, companies have to keep pace with the customers on where and when they want their products or service.

WeChat, founded by Tencent in 2011, has built an infrastructure for mobile commerce within the walls of a single app. It is a one-stop shop for pretty much any need a customer might have, from booking cabs to buying groceries. For WeChat's 600 million monthly users, this seamless experience is a daily fact of life. The real-time instant gratification in connecting with people, brands, places, and things is unparalleled. So much so that in June 2018, WeChat added a one-click divorce option to its services.[14] WeChat is one of the most successful ecosystems available in the mobile format today.

# Economic Value Experience Value Ecosystem Value

## Ecosystem Value

While economic value and experience value have been the core focus of industrial companies for a long time, what is truly unique in the digital age is the concept of ecosystem value. The value delivered by networks and ecosystems is not linear, it is exponential. For this reason, ecosystem value is also called exponential value. What is unique about exponential value is that customers also participate in value creation and benefit economically in the process.

The following are the innovation levers that use ecosystem value:

## 9. Sharing Economy

Sharing Economy is an economic system in which assets or services are shared between private individuals, either free or for a fee.

- Airbnb is a great example for sharing economy where individuals can rent out rooms, homes, or an entire castle.
- DogVacay is a service where dog owners can leave their pets with a host who will take care of the dog. Owners save money, and the dogs still enjoy a caring environment.
- Getaround is a peer-to-peer car sharing service where people can rent cars from their neighbors.
- Lending club's peer-to-peer network allows people to get loans from other network members.

## 10. Augmented Capabilities

One of the key ways in which digital disruptors achieve exponential growth is by leveraging data and capabilities from other providers using application programming interfaces (APIs). This allows the organization to quickly acquire new capabilities without any upfront investment and loss of time. Many online platforms, for instance, use authentication APIs provided by Google and Facebook to capture the social profile of the user during the login process.

## 11. Network Effect

As explained earlier, network effect is a phenomenon wherein a product or service gains additional value as more people use it. Some of the early examples of this include the fax machine telephone and so on. where the value of the device increased with the number of people owning and using the device.

When properly used, network effects lead to a zero-dollar marketing campaign. Unicorns such as WhatsApp and Instagram have built multi-billion-dollar businesses without spending a dime on marketing. Individual entrepreneurs in-turn use these platforms to market their products and services to achieve the viral effect.

Platforms such as Quora, Kaggle, and Innocentive allow companies to tap into the power of large crowds that supply large volumes of data, ideas, and innovative solutions.

## 12. Data Orchestration

Data orchestration is all about how companies leverage real-time data to provide exponential value to ecosystem partners. Using data, customers and partners can take decisions that drive profits for them or help reduce their costs.

John Deere, the global manufacturer of agricultural equipment, has empowered farmers to use real-time data to improve their practices. MyJohnDeere.com offers data not only from the machines that farmers own but also financial and weather data that help them make informed decisions on their farming practices.[15]

Let us now understand how digital businesses are using these 12 innovation strategies in a combinatorial fashion.

Figure 16.9 shows how Uber uses sharing economy (leverage third party assets), data orchestration (real time traffic routes), and real-time pricing optimization (surge pricing) to drive growth.

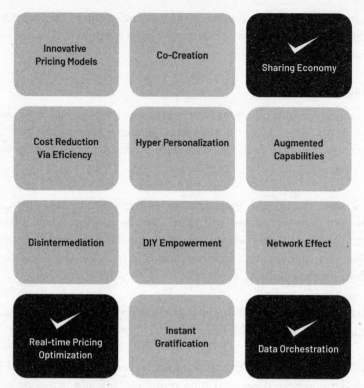

**Figure 16.9** Uber's Innovation Strategy

Figure 16.10 shows how Amazon uses innovative pricing models (Amazon Prime), cost reduction via efficiency (drones for delivery), hyper-personalization (recommendation engines), augmented capability (offering AWS to other businesses) and instant gratification (one-click checkout) to drive growth.

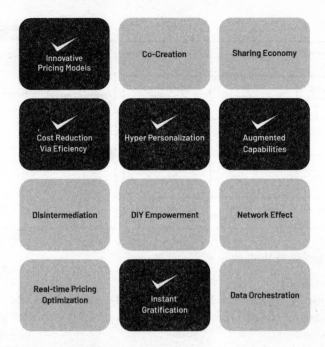

**Figure 16.10** Amazon's innovation strategy

Use Figure 16.11 (a worksheet) to identify design strategies that will help the organization reach unchartered territories. Pick the most relevant innovation levers from the template given in this figure and identify the key value proposition for each ecosystem entity—producers, consumers, and partners.

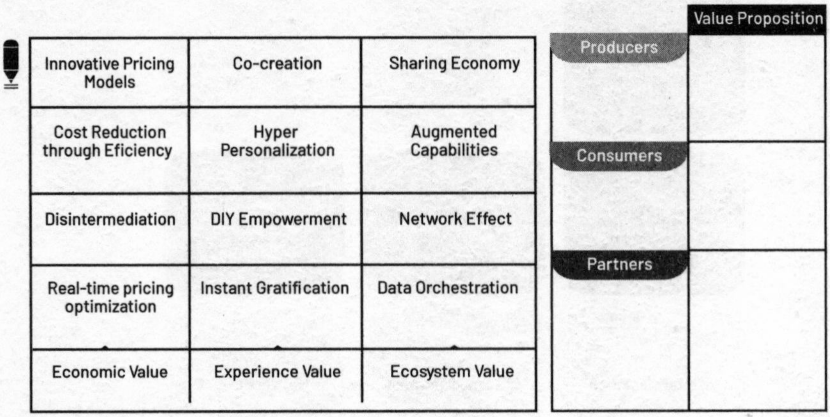

| | | | | Value Proposition |
|---|---|---|---|---|
| Innovative Pricing Models | Co-creation | Sharing Economy | Producers | |
| Cost Reduction through Eficiency | Hyper Personalization | Augmented Capabilities | Consumers | |
| Disintermediation | DIY Empowerment | Network Effect | | |
| Real-time pricing optimization | Instant Gratification | Data Orchestration | Partners | |
| Economic Value | Experience Value | Ecosystem Value | | |

**Figure 16.11** Design as Strategy

In the following Figure 16.12 (a worksheet), summarize the value proposition arising from Design as Strategy for various entities in the ecosystem.

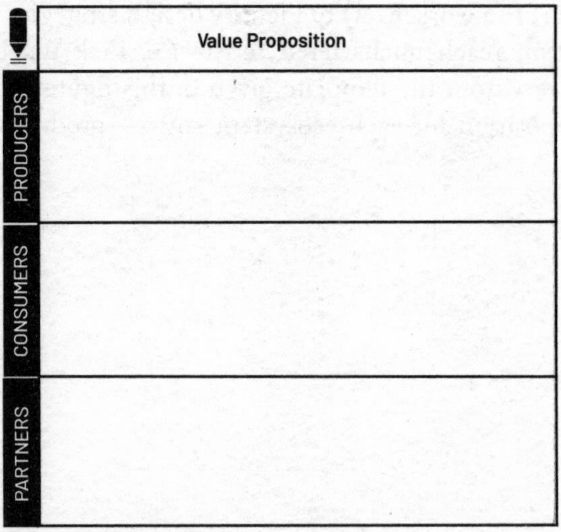

| | Value Proposition |
|---|---|
| PRODUCERS | |
| CONSUMERS | |
| PARTNERS | |

**Figure 16.12** Building Design as Strategy

# CHAPTER 17
# AGILITY AS STRATEGY

"It is not the strongest of the species that survives, nor the most intelligent that survives. It is the one that is most adaptable to change."

—Charles Darwin

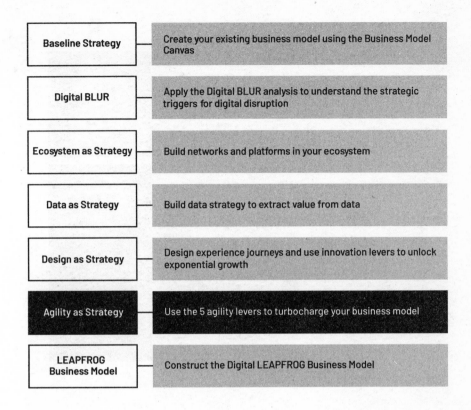

| Baseline Strategy | Create your existing business model using the Business Model Canvas |
| Digital BLUR | Apply the Digital BLUR analysis to understand the strategic triggers for digital disruption |
| Ecosystem as Strategy | Build networks and platforms in your ecosystem |
| Data as Strategy | Build data strategy to extract value from data |
| Design as Strategy | Design experience journeys and use innovation levers to unlock exponential growth |
| Agility as Strategy | Use the 5 agility levers to turbocharge your business model |
| LEAPFROG Business Model | Construct the Digital LEAPFROG Business Model |

This step in the LEAPFROG strategy process is all about responding to the relentless iteration phenomenon by embracing agility as a key strategic response. There are two LEAPFROG levers, as shown in Figures 17.1 and 17.2, that come in handy for implementing agility as strategy.

1. **Obsessive customer centricity:** This is a lever that helps an organization craft the right value proposition for a customer using lean principles.
2. **Game-changing adaptation:** This is a lever that helps an organization navigate the VUCA environment and produce breakthrough innovation.

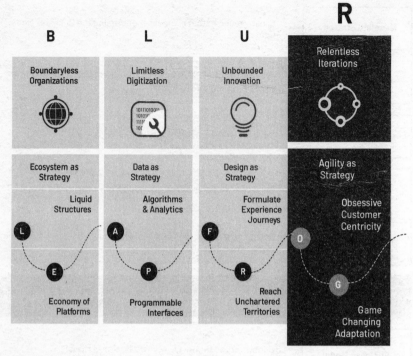

**Figure 17.1** Levers for Agility as Strategy

| Relentless Iteration | | Definition | Examples |
|---|---|---|---|
| **AGILITY AS STRATEGY** | | | |
| **Obsessive Customer Centricity**<br><br>(Use lean principles to craft a highly client centric value proposition) | | Constantly evaluate value proposition using a value canvas | SouthWest Airlines<br>Nintendo |
| **Game changing Adaptation**<br><br>(Thriving in a VUCA environment by building, measuring, learning in rapid iterations) | | Build learning agility, resource agility and change agility to create escape velocity from status quo | Amazon, Google keep re-inventing themselves |

**Figure 17.2** Understanding Agility as Strategy

# Leapfrog

## Obsessive Focus on Customer Value

Agile methodology has been in existence for quite some time in the arena of software development. But now, the concept of agile is spreading across a wide range of industries and functions, including boardrooms.

As noted earlier, there are two kinds of agility that organizations are building. The first is operational agility to ensure that products and services are built and delivered cheaper and better. The next is strategic agility, which refers to the ability of a company to pivot to new business models, new strategic positioning, and produce breakthrough products and services in a flexible, seamless manner.

Agile is a strategic response to many important changes that have happened to businesses in the digital world.

## Connected Customers Demand Real-time Personalization

Customer delight is no longer just a nice-to-have. It is an existential imperative. Organizations must generate real-time, personalized, and frictionless experience at scale. This entails a deep change in the way an organization operates.

## VUCA Environment Leads to Disaggregated Work

The VUCA (Volatile, Uncertain, Complex and Ambiguous) environment has led to businesses adopting a model where small autonomous teams work iteratively in short cycles with tight feedback loops from customers and users. This ensures that teams are always working on value-adding tasks.

# Agile Project Management Enables Disaggregation of Work

Agile is not just an IT change. It is a change in the way the entire organization thinks, decides, and acts. Collaborative agile project management tools allow organizations to chunk up tasks and closely track the progress across multiple teams.

## The Great Unbundling

Due to the unbundling of various industries into many small niches, agile start-ups with maniacal focus on specific areas are innovating at breakneck speed. Larger organizations have no choice but to empower smaller, agile teams to respond faster.

## New Breed of Competitors

Digital native organizations have been built with the customer at the center. Large incumbents, however, have optimized their organizations for operational efficiency. Unless the incumbents learn to offer stellar experience for their customers in real time and simultaneously break the trade-off between internal efficiencies and customer experience, it is going to be a tough fight for survival.

Many organizations, small and large, are now using agility as a source of competitive advantage.

Spotify is a classic example of an 'agile born' company. The 2,500+ employee organization that streams music to more than 100 million people globally, has organized itself into 100-member teams that continuously deliver innovations that customers love.[1]

Ericsson, the 140-year-old Swedish firm, manages networks for the world's telecom companies. Before 2011, the company used to build systems in long five-year iterations. Now, the company has embraced agile methodology and has organized itself into 100-member teams that deliver results in three-week cycles. This has led to rapid development of systems leading to faster realization of revenues.[2]

In 2015, ING Bank went through a massive agile transformation. The transformation had four key pillars[3].

a.  Agile way of working where managerial bureaucracy is removed. IT and commercial teams sit together in the same buildings, divided into squads, constantly testing what they might offer their customers.

b.  Changes in organizational structures with redefined roles and governance policies.

c.  Continuous delivery model where new software releases happen on a very frequent basis (every two weeks rather than having five or six big launches every year).

d.  New people model where a new agile performance management model was introduced. Within this, a manager's salary and bonuses do not depend on the size of the projects or the number of direct reports he or she manages, but on the value that is being delivered to the customer.

The organization has re-structured itself in the form of squads, tribes, and chapters. Squads are the core agile teams, tribes are a collection of squads with interconnected missions, and chapters are teams that develop expertise and knowledge across squads.

To operate in an agile manner, companies need to develop a keen understanding of what their customers really value. This may seem obvious at first, but it is surprising how many business leaders do not have a good appreciation of how exactly they are adding value to their customers. To understand what the customers value, we will use the value curve proposed by W. Chan Kim and Renée Mauborgne in their book, *Blue Ocean Strategy*.[4]

According to the authors, "The value curve or strategic profile is the basic component of the strategy canvas. It is a graphic depiction of a company's relative performance across its industry's factors of competition. A strong value curve has focus, divergence as well as a compelling tagline." Figure 17.3 shows how the value curve of Southwest Airlines looks.

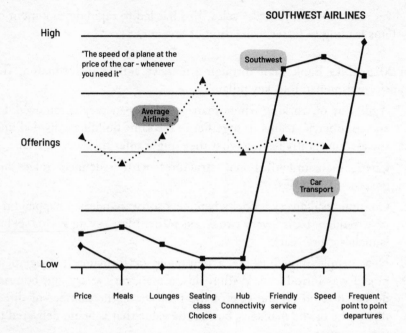

**Figure 17.3** Value Curve of South West Airlines
(Adapted from Chan Kim and Renée Mauborgne's Blue Ocean Strategy book)

On the X-axis, we see the factors of competition and on the Y-axis, we see the value offered by competitors in the industry marked as high, medium, or low. We notice that the value curve of South West Airlines shows the differentiated positioning of the airline in the industry and the catchy tagline says it all: "The speed of a plane at the price of a car—whenever you need it". Blue Ocean Strategy offers a framework, shown in Figure 17.4, for organizations to eliminate, reduce, raise, and create (ERRC) factors of competition to differentiate from the competition and to deliver value to clients that exactly matches their needs.

Essentially, obsessive customer centricity allows an organization to be 'value agile' and 'service agile'. Value agility is all about having the ability to re-configure the value being offered to the customer and service agility is all about doing things in a hyper-responsive manner that delights the customer.

| ELIMINATE | RAISE |
|---|---|
| Which of the factors that the industry takes for granted should be eliminated? | Which factors should be raised well above the industry's standard? |
| REDUCE | CREATE |
| Which factors should be reduced well below the industry's standard? | Which factors should be created that the industry has never offrered? |

**Figure 17.4** The Eliminate-Raise-Reduce-Create grid
(Adapted from Chan Kim and Renée Mauborgne's Blue Ocean Strategy book)

# Leapfrog

## Game Changing Adaptation

While the agile methodology described above is a great way to deal with the product improvement process, what is also equally important is the ability for an organization to produce game changers that are more than just about product improvements.

There are a few key issues to be addressed here:

1. Game changing adaptation happens when market-creating innovations are produced by an organization. Market-creating innovations are essentially about creating new offers or entering new market segments or exploring new channels, or a combination of all the above. It is unlikely for market-creating innovations to happen when individual agile teams are working on features of products or services in a continuous improvement mode. Organizations need a quantum jump.

2. Game changing adaptation is more likely to come from focusing not on the existing customer base, but the non-customer base. Obsessive customer centricity alone cannot do the trick.

3. Game changing adaptation can lead to cannibalization of the company's existing business model. It requires organizational clarity

and leadership will to deal with the conflicts between the now and the next. Uber, for instance, is talking about driverless cabs by 2030 while at the same time, trying to expand its network of drivers across countries.[5] This is a great illustration of simultaneous focus on the 'now' and the 'next'.

4.  Game changing adaptation requires senior leadership commitment for placing a big bet on the unknown and allowing a different time horizon for producing results compared with business as usual.

In the lean start-up model, author Eric Ries talks about the build-measure-learn cycle mainly to establish product-market fitment for early stage start-ups.[6] The same principle can be used by large organizations as well. What is different, however, in the case of large organizations is that there is often a conflict when it comes to resource allocation between the existing business model and the emerging business model. There is also an intense change management challenge that larger organizations must navigate.

Considering the above, the following three-step process provides a good recipe for larger organizations to produce game changing adaptation.

## Step 1. Learning Agility

Adaptation is closely linked with learning. Unless the organization is hyperaware of internal capabilities and external developments it is not possible to evolve. On a continuous basis, organizations must identify the top three hypotheses around their new value proposition, new business models, and new customer segments.

## Step 2. Resource Agility

Once the learning is validated, the organization must find a way to staff, fund, and allocate management time for the adaptation. Resource agility is the ability of the organization to reconfigure systems and rapidly redeploy resources. Without this crucial step, most innovations will languish in cold storage.

## Step 3. Change Agility

Change agility is all about an organization's ability to manage the potential frictions between the now and the next. How will multiple business models coexist within the organization with a clear transition plan from one to another? This has a lot to do with the culture of the organization and the mindset for change.

Figure 17.5 shows how learning agility, resource agility, and change agility drive the overall agility of the organization.

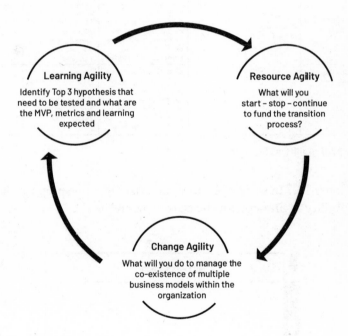

**Figure 17.5** Drivers of Agility as Strategy

Figure 17.6 identifies the five agility areas: learning agility, resource agility, change agility, value agility, and service agility, and the crucial action items for organizations to achieve agility.

| AGILITY AREAS | LEAPFROG LEVER | VALUE PROPOSITION | FOCUS | HOW? | START-STOP-CONTINUE |
|---|---|---|---|---|---|
| VALUE AGILITY | Obsessive Customer Centricity | | Change value proposition to the customer / producer / partner in an agile fashion | Reconfigure Value Canvas on a regular basis | |
| SERVICE AGILITY | | · Rapid Innovation<br>· Reduced Cost<br>· Faster Delivery | Deliver products and services in a rapid fashion | Deliver rapid results to customers through Algorithms and Automation | |
| LEARNING AGILITY | | | Being hyperaware as an organization | Perform BLUR analysis regularly | |
| RESOURCE AGILITY | Game changing adaptation | | Internal capability to reconfigure business systems and redeploy resources rapidly | Use Liquid Networks and APIs to overcome strategic rigidities | |
| CHANGE AGILITY | | | Ability to manage multiple business models at the same time and transition from one to the next seamlessly | Leadership clarity, change methodology and culture wired for adaptation | |

**Figure 17.6** Agility as Strategy

Use Figure 17.7 (a worksheet) to summarize the value proposition arising from Agility as Strategy for the ecosystem entities.

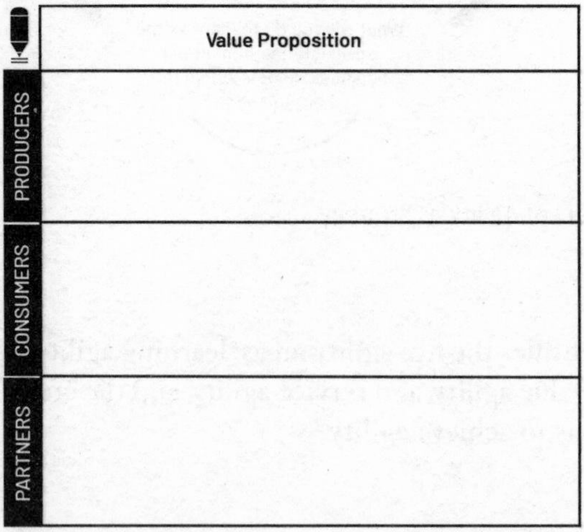

**Figure 17.7** Building Agility as Strategy

# CHAPTER 18

# DIGITAL LEAPFROG BUSINESS MODEL

"In today's era of volatility, there is no other way but to reinvent. The only sustainable advantage you can have over others is agility, that's it."

—Jeff Bezos, Founder, Amazon

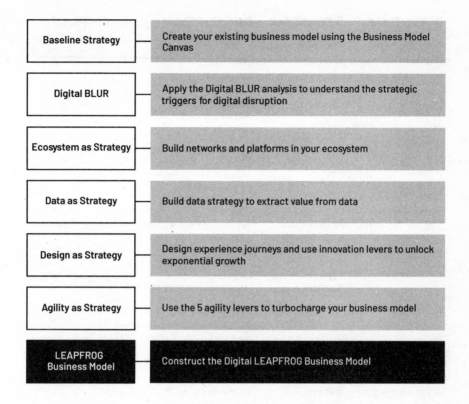

This is the last step of the Digital LEAPFROG process where the inputs from all the previous steps get integrated into a unified canvas.

Figure 18.1 shows a quick summary of the four strategic responses.

In this step, all the inputs from previous steps are aggregated into a unified canvas called the Digital LEAPFROG Canvas, as shown in Figure 18.2.

| STRATEGIC RESPONSE | STRATEGIC LEVER | DESCRIPTION | EXAMPLES |
|---|---|---|---|
| ECOSYSTEM AS STRATEGY | Liquid Structures | On-demand resource pool (People, Technologies and Teams) | Uber Kaggle Innocentive |
| | Economy of Platforms | Leverage External Assets, third Party Apps, Communities, Crowds | GE Predix Philips HealthSuite Wikipedia |
| DATA AS STRATEGY | Algorithms and Analytic | Driving efficiencies and breakthrough insights | Google Adwords |
| | Programmable Interfaces | Loosely coupled connections (often API based) with other systems to acquire new capabilities and drive network effects | Facebook APIs |
| DESIGN AS STRATEGY | Formulate Experience Journeys | Focus on creating experience in the ecosystem | Apple |
| | Explore Unchartered Territories | Achieve exponential growth by unlocking 10x potential | AirBnB WeChat |
| AGILITY AS STRATEGY | Obsessive Client Centricity | Use lean principles to craft a highly client centric value proposition | Zappos DropBox |
| | Game Changing Adaptation | Thriving in a VUCA environment by building, measuring and learning in rapid iterations | Amazon |

**Figure 18.1** Summary of strategic responses to Digital BLUR

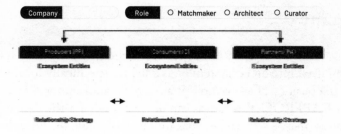

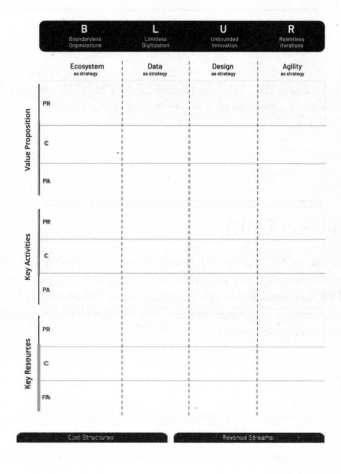

Producers (PR) Consumers (C) Partners (PA)

**Figure 18.2** Digital LEAPFROG canvas

# Company

The canvas can be created either for an entire company that wants to transform itself into an ecosystem or as a hybrid specifically for the digital parts of the business. For example, if a tractor manufacturer wants to do a Digital LEAPFROG, this canvas can be specifically for the digital part of the business (maybe a social network for farmers) while the linear business model of making and selling the tractor can continue.

# Role

The role that the organization wants to play in the networked business model is marked at the top of the Digital LEAPFROG business model. The organization can choose to play one of the following roles:

a.   Matchmaker

b.   Architect

c.   Curator

# Ecosystem Entities

As opposed to the traditional business model canvas where the roles and contribution of ecosystem entities are harder to capture, the Digital LEAPFROG canvas allows you to capture those complexities elegantly. In this section, list down the various ecosystem entities along with relationship strategies for each of them.

# Producers

List down the producers that are part of your ecosystem. For example, for Airbnb, room owners are the producers. For Uber, cab drivers are the producers. For Apple, which uses the hybrid business model, app developers are the producers.

## Consumers

List down the customers that you will focus on. For Airbnb, for instance, room seekers are consumers. For Uber, ride seekers are consumers. For Apple, consumers are the owners of Apple devices.

## Partners

List down the partners that will be part of your ecosystem. For example, payment gateways like PayPal are partners for many digital ecosystems. For Airbnb, housekeeping companies maybe be key partners. For Uber, Google is a key mapping partner.

## Relationship Strategy

List down the ways in which you will attract, retain, and grow the relationship with the producers, consumers, and partners in your ecosystem. The strategy might include offering incentives, discounts, managing the community, customer support, premium plans, and offering tool kits to the ecosystem entities. It is important to focus on the relationship strategy to ensure that the network effects are well established.

## Ecosystem as Strategy

**Value Proposition (VP):** Write down the key value proposition that you will offer to various players in your ecosystem. In the case of Airbnb, for instance, room owners make extra money from their underutilized resource. Room seekers get choice and availability at various price points.

Tip: Transfer the value proposition identified in Figure 14.7.

**Key Activities (KA):** List down the key activities that you will perform to execute ecosystem as strategy. Community management is emerging as a key activity for companies that build ecosystems.

**Key Resources (KR):** Write down the key resources you will need to establish ecosystems. This could be tools that you offer to the ecosystem, data that enables you to deliver value to the ecosystem partners or the liquid workforce in the ecosystem.

## Data as Strategy

**Value Proposition (VP):** Write down the value proposition you will offer to producers, consumers, and partners using core, transaction, and engagement data. Also, identify the value proposition that can be exchanged through APIs with the ecosystem. Facebook, for instance, offers APIs to developers to build apps on top of the platform.

Tip: Transfer the value proposition identified in Figure 15.12.

**Key Activities (KA):** List down the key activities you will perform to execute data as strategy. This might include things like setting up a data architecture to capture data from various channels, establishing data governance within the company, developing APIs to allow others to connect with your systems and using others' APIs to gain capability.

**Key Resources (KR):** The key resources that are needed are the APIs, data architecture, and talented data scientists who can help derive value from data.

## Design as Strategy

Write down the value proposition that you will offer to producers, consumers, and partners using experience maps and the 12 innovation levers. Uber, for instance, can engage its driver community through better incentives for trips and rewards for better feedback score from riders.

Tip: Transfer the value proposition identified in Figure 16.11.

**Key Activities (KA):** List down the key activities you will perform to execute design as strategy. This might include things like setting up metrics to measure customer experience, developing customer journey maps.

**Key Resources (KR):** List down the key resources that are needed to execute design as strategy. These resources typically are customer-centric teams and data to track customer experience.

# Agility as Strategy

**Value Proposition (VP):** Write down the value proposition that will deliver to various ecosystem entities by using agility as a strategic lever. Zappos, for instance, uses agility as a core principle to deliver superior value to its customers.[1]

Tip: Transfer the value proposition identified in Figure 17.8.

**Key Activities (KA):** List down the key activities that the organization will be involved in and key resources that the organization will leverage to execute agility as strategy. Key activities in the context of agility could involve adopting agile project management, embracing agile organization structure, and driving strategic agility through learning agility, change, and resource agility.

**Key Resources (KR):** Key resources for achieving agility will include agile teams and access to resources that can be leveraged on a need basis.

# Cost

Fill out the cost drivers for operating the ecosystem. Some existing cost structures may get eliminated and new costs could get added. For example, production costs could go down because producers in the network foot the bill for actual production. At the same time, costs for managing the ecosystem could go up. Costs for infrastructure development and setting up data architecture might also go up.

# Revenues

List down the revenue streams that power the ecosystem. For instance, data can be monetized in interesting ways to generate more revenues. Transaction fee could be charged for transactions that happen on the platform.

Figure 18.3 shows the Digital LEAPFROG business model for Airbnb.

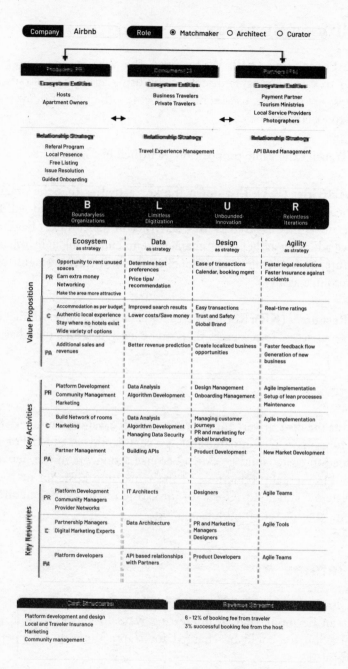

**Figure 18.3** Digital LEAPFROG canvas for Airbnb

SECTION 4

# DIGITAL FAULT LINES

# CHAPTER 19

# FAULT LINES IN STRATEGY EXECUTION

"In some ways, incumbents have a lot of benefits over new players, over start-ups. They have customers, they have great data, they often have a brand. They have financial resources, which a start-up may not have. The question is, can all of those capabilities and assets be deployed in a way that allows you to defend against new attackers as digital disrupts your industry?"

—Paul Willmott, Director at McKinsey

# The Digital Race is On

While digital born organizations are marching towards domination of various industries, many industry leaders such as GE, ANZ Bank, and Walmart are also racing to become technology companies. It is now common for many chief executives of large traditional companies to say, "We are a technology company first". Marianne Lake, the CFO of JP Morgan, an American multinational investment bank and financial services company, says that her firm is more than just a bank. JP Morgan allocates USD 9 billion yearly for technology, spending a sizeable chunk on technology investments, cyber security, and proactive risk management. JP Morgan Chase has a team of 40,000 technologists, including 18,000 software developers creating intellectual property.[1]

Will a digital disruptor go mainstream, or will a mainstream company go digital? This is the key question that will settle the debate on this race.

Here is how the race is stacked up in various industries.

1. Paytm, a Fintech disruptor in India, is learning to become a bank, whereas State Bank of India is learning to become a technology company.

2. Tesla is a technology company learning to become a mainstream automobile company, whereas Ford is an automobile company learning to become a technology company.

3. Apple is a technology company learning to make and sell smartwatches, whereas TAG Heuer is learning to become a technology company in partnership with Google and Intel.[2]

The same pattern is playing out in many industries. The key question from the incumbent standpoint is how they can acquire the capabilities of technology start-ups in an accelerated fashion.

# Digital Fault Lines

Organizations must overcome various fault lines, some internal and others external, to succeed in the digital transformation process. Internal fault lines largely revolve around the structure, process and information flow, goal, and incentive alignment. External fault lines are mainly relating to how the organization manages conflicts that can arise while operating a digital ecosystem.

The following Figure 19.1 shows the internal fault lines associated with each dimension of BLUR. Let's first dig deeper into the internal fault lines.

| **PHENOMENON** | **INTERNAL FAULT LINES** |
| --- | --- |
| BOUNDARYLESS ORGANIZATIONS | Structure and Talent |
| LIMITLESS DIGITIZATION | Streamlining Process and Information Flow |
| UNBOUNDED INNOVATION | Managing the innovation process through goal alignment |
| RELENTLESS ITERATION | Managing the now, next and the new |

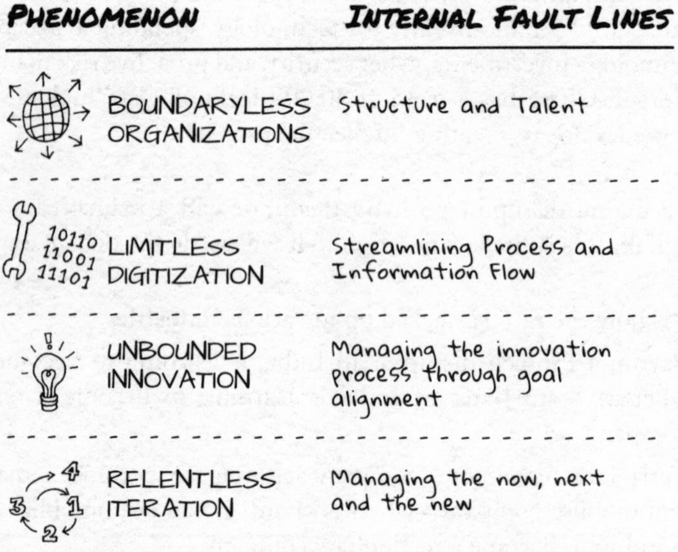

**Figure 19.1** Internal Fault Lines

# Internal Fault Line #1: Structure and Talent

The pyramid organization structure has served well at organizing us in many domains in life from religion to politics all the way to the modern organization. The stability that the pyramid provides helps industrial organizations to minimize variability and ensure execution excellence. In this paradigm, the leader at the top has the vision for the business and the rest of the organization operates in a command-and-control environment to execute the vision.

As critical information became widely available, thanks to the spread of the Internet, employees across the organization started contributing in a strategic fashion. Decentralization of decision making was imperative to keep pace with industry changes. The matrix organization, consequently, was the natural evolution from the pyramid structure. Command-and-control was still the modus operandi but successful organizations learned to instill a culture of collaboration between specialists and generalists to excel in their mission.

In the digital age, however, traditional pyramid and matrix structures are giving way to a more diffused form of organization where teams are self-organized and different specialized teams come together in an on-demand fashion to work on business challenges.

Mozilla develops several world-class products including Firefox, one of the world's top browsers that are offered in the open source format. Unlike a traditional pyramid shaped organization, Mozilla has a diffused structure with a few community managers and thousands of participants, called Mozillians, operating virtually from across the world connected by a common purpose.[3]

Back in the day, organizations were structured around a product in a sequential, value chain format: procurement, production, quality, sales and distribution. To control the value chain, most companies built competencies in-house to gain an edge over competitors. Today, companies are trying to organize around customers, with members from different functions collaborating as one team to serve the needs of the customer in a personalized fashion. This collaboration also extends beyond the boundaries of an organization. For this to work, control mindset must give way to a collaborative mindset. Orchestrating value with diverse teams within and outside the organization has become a crucial success factor.

## Talent Attraction and Retention Challenge

It is hard to attract and retain digital talent in traditional, nondigital cultures. Companies address this challenge through a variety of approaches. Some companies address this challenge by creating group-wide centers of excellence that act as digital hubs for the entire organization. Others create a separate entity to push the digital agenda forward. Some companies acquire smaller start-ups, in a move called acquihire, to build digital talent quickly. Others, like Accenture and Microsoft, support digital start-ups through accelerators and venture funds to gain access to disruptive technologies and teams.

- The UK department-store chain John Lewis bought Buy.com in 2001 to gain digital capabilities and later integrated it with the core business.[4]

- Domino's has focused on technology investments to radically transform its pizza delivery operations. The company has hired 400 software and analytics professionals to explore new delivery capabilities using drones, autonomous cars, and mobile ovens.[5]

- Walmart established Walmart Labs, its digital business, as a separate entity with its purpose to move from BAU (business as usual) to pushing the digital envelope. Walmart Labs built Electrode, an application platform that powers Walmart.com, a site that handles 80 million monthly visitors and offers 15 million items for sale.[6]

## Ownership Challenge

Digital transformation is an enterprise-wide, cross-functional endeavor. In many cases, however, it is not clear who owns digital transformation in an organization. In many organizations where digital marketing is the starting point, Chief Marketing Officers (CMOs) become the de-facto custodian for digital transformational efforts. Over time, when digital projects get kick-started across other parts of the organization, CMOs do not often have an understanding of what digital could mean in those parts of the organization. To deal with this challenge, many organizations are creating a new role called the Chief Digital Officer (CDO). This is also a way for traditional organizations to bring in outside talent with a digital mindset.

Walgreens, the 116-year old US-based pharmacy and retail chain with revenues north of USD 117 billion, hired a digital expert, Ms. Deepika Pandey, to turbocharge digital customer experience.  She has been instrumental in driving omni-channel revenues for the company which has recently topped USD 47 billion.[7] She spearheaded the acquisition of drugstore.com, which still operates as a pure-play e-commerce entity. The acquisition has helped Walgreens acquire critical talent to drive digital initiatives. In addition, drugstore.com shares its digital infrastructure with the company's existing site, walgreens.com. By utilizing common infrastructure between the online business and the offline business, the company is achieving significant operational efficiencies.

Ms. Pandey has been able to successfully orchestrate omni-channel retail for Walgreens using the power of digital technologies. Her finding is that when consumers engage through multiple channels, the customer lifetime value to the organization increases significantly. According to her, while customers who engage with the brand in-store and online are 3.5 times more valuable, customers who engage in-store and online through a mobile device are 6 times more valuable.

The 2017 Altimeter research shows that 28.2 percent of companies have the Chief Information Officer (CIO)/Chief Technology Officer (CTO) spearheading digital transformation in their organizations, compared with CMOs at 22.9 percent. CEOs come third with 20.1 percent. The number of Chief Digital Officers driving digital transformation is at 13.1 percent. The research also shows an increase in companies where digital transformation is driven by the Chief Innovation Officer.[8]

Overall, the issue around ownership of digital transformation seems to be highly contextual to the organization and there seems to be no consensus around who should own digital. Ultimately, this is a crucial decision that has a huge impact on the success of the transformation process.

To sum up, it is important for organizations to design the right structure that promotes collaboration both internally and externally. It is also imperative that they get a clear answer for the question on 'who owns digital' to create ownership and enhance success of digital transformation initiatives.

## Fault line #2: Streamlining Process and Information Flows

The fault line around process and information flows rears its ugly head in the form of turf wars between the business units who may have opposing views on data formats, customer personas, digital infrastructure, and governance policies. To deal with this situation, organizations must develop a clear understanding of their operating models and adopt the right data governance model, without which, there will be no clear game plan for what should be shared and what should be kept independent between various business units.

Building on the research by MIT CISR,[9] Figure 19.2 shows the four digital operating models that companies can use based on the levels of coordination and integration required between their business units.

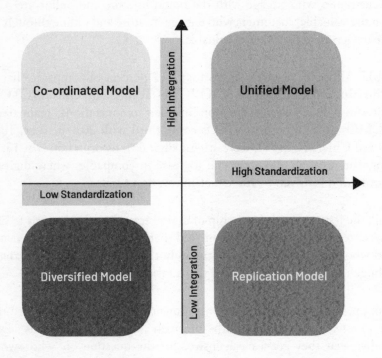

**Figure 19.2** Operating model framework
(Adapted from MIT CISR Research)

Think about a large conglomerate like GE. They have numerous business units, each having its own processes and data sources that have very little in common with the rest. Such businesses are said to be operating in a diversified model, where the business units neither follow standardized process nor do they integrate their data or processes.

Have you ever wondered how after opening a saving account with the bank, the credit cards team gives you a call to make an offer? Although these are two different business units within a bank with different processes, they maintain a single view of the customer by integrating their data systems. Such organizations, said to be operating in a coordinated model, are high on integration and low on process standardization. In these organizations, different business units integrate with each other for accessing common data, but they might follow different business processes.

In the case of franchise-based business, such as Subway or Marriott, process standardization is very high across the board. Every business unit does things the same way across the board. Integration, however, is low because these business units do not share common customers. Such organizations are said to be operating in a replication model.

Finally, there are organizations such as United Airlines, that have highly standardized processes across their businesses and by design, their business units must integrate their systems. After all, when the flight takes off in New York, the London office needs to know about it. Such organizations that have high process standardization and high levels of integration are said to be operating in a unified model.

Based on the operating model, one can come up with the right digital governance model, thereby ensuring that the different business units are aligned during the transformation process and unnecessary conflicts are avoided. Figure 19.3 shows the digital operating model framework.

## Digital Islands

As noted earlier, in a conglomerate such as GE or Proctor & Gamble, business units operate in a diversified fashion where the need for standardization and integration between them is low. In such organizations, digital efforts are typically orchestrated by the center of excellence (COE) team at the enterprise level. The COE is responsible for guiding different business units on their respective digital strategies and establishing best practices for digital governance. Individual businesses may have their own digital teams to address their specific business challenges. This model is referred to as the digital islands model.

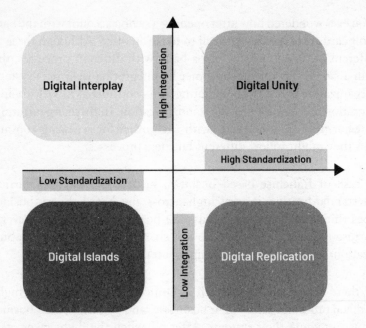

**Figure 19.3** Digital operating models

## Digital Interplay

Amazon has a single view of the customer across its many business units. This allows the company to understand customers' needs holistically and present various recommendations seamlessly. For organizations such as Amazon, that have business units operating in a coordinated fashion where the processes are not standard across business units, but integration requirements are high, the digital interplay model works well.

In this model, business units share data freely between each other through a common centralized data warehouse. They may also share APIs amongst themselves to leverage capabilities across the enterprise. This allows an organization to develop a single view of the customer and paves way for cross-selling and up-selling opportunities.

Jeff Bezos issued a mandate at Amazon in the early 2000s along the following lines:[10]

- All teams will henceforth expose their data and functionality through service interfaces.
- Teams must communicate with each other through these interfaces.

- There will be no other form of inter-process communication allowed: no direct linking, no direct reads of another team's data store, no shared-memory model, no back-doors whatsoever. The only communication allowed is via service interface calls over the network.

- It does not matter what technology they use.

- All service interfaces, without exception, must be designed from the ground up to be externalizable. That is to say, the team must plan and design to be able to expose the interface to developers in the outside world. No exceptions.

The mandate closed with: *Anyone who doesn't do this will be fired. Thank you; have a nice day!* This approach made it possible for teams to have seamless interactions that naturally fostered the culture of collaboration and connection.

## Digital Replicators

For organizations that operate in the replication model, where the process standardization requirement is high, and the integration requirement is low, companies can use digital replicator approach internally to ensure that all business units and functions approach digital in a standardized fashion. In this model, the platforms, tools, and practices are centralized and implemented uniformly across all business units. There is, however, very little integration of data across the different business units.

## Digital Unity

For organizations that operate in the unification model, where the standardization and integration requirements are both high, companies can use the digital unity model to govern their digital transformation. In this model, the entire company uses the same digital backbone for all its operations across business units. Unlike the replication model, in this case, data is shared seamlessly across all parts of the organization. Many banks, for instance, are building a platform that integrates products from various business units onto their platform and the data about the customer is shared seamlessly across the business units of the bank.

If a company is clear on the digital operating model that makes sense at the enterprise level, strategies around information and process flows between the business units can become clearer. The rationale for sharing, integrating, and standardizing is then clear to all the stakeholders. This can go a long way in minimizing the turf wars that can happen between business units.

## Fault line #3: Managing the Innovation Process through Goal Alignment

Major issues can crop up during the digital transformation process when there is poor goal alignment between mainstream business and digital business within an organization.

The performance of most traditional business functions is measured by their efficiency metrics. The industrial model of 'one size fits all' has engendered a set of processes that are geared for scale and efficiency. In the digital world, customer experience comes first. Of course, efficiency is still important, but the organization also needs to find a way to deliver personalized experience at scale. As noted earlier, many organizations are still structured around products instead of customers. Their key performance indicators (KPIs) reflect the product and process metrics instead of customer metrics. Furthermore, many organizations do not have an owner for the customer journey. This results in goal conflicts across the organization.

The suggested approach is to organize the business around customer journeys, having teams responsible for the success of specific customer journeys. This way, both mainstream business and digital business within an organization are aligned on the end goal. This helps shift the focus away from internal functional issues to customer issues.

The other important aspect is about unlocking innovation in large companies. There is a popular notion that large companies are not truly cut out for cutting edge innovation. There are, however, many companies that have dispelled this notion. The much fabled '20 percent time' at Google or '10 percent time at Intuit' empowers an employee to work on whatever they are passionate about in their 'innovation' time.

# Fault Line #4: Managing the Now, New, and Next

It is well understood that digital transformation calls for different sets of competencies, frameworks, metrics, mindsets, and leadership approaches. The real challenge, however, is in creating a digital DNA within the organization while the existing business runs like a well-oiled machine. This is often referred to as the Now-Next-New problem. How should organizations meet the performance requirements of the existing business (now) while at the same time trying to introduce significant changes to the current model (next) and preparing for the quantum jump required for the future state (new)?

This is a key question that Vijay Govindarajan tries to answer in his book, 'The Three Box Solution'.[11] While this book talks about innovation in general, it is highly applicable in the digital transformation context as well. The author introduces the three-box model to help companies channelize their time, energies, and budgets better.

**Box 1: The present:** Manage the core business at peak profitability.

**Box 2: The past:** Abandon ideas, practices, and attitudes that could inhibit innovation.

**Box 3: The future:** Convert breakthrough ideas into new products and businesses.

The three-box framework gives leaders a simple vocabulary and set of tools for managing and measuring these different sets of behaviors and activities across all levels of the organization.

At its core, digital transformation is a human story. It is a story where human behaviors must change for the transformation to happen. As we know from motivational psychology, behaviors change when people believe in the change and there is reinforcement for the change. Often, we see that changes in strategy can happen overnight but behavioral changes to support the strategy can take a very long time.

The following are some reasons why companies struggle with managing the now, new, and the next:

1. Many incumbents are publicly listed companies that obsess over short-term quarterly results. Digital transformation, like any other transformational journey, is a long-term investment that pays off over a long timeframe.

2. Digital transformation is a highly risky endeavor involving uncertainty in technologies, customer segments, skill sets within the organization, and so on. Leadership needs to have deep conviction of the benefits of the digital journey.

3. There could be severe cannibalization of revenues and profits in the short-term during the business model transformation process. Many organizations go into a soft-pedal mode fearing short-term consequences.

4. Organizations incentivize their leaders for managing the status quo and very little incentive is given for path-breaking innovations in the digital space.

5. Leaders must think about the incentive for the frontline workforce to embrace digital. Unless the frontline workforce is enabled, the digital promise may never be realized to its full potential.

6. Companies reward certainty and have an aversion for uncertainty. This prevents capable digital leaders from experimenting with new ideas in the organization.

Companies like 3M and Intuit solve the incentive and motivation problem by aligning the entire organization towards innovation and growth. In these organizations, the mandate is that a significant proportion of the revenues and profits of the organization must come from innovations that were introduced in the last four years.[12] Incentives are well-aligned across the board to meet this goal.

# External Fault Lines

In addition to the internal fault lines, companies that build digital platforms must also wrestle with external fault lines, as shown in Figure 19.4.

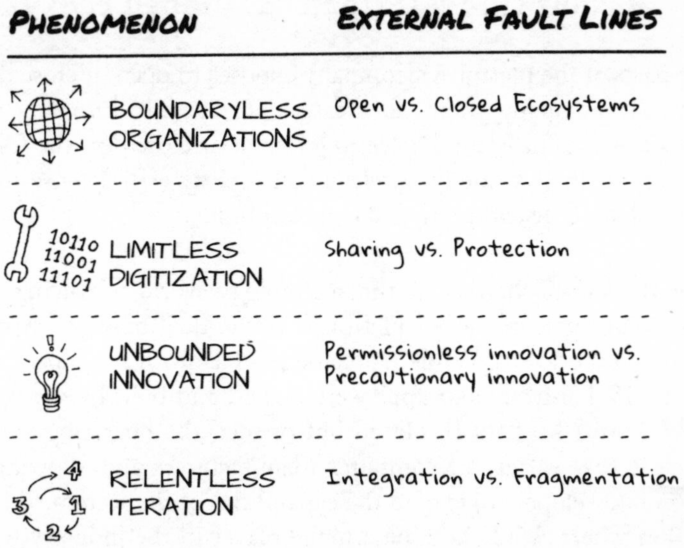

| PHENOMENON | EXTERNAL FAULT LINES |
|---|---|
| BOUNDARYLESS ORGANIZATIONS | Open vs. Closed Ecosystems |
| LIMITLESS DIGITIZATION | Sharing vs. Protection |
| UNBOUNDED INNOVATION | Permissionless innovation vs. Precautionary innovation |
| RELENTLESS ITERATION | Integration vs. Fragmentation |

**Figure 19.4** External Fault Lines

When companies become boundaryless, with their platforms powering growth, there is a crucial decision to be made on how open or closed the company wants the platform to be. This decision has a deep impact on how the ecosystem will grow over time.

Limitless digitization produces enormous amounts of data from which the organization can derive value. There are plenty of risks that the organization needs to protect itself and its community from. How the organization governs its data sharing and protection policies has an impact on the trust the platform will engender with its constituents.

Unbounded innovation processes encourage companies to venture into unchartered territories. Sometimes this might entail adopting a radical approach to innovation where regulations are not clear on what is right and what is not. Companies must perform a careful balancing act while pushing the boundaries on innovation.

Relentless iteration introduces challenges around managing product or service diversity. Companies must develop a clear strategy for managing the fragmentation of product versions.

# External Fault Line #1: Open vs. Closed Ecosystems

Which parts of the platform a company chooses to open or close depends on how the company wants to create, deliver, and ultimately capture value. Companies have the choice to go open or closed on the following depending on their strategy: intellectual property (IP), license to create variant and apps, distribution, and consumption.

One of the classic battles in the technology world, revolving around the theme of open vs. closed platforms is the duel between Apple and Microsoft in the 1980s. While Apple built Macintosh as a closed system, where the IP, hardware and apps were owned and built by the company itself, Microsoft kept its IP closed but opened the operating system by licensing it to a variety of computer manufacturers and allowing other application developers to extend the capabilities of the system. This led to a situation where Apple became a niche player in the industry with less than 10 percent market share, whereas Microsoft started dominating the industry with a near monopoly situation.[13]

Apple seems to have got its act right with iPod and subsequently with iPhone in the 2000s. While the IP and the hardware are still closed, Apple opened its operating system for other developers to build apps on top of; it also ensured that its iTunes software works on the Windows platform.

In contrast to both Apple and Microsoft, Linux is considered a completely open system where the IP, license to create variants and apps for Linux, distribution, and consumption are all open. Google's Android OS also qualifies as a largely open system, although some crucial applications of the system, including search, music, camera, and so on are created by Google. Google also encourages mobile handset manufacturers to be part of the Open Handset Alliance, a forum that's committed to creating and maintaining mobile hardware and software standards.

In the game console space, the PlayStation, Xbox, and Nintendo consoles are currently all closed platforms. Game developers license their games with the console's manufacturer who then sells the console to the end user with the games on top of their platform.

HP's 3D printing business is built on top of the open materials platform model. The USD 12 trillion global manufacturing industry presents a massive opportunity that a single company cannot completely disrupt. Keeping this in view, HP has forged a partnership with manufacturing companies around the world to develop 3D printing materials and make them all available on a collaborative open platform.

"An open ecosystem of industry leaders is critical for greater innovation, breakthrough economics, and faster development of 3D printing materials and applications. Our growing certified partner network and leading-edge lab facilities are a testament to the progress we are making in spearheading a dynamic community of collaborators focused on delivering the most innovative and production-ready 3D printing solutions," says Tim Weber, HP's Global Head of 3D materials and advanced applications.[14]

Open platforms attract users that do not have to worry about being locked in behind the secret walls of a proprietary platform. With more users joining the network, the addressable market grows, which then attracts more innovators and providers who create better experience with their new applications. The choice and variety of these apps then attracts more users. In effect, open platforms typically enjoy the benefits of network effects.

If openness has such a compelling value proposition, why might companies consider closing their platform off? First, openness can take a toll on user experience. In the early days of Windows 2000 OS when the APIs were limited, application developers resorted to hacks to extend the platform's capabilities. This led to a lot of stability issues in the platform and resulted in the infamous Windows 'Blue Screen of Death' problem where the user sees a blue screen with unintelligible characters on the screen. Apple, however, enjoys a better reputation when it comes to seamless user experience and stability.

In many cases, certain apps become so popular that they end up creating a power tussle between the platform and the apps. As a response, the platform either buys the app or closes that category in the platform or replaces it with their own. The spat between Apple and Google over maps is a legendary case study that illustrates this point. Apple pulled Google Maps (and YouTube) from iOS stock apps in 2016 and replaced it with their own Apple Maps app. The inferior quality of Apple maps became a subject of mockery and Tim Cook had to apologize publicly. The company, however, kept its focus on improving the app. A year after its release, it is reported that three out of four iOS users use Apple Maps over Google Maps. For Google, gaining access to Apple's user base is extremely crucial. Google continues to pay USD 1 billion to Apple for maintaining its status as the default search engine. Google reportedly makes USD 8.85 billion from mobile ads on Apple iOS and 75 percent of its mobile ad revenue for 2015 came from iOS.[15] Managing such conflicts is a core part of leading a platform business that a company needs to master.

## External Fault Line #2: Sharing vs. Protection

There is a famous maxim about internet-based business models that goes like this: 'If you are not paying for the product online, then you are the product'. The idea is that the user's data will be monetized through ads or other means. This popular online business model came in direct collision with regulators during the congressional testimony of Mark Zuckerberg, the Founder-CEO of Facebook. Responding to a question by U.S representative Ben Luján, Zuckerberg said that for security reasons, Facebook also collects "data of people who have not signed up for Facebook."[16] Data privacy concerns have dogged Facebook ever since it acknowledged that information about millions of users had been wrongfully used by a political consultancy called Cambridge Analytica, a firm that was supposed to have played a significant role in Donald Trump's electoral campaign.

How a platform strikes the right balance between sharing and protection and between security and privacy is a topic of intense debate.

With the growth of the digital economy, data has become the lifeblood of organizations and ecosystems. Leveraging digital entails sharing data within and outside the organization. Sharing unlocks value from existing data by enabling new insights and innovations. Herein lies the crucial insight. Data sharing is not simply about the sharing of data, it is also about sharing the interpretation of that data. How data can be interpreted cannot be foreseen when it is being shared with various actors within the ecosystem. This introduces significant risks—privacy, security, ethical and economic.

In response to growing concerns around data privacy, regulators in Europe have enacted a new European Union law, known as the General Data Protection Regulation (GDPR). According to eugdpr.org, the regulation was designed to harmonize data privacy laws across Europe, to protect the data of all EU citizens from misuse and to reshape the way organizations approach data privacy. Under the regulation, individuals will have various privacy rights including the right to be forgotten, which is to say that they can demand the data controller to erase their information.[17]

The fault line between sharing and protection has far reaching consequences for the organization's business models, for regulators and ultimately individuals in the digital age.

## External Fault Line #3: Permissionless Innovation vs. Precautionary Innovation

Permissionless innovation is all about a liberal approach to experimentation with new technologies and business models. The idea is that innovation should generally be permitted by default unless a compelling case can be made that an innovation can bring about serious consequences. Problems, whenever and if they happen, if at all they do, can be addressed.

This idea runs counter to 'precautionary innovation' where developers of innovative ideas are expected to prove that their innovation will not cause any harm. Precautionary innovation, as the name suggests, tries to encourage a conservative approach to innovation.

In many industries where disruptions have happened, one would notice that the disruptors have used the permissionless approach to innovation. These companies expand at a pace that is far more furious than regulation can keep up with. As mentioned earlier, it takes an average unicorn 4.4 years to reach the billion-dollar valuation status. Within this time, they manage to disrupt many companies and industries. Beyond a point, it becomes difficult to regulate them away because by then, they would have become mainstream.

According to permissionlessinnovation.org, the sharing economy is one of the best examples of permissionless innovation or unbounded innovation in action today. The term 'sharing economy' refers to any marketplace that brings together distributed networks of people to get more value out of underutilized assets for both profit and fun. Uber is a company that has benefitted from the shared economy model. Regulations in many countries have difficulty in creating a level playing field for incumbents such as taxi companies and technology-driven disruptors (Uber and Lyft).

Even as regulators figure out the future of connected cars, Waymo, formerly called the Google self-driving car project, has already made significant progress. As of April 2017, Waymo had started offering free car rides to passengers in Phoenix, Arizona.[18]

Permissionless innovation creates an uneven playing field between disruptors who are unregulated and incumbents who are bound by regulations. The key question before the incumbents then is: How do they start embracing uncertainty and start pushing the boundaries of innovation without creating regulatory risks? Many large organizations have come up with a variety of strategic responses. Some of them launch an accelerator to incubate many disruptive start-ups, providing access to market for smaller organizations and acquiring capabilities in return. Others invest in disruptive companies to get a share of the pie and there are others that build capabilities internally.

## External Fault Line #4: Integration vs. Fragmentation

What is common to Jelly Bean, KitKat, Lollipop, Marshmallow, Cupcake, and Donut? Yes, they are all delicious but, in the digital context, these are names of some of the Android versions that are out there in the market.

With well over a billion phones made by a variety of device manufacturers running on wireless networks across the world, Google's Android operating system has grown into the most widely used mobile OS. One of the crucial decisions Google made very early on is to make Android open source and give manufacturers the opportunity to create their own versions. It is this very decision that convinced so many different manufacturers and carriers to adopt the platform early on. This was Google's necessary move to gain momentum and challenge Apple. The same flexibility now comes back and bites Android in the form of platform fragmentation. Fragmentation of the platform is happening because wireless carriers and device manufacturers, and not Google, are the ones who control the timing of the Android versions sent out to different devices.

What is the problem with this? The relentless iteration that pushes Google to release updates to its OS, to keep satisfying its users expectations, does not, however, sync with the upgrade cycle of the device manufacturers. Android device manufacturers have an incentive to customize Android OS to create differentiation in the Android marketplace. Device manufacturers have an even bigger incentive in upgrading their hardware and enticing users to buy new models rather than upgrading the software.

Figure 19.5 shows how severe the level of fragmentation is on the Android platform. The figure shows that 35.6 percent of Android smartphones are using Lollipop, which came out in late 2014, and 32.5 percent are still stuck on the even older KitKat version of Android.[19] This is not an unusual situation in the world of software. Microsoft Windows also has very old versions of the desktop OS still running. What is different about mobile fragmentation is that several million people and app developers that are participating in droves in the mobile ecosystem have trouble making sure that their apps work on multiple versions of the software. When an app is not supported in a particular version of the OS, user experience takes a severe hit.

Apple, however, is in complete control of when iOS updates are made to iPhones.

Apple indicates that 84 percent of its iOS users are on its most recent version, iOS 9, 11 percent are on iOS 8, and 5 percent are using older software.[20]

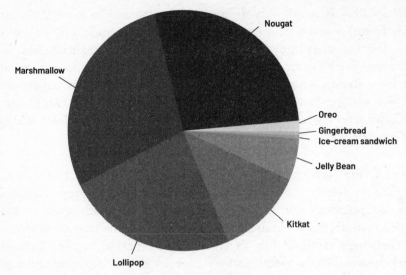

**Figure 19.5** Fragmentation of the Android platform

The ability to manage relentless iterations is a challenging enough, but managing relentless iterations that are rolling out in different phases is an even bigger challenge. The ability to manage the now, next, and new for the platform is crucial to develop a coherent ecosystem that works for all the stakeholders.

# Reflect and Share

1. The digital race is on. The question is whether digital born organizations will become mainstream first or will incumbents acquire digital capabilities first.

2. There are four internal fault lines and four external fault lines that organizations must deal with in their digital transformation journey.

3. The internal fault lines revolve around structure and talent, streamlining process and information flow, managing the innovation process through goal alignment and managing the now, new, and the next.

4. The external fault lines revolve around open vs. closed ecosystems, sharing vs. protection, permissionless innovation vs. precautionary innovation and integration vs. fragmentation.

# Key Questions

- Do you have clear owners for digital initiatives in your organization?
- Does the business team have digital acumen to leverage the internal digital team?
- Does the digital team understand the business context well enough?
- Are incentives for managers and leaders aligned with digital milestones?
- Does the organization have a game plan to manage multiple business models playing out at the same time?
- Do you have a mature governance plan for managing the complexities of leading or being part an ecosystem?

# CHAPTER 20
# LEADERSHIP FAULT LINES

"Anyone should be able to tell me anything, that's the culture we strive for."

—Satya Nadella, CEO, Microsoft

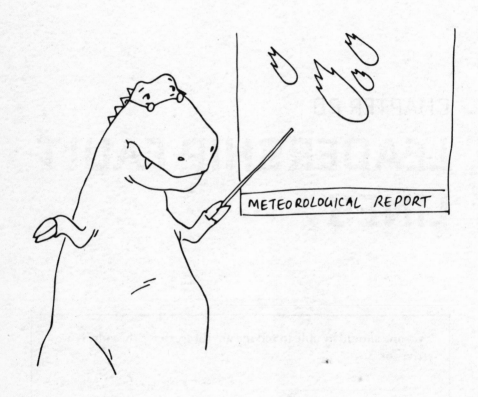

# Leadership Lessons for the Digital Age

Rapid mortality rate of companies in the digital age is ultimately a leadership issue. The success of digital transformation of organizations depends on how well leaders transform themselves first. Along with a healthy dose of optimism, leaders need to demonstrate unprecedented levels of learning agility. This is crucial because the very survival of their organizations is at stake.

How does a leader develop clarity in the age of the Digital BLUR? By unlearning, re-learning and learning; not just technologies but more importantly, mindsets and behaviors.

# Leadership Unlearning

In the era of Digital BLUR, there are quite a few things that leaders must unlearn.

### Digitalization Demands a New Leadership style

With the emergence of boundaryless organizations and the proliferation of stakeholders, leaders must unlearn old leadership habits anchored around command and control. Leading with authority is passé. Leading without authority is very much in vogue. An industrial-age leader's natural response to valuable resources is to hoard. Digital leaders' natural response is to share. It is in fact by sharing that digital leaders gain their license to influence others without authority.

Continuous collaboration and real-time dialogue between leaders, managers and frontline employees is a crucial success factor in the digital age. Leaders must architect a collaborative, networked organization that responds to internal and external changes in an agile fashion. Digital also forces leaders to be much more engaged with the external environment of the organization, be it with governments, NGOs or consumer groups.

## Digitalization Requires a Complete Re-think of the External Business Environment

The companies that are likely to disrupt the industry are increasingly unlikely to come from the same industry. The ones that are armed with a digital arsenal from different industries are becoming threats to incumbents. To develop foresight, leaders need to develop a clear understanding of the forces that are shaping not just their industries but also other industries.

Additionally, be it the 4Ps of marketing or Porter's 5 forces, the traditional lenses for analyzing the external business environment have become less relevant in the digital age. It may be useful for business leaders in their respective industries to ask, "What would Google do"? This question brings to sharp focus the rethinking that needs to be done to be relevant in the new age.

## Organizational Mission and Purpose to be Revisited

Leaders may need to revisit the "Why" question for their organizations and question assumptions behind the business model of the organization and the industry. To adapt, they would need to bring the risk of disruption into business planning, no matter how comfortable they may feel at this point about their business performance. The single most important factor that galvanizes the ecosystem partners, customers and employees of the organization is the overarching organizational mission.

# Leadership Re-learning

In the era of Digital BLUR, leaders must renew their focus on certain key aspects.

## Digital is an Organizational Capability

Digital is not just a senior leadership topic. Digital capabilities need to be built from individual contributors all the way up to the board, failing which, severe gaps would likely rear their ugly heads between strategy and execution. To add to this, capability building needs to be an agile, continuous process. Nothing captures this better than Peter Senge's timeless quote, "The only sustainable competitive advantage is an organization's ability to learn faster than the competition."

## Change Must be Built into the Organizational DNA

The operating principle in the digital world is that if something can be disrupted, it will be. Adapt or perish, the inexorable law of nature is truer today than ever before. As noted earlier, digital has caused tectonic shifts that have displaced individual companies and even industries. Change management used to be a program management activity for companies faced with a massive transformation. Today, leaders must ensure that the capability and motivation to continuously change are built into the very DNA of the organization.

Digital revolution is not so much a technology revolution, as it is a cultural revolution. Organizations that have an agile, open and learning culture will thrive and others will fall by the wayside.

## Strategy at the Speed of Digital

There used to be a time when leaders could lock themselves up for weeks on end to come up with their five-year strategic plans. Today, the shelf life of strategy has been drastically reduced, and more importantly, strategy and execution happen "in sync" in a tight feedback loop on the job. It is no longer a closed room exercise. The 'Build, Measure, Learn' cycle advocated by Eric Ries in his book, "The Lean Startup" for product development is also very much applicable to business strategy.

# Leadership Learning

To master the rules of the digital age, leaders need to develop a few new areas of expertise.

## Design Thinking: From Economies of Scale to Economies of Experience

Leaders who have earned their stripes in the industrial era need to pay attention to Design Thinking. In the industrial age, business decisions were geared towards achieving economies of scale by optimizing operations through a one-size-fits-all approach. Today, digital has empowered individuals in an unprecedented fashion. Consequently, hyper-personalization is expected in every offering, be it to consumers or employees. In other words, one-size-fits-none.

By following a structured Design Thinking process, leaders can create differentiation for their businesses by crafting exceptional personalized experiences for their stakeholders.

## Agility: Fast Fish Eats the Slow Fish

In an on-demand world, if organizations are not agile, irrelevance is imminent. To succeed in this new environment, leaders need to empower their managers and frontline employees with enough avenues to take agile decisions and bring information back to the organization to learn about the outcomes.

## From Educated Guesses to Data-driven Insights

Business leaders need to ensure that decisions across levels are guided by data and insights. The successes of many new-age digital organizations show that an organized data-driven trial and error process is guaranteed to produce better results at an organizational level than the educated guess of a lone genius.

## In Constant Search of Blue Oceans

Innovation cannot just be a buzzword. Leaders must champion bold experiments on a continuous basis and help organizations learn faster. This requires leaders to prepare themselves and others for embracing volatility, uncertainty, ambiguity and risk. Searching for blue oceans is no longer a one-off activity; it is part of the daily agenda.

# Industrial Leadership vs. Digital Leadership

Leadership in the digital age is markedly different from leadership practices of the industrial age. While in the industrial age, command and control was the dominant mindset; in the industrial age, collaboration is the operating principle.

Figure 20.1 outlines the differences between Industrial and Digital leadership.

| PHENOMENON | INDUSTRIAL LEADERSHIP | DIGITAL LEADERSHIP |
|---|---|---|
| BOUNDARYLESS ORGANIZATIONS | → Leaders operate with a control mindset within the organization. | → Leaders operate with a collaborative mindset in ecosystems. |
|  | → Leaders use command-and-control leadership style with formal 'authority as the main currency. | → Leaders focus on leading without authority using influence as the main currency. |
|  | → Leaders demonstrate hoarding mindset to gain power. | → Leaders demonstrate sharing mindset to gain influence. |
| LIMITLESS DIGITIZATION | → Leaders resort to personal experience and intuition for decision making. | → Leaders find a way to integrate data and intuition to hone decision making. |
| UNBOUNDED INNOVATION | → Leaders operate with a constraint driven mindset. | → Leaders demonstrate an abundance mindset to drive exponential growth. |
|  | → Leaders use process thinking to drive efficiency gains in the organization | → Leaders use design thinking to create exceptional experience for customers. |
| RELENTLESS ITERATION | → Leaders demonstrate a stability mindset that promotes the status quo. | → Leaders demonstrate an agile mindset to rapidly innovate. |
|  | → Leaders place products at the centre with a one-size-fits-all approach. | → Leaders place customer at the centre with a one-size-fits-none approach |

**Figure 20.1:** Differences between Industrial and Digital Leadership.

# New Age of Leadership Development

Traditional approaches of developing leaders are outdated. Companies need to reinvent their approach to identifying, selecting and developing leaders for the digital age.

Figure 20.2 outlines the key differences in the approaches used for building industrial leaders versus digital leaders.

| LEADERSHIP DEVELOPMENT PROCESS | INDUSTRIAL LEADERSHIP | DIGITAL LEADERSHIP |
|---|---|---|
| IDENTIFICATION | → Leaders are identified based on their experience, tenure and past performance.<br><br>→ Leaders are expected to work their way up the leadership pipeline over a long period of time. | → Leaders are identified early in the careers for agility, problem solving and growth mindset.<br><br>→ Leaders are given early, stretch responsibilities to test and develop leadership skills |
| ASSESSMENT | → Leaders are expected to have ready answers and bring their experience & judgment to solve business challenges<br><br>→ Leaders are assessed for their personality traits and competencies | → Leaders are expected to collaborate and innovate with internal and external stakeholders to find solutions to business challenges<br><br>→ Leaders are assessed for their cognitive skills and practical problem-solving ability |
| DEVELOPMENT | → Leaders are developed through formal training process focusing mainly on education<br><br>→ Leadership is considered as a sacrosanct role in an organization<br><br>→ Leaders are developed to lead organizations and functions | → Leaders are developed through education, exposure, experience and enablement.<br><br>→ Leaders are developed at all levels within the organization.<br><br>→ Leaders are developed to lead ecosystems and networks. |

**Figure 20.2:** Differences in leadership development approaches between the industrial age and the digital age.

# Reflect and Share

1. Digital leadership is markedly different from industrial leadership.
2. While industrial leadership thrives on a command and control model, digital leadership thrives on leading without authority.
3. Leaders must go through a process of unlearning, learning and relearning to stay relevant in the digital age.
4. Organizations must use a different model for identifying, assessing and developing digital leaders.

## Key Questions

- Do your leaders have a boundaryless approach to leadership?
- Are your leaders data savvy?
- Are your leaders adept at using design to create breakthrough experiences?
- Do your leaders embrace agility both at the strategy as well as the operational levels?
- Do you have a success profile for a digital leader in your organization?

# CHAPTER 21

# CULTURAL FAULT LINES

"Culture is to recruiting as product is to marketing."
—Dharmesh Shah, Co-Founder and CTO, Hubspot

# The Digital Culture Code

McKinsey's research shows that organizations that focus on transforming culture and building capabilities during a transformation are 2.5 times more likely to succeed.[1] Attempting to introduce digital transformation with an industrial organization culture is a sure-fire path towards failure. Figure 21.1 shows some key differences between industrial culture and digital culture.

| PHENOMENON | INDUSTRIAL CULTURE | DIGITAL CULTURE |
|---|---|---|
| BOUNDARYLESS ORGANIZATIONS | → Companies operate in a closed, silo-ed fashion, protecting their work from external entities. Control is the operative word. | → Companies operate in an open, networked fashion sharing their work with external entities. Collaboration is the operative word. |
| LIMITLESS DIGITIZATION | → Companies hoard data from external entities and even within the organization. Decision-making is predominantly centralized. | → Companies share data both with external entities and within the organization. Decision-making is decentralized and happens at all levels. |
| UNBOUNDED INNOVATION | → Companies rely completely on their internal R&D teams to produce innovative ideas and solutions.<br><br>→ Companies tend to be risk-averse and have an aversion for ambiguity.<br><br>→ Compliance is rewarded, failure is not. | → Companies believe in building an inclusive culture and promoting peering with partners from within & outside the organization.<br><br>→ Companies are open to ambiguity and uncertainty and take on risks in a data-driven manner.<br><br>→ Fail-early, Fail-Fast culture. |
| RELENTLESS ITERATION | → Stability is rewarded<br><br>→ Intense product focus<br><br>→ Most organization processes, such as employee feedback, performance appraisals etc. tend to be annual. | → Agility is rewarded<br><br>→ Intense Customer Focus<br><br>→ Organizational processes tend to be real-time. |

**Figure 21.1** Differences between industrial and digital cultures.

# Building a Boundaryless Culture: Teaming, the New Way of Doing Work

Imagine that you are the head of research at a detergent company and you are faced with the daunting task of finding a formula that will remove the toughest red wine stain from clothing. How would you go about solving this challenge? Chances are that you might give the problem statement to a select group of smart scientists in your organization, give them a budget and a timeline and expect them to solve it for you. As it turns out, that is the industrial way of doing it, wherein the organization tries to solve challenges by doing it all through thoughtfully composed in-house teams. In the digital age, however, problem solving is everyone's job and the approach is to collaborate with anyone in the world who has the answers, through a process called 'Teaming'.[2]

Amy Edmondson, the author of "Teaming: How Organizations Learn, Innovate and Compete in the Knowledge Economy", defines teaming as teamwork on the fly. She says that leaders need to stop thinking of teams as static groups of individuals who have ample time to practice interacting successfully and efficiently.

Traditionally, corporate teams, sports teams, music bands have all operated as a static collection of individuals inside stable boundaries. These individuals develop trust over time, collaborate on well-designed tasks, and understand each other's roles well. But today, teams are becoming increasingly boundaryless and dynamic. The new reality in the digital age is that businesses operate in an environment where the problems are new, big, urgent, or unprecedented. Paul Polman, the CEO of Unilever says, "The issues we face are so big and the targets are so challenging that we cannot do it alone, so there is a certain humility and a recognition that we need to invite other people in."[3] This calls for people, from within and outside the organization, to come together quickly without any formal supporting structures, learn to coordinate across boundaries, such as expertise, time zones, and languages, take decisions and achieve results.

The extraordinary rescue of all the 12 Thai football players and their coach who were trapped deep inside the Tham Luang cave complex is a case in point. The rescue team had Thai Navy SEALS, Australian divers, British divers, and doctors from various countries. They teamed up on the fly, learned to collaborate seamlessly without any formal structures, found innovative solutions, and ultimately emerged victorious in their mission.[4]

Just to be sure, teaming does not just happen during accidents and matters of life and death. It can happen in a corporate setting too. With gig economy on the rise in the digital age where professionals choose freelancing arrangements over formal long-term contracts, it is imperative for organizations to embrace teaming. Teaming can also happen internally in an organization. Publicis, the French multinational advertising and public relations company, has recently unveiled Marcel, an AI driven platform that promises to bring all its 80,000 employees to a common platform to break all silos. On Marcel, employees can bid to take part in client projects, team up, get work done, and disband themselves. This enables the organization to tap into their wide network of talent that exists across boundaries and serve the unique needs of its customers in innovative ways.[5]

What can leaders do to enable their organizations to practice teaming effectively?

1.  As Daniel Coyle says in his book, "The Culture Code", leaders need to instill the power of vulnerability in their teams. Everyone in the

organization should feel psychologically safe to be able to say, "I don't know the answer, let me seek help".

2.  Leaders may want to remove barriers to effective collaboration within and outside the organization.

3.  Leaders must empower employees to seek the best possible solutions irrespective of where it was created. The 'not invented here' mindset has to give way to 'awesomely created elsewhere' mindset.

4.  While in the industrial age, we hoarded valuable resources to gain influence, in the digital age, the instinct is to share the resource widely to achieve the same result. Leaders must foster a culture of sharing ideas, products, methods, and best practices to build a thriving community of problem solvers that support the company.

So how do modern workplaces solve the challenge of red wine stain on clothes? Procter & Gamble, the global consumer goods company, offers a great idea to get this done. When A.G Lafley became the CEO of Procter & Gamble, he quickly understood that the 'do-it-yourself' model of innovation had run its course for the large multinational. To turbocharge the innovation process, he embraced the open innovation model. He renamed the Research and Development (R&D) function to Connect and Develop (C&D). The idea was to connect with anyone outside the organization that had answers to the tough problems that the company was trying to solve. The goal of the rechristened team was that 50 percent of the innovation must come *from* them and the remaining 50 percent should come *through* them. Today, the company leverages 7,500 of its internal researchers and 1.5 million people outside to create innovative products.[6]

# Mastering the 5As to Establish Data Enabled Culture

It would be safe to say that organizations today have more data than ever before. But deriving actionable insights from the data and converting the knowledge into value proves to be a daunting task for most companies. Often, it is not the lack of technologies that causes the problem. In many cases, it is the culture and inertia carried over from the industrial age that does the damage.

Uber uses real-time demand and supply data to arrive at surge pricing to optimize its revenues. With many million active users, Twitter has made a business model out of breaking news and live trends. Spotify offers music on demand to more than 75 million users using real-time personalized data. These digital born organizations are built with data right at the center of the organization.

Industrial organizations, on the other hand, struggle with data. There are five systemic challenges, called the 5As of data, that these organizations must overcome to derive value from data. As shown in Figure 21.2, the 5As are availability, access, accuracy, analytics, and agility.

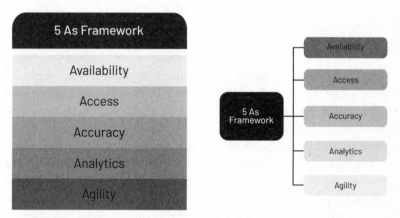

**Figure 21.2** 5As of Data.

## Availability

"Forty million shoppers buy our products in a year, but we do not know who these shoppers are". This is one of the classic woes you might hear at an organization that faces the availability challenge. The crux of the challenge is that the organization has incomplete internal and external data sources. An example of internal data that may not be easily available is the health record of employees. An example of external data could be the biometric data of all customers in a retail bank. Decisions in these organizations tend to be made based on limited data or personal experiences of decision makers.

## Access

You know that you are witnessing the access challenge if you hear something like this from an organization: "We have identifiable data of all our 10 million customers, but the commercial bank division cannot access the data from the retail bank database." Access challenge happens when the data sources are available but not everyone in the organization has adequate rights to access the data. This could be an intentional design to control access to sensitive data. In many cases, however, the sheer complexity of data systems prevents employees from one business unit from accessing the data from another. These organizations experience a lot of frustration because duplicate systems emerge over time, costs escalate, and a lot of time is wasted on just tossing around data from one system to the other.

## Accuracy

When an organization faces the accuracy challenge, you might hear something like this from them: "We have 10 different data systems within our organization that capture customer data, each speaking its own version of the truth. It takes fifteen days to produce a comprehensive business dashboard." Accuracy challenge happens when the data is available and accessible, but it is of poor quality. This could happen because of a variety of reasons: improper training of data entry staff, incoherent data coming in from different channels, inaccurate machine data making its way into the organization without any data processing and so on.

## Analytics

When an organization faces the analytics challenge, you might hear this from a leader: "We have invested in acquiring the latest technologies for data analytics, but we don't have the right data analytics capabilities to leverage them for achieving results". Organizations are spending a lot of money in acquiring software tools for data analytics but the capabilities of employees in converting data to insights still lags.

## Agility

At the highest level, data savvy organizations perform analytics on-demand and in a real-time fashion. You might hear this from an organization that faces the agility challenge: "We have the right data systems, but we are unable to make use of the data on a real-time basis to maximize outcomes". The root cause of the agility challenge lies in the way work gets done in the organization. If the organization's work practices are not agile, agility in data is not achievable.

What can leaders do to enable a data-driven culture?

1. Without a single view of the customer, organizations cannot really do justice to customer experience in the omni-channel-driven digital age. Leaders may want to design their businesses in a way that data flow between different units is seamless.

2. Leaders will benefit by investing in building data capabilities in their teams, sensitizing them to the opportunities and risks.

3. It is important that in addition to creating new value from data, leaders must also be mindful of safeguarding existing value through strong data protection and ethical practices around data usage.

4. Leaders may want to embrace agility in data-based decision-making so that their businesses can maximize opportunities and reduce risks.

5. Data-enabled culture does not mean that we ignore humanities. Often, the best data comes in the form of stories and qualitative inputs from ethnographic studies. It is important that leaders find a balance between 'thick data' (data derived from human experiences and, hence, contextually rich) and 'thin data' (large data without contextual richness).

While there are many technology tools to help with the 5As of data, ultimately the challenge lies in the capabilities, culture and mindsets of the people of the organization. These will hold the key for determining whether organizations can derive value from data and stay ahead in the digital race.

## Busting Biases to Build a Great Social Culture

Social media can be a great force for uniting people to achieve extraordinary results. On August 1, 2015, the ALS ice bucket challenge was launched with a goal to raise money for research into ALS, also known as Lou Gehrig's disease. The challenge encourages nominated participants to share a video clip where they pour a bucket of ice water on their heads and then nominate others to do the same. The nominated participants have 24 hours to comply or forfeit by way of a charitable financial donation to the cause. The challenge took the internet by storm. More than 2.4 million participants shared video clips and the ALS association received USD 115 million in donations.[7] The initiative succeeded because of a combination of social proofing, altruism, fun, competitiveness, and social media pressure. The designer of the challenge clearly had a great sense of how to raise awareness and promote positive action for the cause.

Social media can also lead to intense polarization. Wael Ghonim helped spark the Arab Spring by setting up a Facebook page that galvanized the people of Egypt to raise their voice against the Government. Once the revolution spilled over to the streets, it started becoming unmanageable with people pulling apart in different directions. The effect was immediately seen on social media. The very platform that enabled the organizers of the movement to engage people, crowdsource ideas, and build a strong community quickly became an intensely polarized battleground. Hate speech and negative sentiment quickly spiraled out of control. Wael Ghonim in his TED talk, "Let's design social media that drives real change", makes a plea to design social systems that promote civility and reasoned argument.[8]

In the digital age, leaders play an active role in building communities, promoting action and ensuring sustenance of the community. To do this successfully, leaders need to understand how social media amplifies the biases we all carry. This understanding is important for leaders to design sustainable social systems within and outside the organization.

First, fake news is dished out to us daily through messaging apps, social media platforms, and even mainstream media. We are constantly consuming conspiracy theories, partisan content, and questionable science packaged as facts. In December 2016, a WhatsApp message claiming that the Reserve Bank of India has cancelled Axis Bank's license went so viral that it led to people withdrawing all their money from their Axis Bank account.[9] In absence of fact-checking on the part of the readers, we witness knee jerk reactions en-masse. Fake news stokes our confirmation bias, the cognitive blind spot that makes us seek out evidence that matches our belief and disregard evidence that does not fit.

Second, technology serves news feeds based on our preferences captured through our online activity. We inadvertently create a filter bubble for ourselves and end up cutting ourselves off from diverse information sources. Information coming from similar sources tends to reinforce our already existing beliefs. It also makes us believe that certain events are happening more frequently than the norm. This leads to availability bias, a mental shortcut that relies on recent examples while we evaluate situations.

Finally, content producers are incentivized today for maximizing clicks and views. Hence there is an implicit push towards creating click baits and sensational news. Sensationalism leads to greater collective attention which then leads to social proof. Critical thinking and civilized conversations are lost in the bargain as collateral damage.

What can leaders do to build a great social culture?

1.  Within the organization, leaders can promote a culture that encourages diversity in the team and urges people to stay open and to reconcile with conflicting ideas. Chances are, employees will use the same values when they deal with the community outside the organization.

2.  Leaders need to recommend seeking disconfirming evidence for beliefs. To do this, leaders must establish a hypothesis driven culture, where team members are encouraged to build prototypes, prove or disprove their hypothesis before decisions can be made.

3.  Leaders also need to encourage critical thinking and thoughtful action in everything that the organization does.

4.  Outside the organization, leaders need to build a community based on the higher purpose of the organization and inspire positive action.

5.  Social media interactions need to be human-centered and empathetic.

While algorithms are great for driving efficiency in interactions, we are still some time away from effectiveness and empathy. The recent Facebook fauxpas in Indonesia is a case in point. After the 6.9 magnitude earthquake in Lombok, Facebook users wrote 'I hope people will survive'. They used the word 'selamat' in the sentence, a word in Bahasa Indonesia that means both congratulations and survival. Facebook received a lot of flak when its algorithms interpreted 'selamat' in the positive context and started showing some balloons and confetti on the user's page.[10]

Social media is a powerful platform for achieving extraordinary things that are not usually possible with small groups of individuals. At the same time, there are dangers of manipulation, misinformation, and polarization that leaders and organizations need to watch out for. Leaders must strive to set up social systems that leverage the power of conversations and mindfulness to create positive impact.

# Fostering Growth Mindset for Building Agile Teams

Satya Nadella, the CEO of Microsoft, says that Microsoft has moved from a know-it-all culture to a learn-it-all culture.[11] The implications of this transformation are profound. In the know-it-all culture, individuals try to act intelligent and invincible. The problem with this is that over time, this leads to a fixed mindset culture where individuals avoid challenging tasks to stay away from failures. They also put in suboptimal effort because of the belief that their abilities are great already and that there is no room for further improvement.

Carol Dweck, the author of Mindset: The New Psychology of Success, coined the terms 'fixed mindset' and 'growth mindset' to describe the underlying beliefs people have about learning and intelligence. When people believe that they can get smarter, they understand that effort makes them stronger. Therefore, they put in extra time and effort, and that leads to higher achievement. This mindset is called the *growth mindset*. When a person demonstrates growth mindset, there is a tendency to accept challenges because of the learning opportunity. Tough situations offer a path towards mastery in the eyes of a person demonstrating growth mindset. They persist in the face of setbacks and are keen to receive feedback to improve themselves further.[12]

Growth mindset is the very essence of a successful agile culture. Without growth mindset, individuals and teams will not have the motivation to pursue relentless iteration on value creation activities for the customers. They will not have the urge to question the status quo and to improve things.

So, what can leaders do to establish an agile culture enabled by growth mindset?

1. Create an environment of psychological safety where employees can ask questions and challenge status quo. In a learn-it-all culture, it should be okay for an employee to say, "I don't know" and seek help to find answers, without feeling judged.

2. Revisit the role of managers in the agile ecosystem. Essentially, managers become coaches and focus on capability development and continuous learning.

3. Provide frequent, meaningful feedback that allows employees to do quick course correction.

4. Reward smart failures.

5. Establish small execution teams that are empowered to learn and find their own answers. With increased ownership, individuals and teams start to find innovative ways to solve problems.

6. Reframe work as not an execution challenge but a learning challenge.

# Reflect and Share

1. There is a marked difference between industrial and digital cultures.
2. Digital culture is all about being open, peering, sharing, becoming data-enabled, design driven, and agile.
3. Teaming is increasingly the new way of working in the boundaryless organization model.
4. Organizations must evaluate themselves on data maturity model by using the 5As framework.
5. Organizations must foster growth mindsets to build agile teams.

---

## Key Questions

- Do your leaders have a 'Not invented here' mindset?
- Does your organization promote sharing and peering within and outside the organization?
- Does your organization take decisions enabled by data?
- Does your organization have a strong diverse workforce and an inclusive culture?
- Do leaders in your organization promote the fail-early / learn-fast culture?

---

# SECTION 5

# REFLECTIONS ON DIGITAL BLUR

# Perspectives from a Board Member

## Ravi Venkatesan

Banking industry has undergone massive digital transformation in the last few years. The industry has become unbundled and smaller and agile Fintech companies are nibbling away at niche segments within the industry. In this interview, Ravi Venkatesan, the ex-Chairman of the board at Bank of Baroda, a leading Indian public sector bank, shares his perspective on digital transformation and talks in-depth about the response from Bank of Baroda.

Ravi Venkatesan, a business leader with diversified experience, until recently was also the Co-Chairman on the Board of Directors for Infosys, India's second-largest IT services company. He is a member of Board of Trustees of Rockefeller Foundation; the Founder-Chairman of Social Ventures Partners India and a Venture Partner in Unitus Ventures.

Ravi Venkatesan has a wealth of experience in corporate leadership, globalization, innovation, and the private sector. His experience and insights have culminated in a book titled 'Conquering the Chaos: Win in India, Win Everywhere', published in 2013 by Harvard Business Review Press.

An MBA from Harvard Business School with a Master of Science degree from Purdue University, and Bachelor of Mechanical Engineering from IIT Bombay, Venkatesan has served as a Chairman of Cummins India, Chairman of Microsoft India (BMSI), and on the board of AB Volvo.

**RJ: When you hear the word 'Digital', what comes to your mind?**

**RV:** Everybody is talking about Digital. But, if I had to explain what I think of business and digital, I think of it in three ways:

1. It's a channel. It's one way in which we engage with customers and the people outside. Customers get information, engage, transact through digital channels. It is very important and useful, particularly in a world where everyone has a smart phone and internet access. Digital becomes a very powerful, low cost and high engagement channel.

2. The second thing about digital is that it is all about how you design, enable, and control your internal processes, and how do you enable productivity for your own employees. It's about using technology to enable all your processes, automate as much as you can so that employees are truly doing work that only humans can do. That way, you are taking off cost, speeding things up, and you have much more effective workflows.

3. The third thing is all about data. As you transact more and more digitally, you're generating huge amounts of data. This can be used in extraordinary ways, for example, open new opportunities, create new business models, among others. For instance, in Bank of Baroda, we found that we had a treasure trove of data we weren't using. Historically, we wouldn't lend to a person unless he had a credit history and assets to offer as collateral. For people who don't have great assets but have a lot of transaction history from paying bills and such, we can determine their credit worthiness from their transaction history. That's how we would lend. This is true of every business. When you generate vast amounts of data, you can generate insights from it. Data enables you to do wonderful things.

**RJ: What are some of the myths that you hear about digital?**

**RV:** Bill Gates said that we overestimate change in the short run and underestimate its impact in the long run. I think people are confused about the timelines in which things are going to happen. For instance, some prominent people are saying that because of digitization, banks are toast.

I think you should understand that no matter what science fiction writers say, big banks are not going to get disrupted and disappear overnight. Temper your expectations about the rate at which things are truly going to change. Things will change, and they are changing faster and faster, but it is not going to happen anywhere near the speed at which we expect.

**RJ: What, according to you, is the future of banking?**

**RV:** I think the nature of banking, particularly in a country like India is changing quite a lot. India is a microcosm of the whole world. You have a small, highly affluent population, about the size of Australia. Then, you have a reasonable middle class which is probably the size of Vietnam, and an Africa-sized population at the bottom.

The big challenge, when you think about India, is not dealing with the affluent. If anything, they are overserved. I think that the big need is as you start drilling down the pyramid.

Technology is the only way that you can reach these segments and serve them in a financially sustainable way. We're just scratching the surface when it comes to that.

The second big idea is around FinTech companies who are using technology to gather information and put it together in extraordinarily interesting ways. So, think about offering educational loans to people, or credit to SMEs that don't have a credit history. It's about how you use credit data from social media, how you're able to use transaction data to put together the credit-worthiness or the risk of various customers and then serve them in an economical way.

I think that technology today enables you to think about these things and do them in a profitable way, which you could not earlier.

For instance, one of the more successful products that Bank of Baroda has recently launched is supply chain financing. In the past, you used to lend to a small company, say a machine shop making some widget or part. Usually such a company would struggle to get credit. If you think about it, this company is supplying an automotive subsupplier who is supplying to Maruti, for example. When a fuel system gets installed in a Maruti, all these companies get paid over time. If you integrate this supply chain, you can start lending to this guy based on his receivables. Using this new solution we've built, we're now able to give credit to manufacturers and their supply chains as well as their distribution chains. So, we can attract a whole new vast segment of customers. That's a win-win, and we couldn't have done this without technology.

**RJ: Fintech and other technology companies are trying to commoditize the banking industry. How do you see this playing out?**

RV: First, technology has always been a commodity. There are plenty of companies who sell all the technology you need and some more. That is an enabler, but it is not a differentiator. It all comes down to the way you think about applying technology to your business to get an edge, and then figuring out who are the right technology partners who will help you get there.

In Bank of Baroda, we recognize that this is a bank and not a technology company. We created a subsidiary and brought in both IBM and Accenture, almost like joint-venture partners; IBM to deal with the core technology, including the customer engagement piece, among others, and Accenture just to focus on the data and analytics. With this, a bank like Bank of Baroda has every opportunity now to be a disruptor.

With the FinTechs, the theory is that they are going to disrupt the established banks. I don't think so. The way I see it is that FinTechs have certain things that we will never have:

1. An entrepreneurial spirit
2. Speed
3. They are tech savvy
4. They have lower costs and can access customers more efficiently

On the other hand, there are certain things they will never have:

1. Access to low cost capital
2. Brand value and trust that a 100-year old government backed bank has

We need each other. So, it is a win-win when we can collaborate.

In doing so, we are gradually moving Bank of Baroda towards thinking about platform banking. Can Bank of Baroda become a platform? Can we open our APIs so that Fintech companies can build their solutions on it, and engage and transact with us in a seamless way? Can we put together an economic model that is a win-win? That is how we are now working with some 30 companies.

**RJ: For banks to operate in a boundaryless model, what kind of leadership mindsets need to exist within the organization?**

RV: As per me, these are some of the challenges of leadership going forward:

1. **Outside-In Orientation**
   Whether it is a bank or any other business, it is less and less likely to succeed if you're inwardly focused. I think that things are changing fast, and you must be incredibly customer-centric, market focused, aware of trends, talking to possible partners, and stitching together coalitions. That external orientation is key for getting a sense of where you want to go and how to be ahead of the rest.

2. **Speed**
   How do you shape the culture of the organization, so it can respond and move quickly? This is a hugely important task for leadership.

3. **Creating an environment without fear, without hierarchy, and with a high degree of trust**
   If people must go up and down the hierarchy, it is not going to move fast. If people don't trust the chain, it is not going to work fast. So, you must do an enormous amount of work on the soft stuff to move fast. It is not a technology thing alone. In fact, technology is a very small part of it. Trust and relationships are much more important.

4. **Innovation**
   The ability to try many things, fail fast, scale up the few things that show potential, and the ability to do this, not just a one off, but as a way of life is crucial.

5.  **Learning agility**

    Getting everybody to learn is hugely important. You must create a culture where the onus of learning is on the employees.

**RJ: How can board members help CEOs navigate challenges in the intelligent age? What will be your advice to CEOs?**

**RV:** Get the right people on board. These are not normal, peaceful times so you need a board that has people who have lived through and led transformational change. At least a couple of directors should be very familiar with doing business digitally. The board must be engaged in the business and the transformation, so you need directors who will make the time to understand what's going on and be a sounding board for the CEO and the management team. The board must understand that doing nothing, staying in place, is the greatest risk of all and be supportive of the CEO taking some big bets. Most of all, the board needs a strong Chairman who has wisdom, the courage to make tough decisions, and can be a good partner and coach for the CEO.

# Perspectives from a Leader in The Agriculture Business

## Surampudi Sivakumar

It is quite common to quote examples of companies such as Uber, Airbnb, and Amazon when we talk about digital. Here is a company that has been applying the idea of digital ecosystems from way back in 2000: ITC, a leading Indian conglomerate. Mr. Surampudi Sivakumar shares with us the evolution of ITC e-Choupal, the breakthrough platform that has revolutionized supply chain in the Agriculture industry.

Mr. Surampudi Sivakumar serves as Group Head of Agri and IT Businesses at ITC. The e-Choupal initiative was developed and executed under Sivakumar's leadership of the Agri Business Division. Topper of the Class of 1983 from the Institute of Rural Management Anand, (IRMA), Sivakumar worked with a farmers' cooperative for six years before joining ITC in 1989.

Sivakumar is also Vice Chairman of ITC Infotech India Limited and its subsidiaries in the UK and USA, Chairman of the National Agricultural Council of the Confederation of Indian Industry (CII), Vice Chairman of the World Economic Forum's Global Agenda Council on Social Innovation, and a member on the Board of Governors of Institute of Rural Management, Anand (IRMA).

Among other organizations, Sivakumar has served on the Boards of India's National Bank for Agriculture and Rural Development (NABARD), and Indo US Knowledge Initiative on Agriculture, the Private Sector Committee of the Consultative Group on International Agricultural

Research (CGIAR), and UN Global Compact's Core Advisory Group to develops sustainable agriculture business principles.

**RJ: What does digital mean to you?**

**SS:** That is a very interesting question, because digital means different things to different people. To me, digital is the convergence of many different pieces. There is technology, Big Data, analytics, among others. When you integrate all of them into a business system to create value, that to me is digital. Look at it this way:

1. There is a microscope, which allows you to look at the finer details.
2. There is a telescope, which allows you to look at things from the outside and from afar.
3. There is a remote, which you use to control these other systems.
4. There is a processor, which allows this process of control and action.

Historically, these are all separate entities. When you combine them together, you embed intelligence into things. Take a chair for example. Historically all we did was sit on it, or perhaps stand on it. It served a unidimensional function. Now put a microchip into it. You can collect and analyze several kinds of data:

1. How often do people sit on the chair?
2. In what position do they sit?
3. How heavy are the people who sit on the chair?
4. What periods of time do people sit on the chair?

These are only some of the data points that the microchip can provide. That is not as important as the economic relevance of this information. You have taken a seemingly simple object and made it incredibly valuable.

In other words, digital is about integration. Integration creates intelligence, which adds value.

**RJ: e-Choupal is viewed as a successful case study of an organization becoming boundaryless. How did that idea come about?**

**SS:** In the 1990s, the agricultural world opened up for global trade. As both an importer and exporter of goods and services, India was not competing in a global market, against the likes of the US, South America, Australia, and others, who had far superior infrastructure than we did. We had all kinds of broken infrastructure at the time— farm lands less than 1/1000th the time of our competitors, seaports no larger than swimming pools, relatively primitive tools with which farmers farmed their lands, inferior quality for cost saving, and so on. In a sense, India was competing with world players in agriculture with both hands tied at the back. In such a context, how do you compete, export, and succeed?

A key insight we took away from analyzing this scenario was that to be able to compete and win, we had to raise the bar within our boundaries. This was what we could see at that time. However, we soon realized that for us to be able to compete in the global market, the entire value chain had to evolve, not just one part of it. The realization that an enterprise's competitiveness is not within the boundaries was the trigger which created e-Choupal.

**RJ: e-Choupal, as an idea and concept has evolved over time. Can you take us through the journey?**

**SS:** We did have a hazy idea of what we would be doing at the end of a long period of time when we first conceived this idea. As we evolve to a new stage, what we are essentially doing is reorganizing the supply chain to make it more efficient, more aligned with the market, and offer the producer a fairer share. The efficiencies we have managed to bring in by way of digital are:

1. Allowed producers to understand and derive appropriate value for their goods in comparison to larger domestic terminals and international markets.

2. Measured and elevated the quality of the produce being sold by the farmers.

3. Eliminated the intermediaries in the distribution process.

4. Catered to the specific needs and preferences of the diverse consumer market.

Every commodity value chain has its own dynamic. Therefore, we need to reorganize to create new value. Historically, I would work with the farmers and give them information and knowledge at a cost based on their financial sustainability. In the case of e-Choupal, all the information and knowledge were given free of cost. All the transactions on the platform were based on the freedom of the farmers' choice.

Identifying a market inefficiency and making it efficient is what created the financial success of the e-Choupal platform. In the process, we noticed that all the pieces that were put together were like a platform that consisted of multiple layers with multiple levels in each layer—a 3 × 3 platform. This essentially involved unbundling the whole value chain and making each piece separately available to different stakeholders to bundle it the way they like it. The freedom to unbundle along with the choice of an already bundled offering, and bypassing information flow and market signals is what digital has enabled us to provide the various stakeholders within the agricultural value chain.

To allow this the layers built were:
1.  Digital infrastructure, by way of internet to the farmers with assisted human interfaces to operate the internet
2.  Physical infrastructure, by way of e-Choupal Sagars with human interfaces that traditionally played the roles of the intermediaries
3.  Collaborative ecosystem of people—weather forecasting companies, seal companies, nutrient companies, agri extension companies among others.

All of this was orchestrated by ITC. These three layers with their components could unbundle any value chain originating in the village and make it available for all the participating stakeholders to bundle as they wanted. That capacity of the platform became an opportunity to create a two-way flow of goods and services.

Eventually, we became an ecosystem as a service, focusing on a larger bundle of offers beyond just connecting farmers to consumers. As cloud, mobile, and other technologies became more pervasive, we saw an accelerated development in the consumption of our platform service, making the platform more robust and comprehensive.

The digital age made the platform more plug-and-play ready, adding a fourth layer, scaling beyond the human intervention necessary for the other three layers. This generates more data, allowing us to personalize the offerings to all our stakeholders. That is how far our journey has come now.

**RJ: You had the vision to set up a platform in the year 2000 much before many of these digital born organizations even existed. What would be the primary differences between a digital platform like Amazon or Uber and what you have envisioned for e-Choupal?**

**SS:** Platforms, at a generic level, are pretty much the same. A platform is something where you create an engagement among multiple players, including yourself because you may also be a player besides just sharing the platform. The participants continuously discover problems and solutions in an iterative fashion. It is a combination of many different applications and interactions across a host of players who will constantly resolve problems for everyone in the ecosystem. I think that is the distinction as to what a platform is versus anything else.

The interesting difference of the e-Choupal platform is that there is no such one-way flow, of saying here is a producer and here is a consumer, and I am moving goods and services from one end to the other. For me, a farmer is a consumer as well as a producer. Someone who is selling a seed or a nutrient to grow the produce would in turn receive something from the farmer for his or her consumption. In some sense, e-Choupal is a barter system.

**RJ: What would be your advice for all organizations belonging to a traditional sector trying to become an ecosystem leader?**

**SS:** With the consumer mind now accessible through data, platforms can now create solutions that are more apt than individual products and services that each of these companies is currently producing in silos. Therefore, platform providers must develop extraordinary empathy with the consumer. That is the first step. It's not about 'how do I maximize the sale of my product', it's more about 'what does it mean in the continuum in a product or service to solve a problem'; the problem could be a new opportunity or a new experience.

The second important thing is that the conventional value thinking, that is, 'I create value within the boundaries of my organization' must change, because, today, there are multiple players who are creating value for the consumer together. Therefore, as a platform provider, you are an orchestrator ensuring that consumers' evolving needs are uncovered and catered to. Essentially, in the end-to-end model, you have to convince everyone in the value chain. If you are missing some piece, it cripples the whole value chain. It is not a complete solution for the consumer. A platform is very different from an enterprise that is creating a product or service in a linear fashion. A change in the mindset and conception, with consumer centricity at the core is fundamental.

**RJ: What changes are necessary internally to pull off a change in the end-to-end platform story?**

**SS:** One of the most critical elements is building trust. For farmers to feel that the e-Choupal platform is their platform and not an ITC shop, they should feel that they are a part of it and that they own it. The first step to creating that feeling of security is the foundation of trust.

You also have a buyer who is looking at low cost, and a seller who wants to make higher profits. How do we work together to ensure that you make more profits while I produce at a lower cost? That engagement is merely possible with trust. For us, as the different stakeholders in the value chain started trusting each other, we were able to work more closely and efficiently to figure out the win-win situations all around.

The second critical element is from a management perspective—the element of collaboration, and managing expectations. Organizations typically work on a command and control model. However, when you are working through a platform, with multiple stakeholders who have their own set of expectations, how do you gain clarity on the expectations from both ends and find a middle ground together that is beneficial to everyone? Modeling those expectations and subsequently the behaviors is crucial, because many of these partnerships for us are social contracts. Therefore, we must find a way to blend the commercial and social aspects of these partnerships.

These are the things we had to think about, change, and evolve as we went through this journey.

**RJ: How do you view the data coming out of e-Choupal? What are some of the opportunities that you feel are waiting to be tapped?**

**SS:** The information that is very useful in predicting what might happen is:

1. Selling intention is an enormous amount of intelligence.
2. Selling behavior, such as what kinds of crops have been sold at what points of time, when is something going to be harvested, what will be the output curve per day and so on are crucial data points that we have today.

**RJ: What is the biggest innovation that has happened as part of the e-Choupal initiative?**

**SS:** At one level, we couldn't have moved at all without internet being brought to the villages and all the related technology innovation it engendered: where you get power, how do you get access to bandwidth and so on, all in the days where 2G/3G/4G didn't exist. That was one kind of technology innovation.

The most critical part, however, was the whole institution of 'Sanchalan' that was created—digital within walking distance that was managed by a local person (Sanchalak) from within the community. For many decades, companies had their own agents in the village. For the first time, we created a unique institution which bridged the gap between ITC and the local community. This institution is seen as a part of the community, as opposed to an outsider catering to a large corporation. The conventional system of an agent on either side led to mistrust and a sense of alienation, something that the 'Sanchalak' system eliminated. That is a unique innovation, and a crucial pillar in the success of e-Choupal.

# Perspectives from a Technologist

## Avnish Sabharwal

In this interview, we will focus on the perspectives of a leader from Accenture, one of the leading providers of digital transformation services to some of the largest companies in the world. Avnish Sabharwal will share with us his perspectives on digital and what companies can do to succeed in the digital transformation journey.

Avnish Sabharwal is an innovator, strategist and a technology evangelist with 25 years of extensive experience and track record around market making, growth hacking, corporate innovation, digital transformation, and leadership development for Top 500 Fortune clients in both mature and emerging markets.

He is a mentor for Change for Atal Innovation Mission in India and part of the advisory board of the Israel CoE at IIM-B. He was voted as the most Innovative Leader for 2018 by World Innovation Congress.

He has also served in the Indian Armed forces for seven years and has performed the role of aide de camp of the Governor of Madhya Pradesh.

**RJ: What exactly is digital?**

**AS**: Every organization has a different way of defining digital. From my perspective, first and foremost it is a mindset shift of doing things differently–unlocking values from the physical world by creating a virtual twin by leveraging digital technologies like interactive, cloud, and cyber security.

It is also a big cultural transformation. A lot of attention must be given to what the impact of digital will be, or how digital will be leveraged by people, because the 'human' is in the middle of all this transformation, and if we don't pay enough emphasis on that part, most of the digital transformations are liable to fail.

A more transactional focus on digital would be in three key areas:

1. Improving customer experience: digital customer
2. Improving internal structures and processes: digital enterprise
3. Building new business models: digital innovation

These three would be the key components of any digital implementation in a larger enterprise.

**RJ: In the same breath, can you also define what digital is not?**

**AS:** It is not independent technologies and initiatives. Digital is an enterprise wide transformation, right from the leadership to the workers on ground or factory floor. If things are happening in pockets and silos, then it is not digital. That's the first thing.

Second, if digital is happening in a few of your processes and touching just a few of your systems, that is not digital. For example, just by building a few apps you can't call yourself a Digital enterprise. Digital needs to be applied to your core business as well help you launch new businesses. As I said earlier, digital touches three important elements—business model, customer experience, and internal processes.

Third, it certainly is not about IT and technology. Digital is much more business than anything else. It is a key strategic imperative for all business leaders. So, it is much more a business issue than it is a technology issue. The entire organization strategy, culture, structure, and investments need to be aligned to make a digital transformation successful.

**RJ: In the industrial age, companies used to have a linear business model, where the focus was on the product, whereas, today, becoming a platform is important. Why do you think that becoming a platform is important in the digital context?**

**AS**: If you look at the Fortune 500 companies now, at least 60-70 percent of them are platform companies. These organizations did not exist even 10 years ago. But the kind of speed at which they have grown, and the market capitalization that they are showing pushes them much ahead of the value chain pipeline companies.

What happens in a value chain organization is that you have several different inputs and in the end, you have an output. Something happens in the middle, where you work on those inputs. That's a traditional pipeline business. Platform business is different in that it basically works on the 'network effect' where you have multiple buyers and/or sellers and you have people who are controlling the platform. It is the power of networks that makes this business model favorable over the pipeline business.

Studies have shown that whenever there is competition between a pipeline business and a platform business, a platform business will always win; which is why traditional organizations are trying to reinvent their businesses. They are trying to build platform businesses in addition to their traditional value chain business.

**RJ: How are companies deriving value from data?**

**AS**: I think it's a common saying that 'data is the new oil', and 'AI is the new electricity'. Earlier, we didn't have the technology or the computing power to extract the data. Now, if you look at the kind of things that are happening from the connected world point of view and IoT, we have about 50 billion, or maybe even more devices which are connected. The volume, veracity, as well as the velocity of data has significantly increased. The ability of organizations to use different technologies to make sense of both structured and unstructured data is giving them insights which they never had earlier, and that is what is creating value.

But I think that is also the limitation of most of the organizations that unless they have the data layer fixed, no amount of digital technology is going to work. Most of the organizations are struggling with that. If you go to a manufacturing company which has been using traditional machines for a very long time, it is very difficult to extract data from those machines. And if you can't do that, obviously the analytics, or the rest of the artificial intelligence or machine learning which you want to use will be limited at best. Also, the authenticity of the data will be key determinant of enterprise value.

Therefore, many organizations are using significant amounts of resources to first build their data layer. Once done, they then start planning what kind of digital services they would provide leveraging the data and insights. But getting the data layer right is the first and critical step towards your digital transformation.

**RJ: While agility in project management is well understood, how do organizations become agile from a strategy point of view?**

**AS:** I think that is a key question for big organizations. As organizations become bigger, complexity increases, and agility reduces. Agility should be a key part of an enterprise's future strategy, because it is a mindset, in terms of how quickly an organization can pivot to new opportunities in the market.

The bottom line is, whether it is product development, or it is strategy, we no longer have a 1-2 year time frame. It's all very dynamic and fluid, including strategy. It changes as the environment changes, which is constant. So, we no longer do those big exercises of conducting annual strategy summits and developing a three-year strategy, because those things are irrelevant now. We need agility, and that is why agility becomes an intrinsic part of an organization's strategy formulation.

# Perspectives from a Banking Leader

## Maaike Steinebach

In this interview, we will delve deep into the disruption brought to the fore by Fintech companies. Maaike has had deep experience working with large banks and is also part of the Fintech association of Hong Kong. She brings together insights from both the banking as well as the Fintech industries to give us a comprehensive view.

Maaike has been in the banking industry for 20+ years and has worked across multiple jurisdictions in Europe and Asia and has held senior positions in financial institutions including CBA, Fortis Bank and ABN AMRO.

Most recently she was Chief Executive of Commonwealth Bank of Australia where she managed Institutional Banking & Markets and provided oversight for the Private Bank, supported the bank's business development in China and was instrumental in setting up the first overseas Innovation Lab for CBA in Hong Kong for which she was the executive sponsor.

She is passionate about technology and inclusive leadership. She is a board director for the Australian Chamber of Commerce for Hong Kong and Macau, where she sits on the Women in Business Committee. She started work on the FinTech Association of Hong Kong in 2016 which was officially launched in June 2017. She is also one of the founders of Women in Tech Hong Kong and Women Chief Executives, a network of 16 female CEO of Financial Institutions in Hong Kong.

**RJ: One of the things I hear about often is the great unbundling of the Banking, Financial Services and Insurance Industry. What does it exactly mean and how is it happening?**

**MS:** The banking industry has largely remained unchanged over the past few years. Barring a few changes in payments or trading, it is still very traditional and still organized with the same distribution channels as it has been for the last 20 years. This unbundling is happening because of the customer experience:

1. It's either through the consumers who are not happy with the way they are engaging with the financial institutions, or

2. It's the people from within the industry who are recognizing that there are now different ways in which they can improve the customer experience.

This leads the industry to find alternative ways to improve customer experience. The big unbundling is happening because new solutions are coming from outside the industry for people to do their banking business.

**RJ: How are traditional banks responding to this?**

**MS:** Banks are currently looking at how they can improve the customer experience and, obviously, there are different ways in which they can do that:

1. Innovation coming from within the organization, where they come up with their own solutions. However, I see a lot of the global banks struggling with curating the solutions internally or coming up with a solution that can be implemented globally:

    a. For example, the bank I use in the Netherlands has a great way of making peer to peer payments but its only available with a Dutch phone number;

    b. Or a local bank in Hong Kong has a new peer to peer payment app but you can only download the app from the HK Apple Store and you can only pay other customers of the bank.

2. Enforcing solutions from Fintech, through integration and creation of an ecosystem where there is a strong co-operation with Fintech companies. The only bank in Asia that seems to be able to do this successfully to date is DBS from Singapore that has just been named one of the best digital banks in the world. Embracing FinTech and putting customer at the center of it has changed the culture of the bank and enabled a better customer experience.

A lot of Fintech start-ups have founders that are ex-bankers wanting to improve the customer experience. But the success rate is still quite low in Asia because banks either don't have the infrastructure to support and integrate this, or they don't have the proper culture and talent to handle the on-boarding and integration. Some of the Fintech companies go through procurement teams to be onboarded, while others may be onboarded by the IT department. We are now slowly seeing banks implementing onboarding protocols.

What I also hear from the Fintech companies is that the lead time on a deal with a bank is very long and they also have issues with who funds what, particularly when it involves a proof of concept. Boot strapped start-ups obviously are looking for a quick success, so it is problematic. Also, most of the start-ups begin with an idea to improve a banking product because they feel that they could improve the customer experience. But sometimes they work on their solutions for so long that by the time they come to market either the solution is outdated or the founders, instances of which can be seen when they prove to be very inflexible and unable to make bespoke solutions for the banks. So far, I've only seen very limited successful cooperation between banks and Fintech companies. I am, however, optimistic about the future.

**RJ: Given your experience in Asia and Europe, is there anything unique about digital in Asia? What are some differences that you see about banking in Asia or digital in Asia?**

**MS:** Whilst the success rate might not be very high, the cooperation between banks and Fintech companies seems to be quite good in Asia. There is a lot of mutual respect. In other parts of the world, it seems to be more competitive. They also seem to be sharing much more big opportunities amongst each other. This doesn't seem to be the case elsewhere. I think that's a positive.

Across Asia there seems to be a better platform for banks and companies to share, but I do think that the success rate is equally bad in Asia as it is in Europe. I am however noticing a more positive trend in Asia, maybe also shaped by the rise of the Chinese Fintech giants like Tencent and Alibaba.

**RJ: What do you see as the biggest roadblock when it comes to digital transformation?**

**MS:** I think it starts with culture and the tone from the top. If the CEO or the executive committee of the financial institutions are not themselves fully prepared or open to believing that there is need for change and a need for them to be a change within the company, it's not going to happen. It is rare to see that the CEO has embraced innovation, customer centricity and digitization as a priority. It is very rare that the entire organization understands the importance of the customer experience.

In my view, only if the people at the top are supportive, this will be successful. Because I have also seen the opposite, where an appointed Head of Innovation or a Head of Digital would come for help on senior management education. It really needs to be full buy-in from the top; one person won't be able to make the difference.

**RJ: A lot of companies have embraced agile project management, and that area is well understood. How do organizations become strategically agile, like the way Uber gets into Uber Eats or Amazon gets into many different industries in a very agile fashion?**

**MS:** This is a very difficult question because I've never worked in an organization that has succeeded in embracing agile project management. At CBA, we had just started this through productivity. I think start-ups are better at it but don't call it agile. They are agile by default. I think traditional companies interact with clients and models in ways that were working 25 years ago. These ways are very command-driven, hierarchical, highly structured and organized. I think because of the speed of change globally and the complexity of what the world looks like, we require different ways of working and leadership that is focused around purpose and compassion. It's the only way organizations can succeed going forward.

It is about trying to work as flexibly as possible, to be able to adapt as quickly as possible to the changes that are coming your way. To do that, people really need to rethink the way their organizations are structured. This depends on the type of leaders and the kind of corporate governance structure you have. That's why I really like the Netflix example where they have completely changed the way they organize their board meetings. They don't have physical meetings but have the board members go and visit the work floor to learn from people in the field how the company is doing.

The struggle that people have is becoming more agile because it requires an inherent change which people just naturally resist. I think without leaders who are embracing that change and are looking forward to change, becoming agile as an organization is almost impossible.

**RJ: How do you enable a culture of experimentation and failing fast, especially in a context that is regulation heavy?**

**MS:** I think that's hard. It is very difficult to get people to experiment because people are quite risk averse by nature. Anything that goes wrong in the banking scenario has regulatory consequences. Finding ways in which you can encourage people to experiment in a safe environment and show them that there are learnings from failures, that it is okay to fail, and that experimenting would benefit their own work is quite crucial. That's the only way to ensure they continue to upskill and learn and move the organization forward.

# Perspectives from an HR Leader

## Prabir Jha

All said and done, Digital is very much a human story. While everything around us is changing in the digital world, one thing we will still need in abundant measure is leadership at various levels to channelize people and resources towards solving massive challenges that we face. In this interview, Prabir Jha shares with us his insights on the future of work, leadership and culture.

A #LinkedIn Power Profile, TEDx speaker, columnist and active tweeter are just some of the hats worn by the President and Chief People Officer of Cipla Pharmaceuticals, Prabir Jha. In addition to leading the global human resources function for the company, Prabir also leads the corporate communications and administration functions.

After a decade long tenure as a civil servant, Prabir made the shift to pursue a corporate career in human resources, serving as the Chief HR Officer at some of India's leading corporations like Dr Reddy's, Tata Motors and before his current assignment, Reliance Industries.

Prabir has built a solid reputation as an organization transformation strategist and a very progressive HR thinker and practitioner. His strengths lie in Strategic HR, Change Management, Leadership, Organizational Transformation, Talent Management and Coaching and Training, allowing him to lead large-scale HR and organizational transformations.

Prabir earned his B.A. and M.A. degrees in History from St. Stephen's College.

**RJ: From an HR standpoint, how should organizations think about the new way of organizing themselves, in terms of organization structure? Do you think anything should change in response to digital?**

**PJ:** First is how is the organization architecture going to look? Then, how is the HR architecture going to look? I will try and respond to both.

In my understanding, if we believe in the power of digitization, and are clear in how we want our organizations to grow to become digital, many things will change. One of the big things that will happen as part of this exercise is what is called 'information democracy'. Digital will enhance transparency and accountability in a manner that we have never seen before. You cannot hide behind an excel sheet or PowerPoint and deck it up to look nice.

Information democracy will:

a.  Allow organizations to reach out and communicate with all stakeholders almost any time and anywhere.
b.  Eliminate many levels of hierarchy.
c.  Replace aggregating roles with centers of expertise.

In other words, Digital will enable people to be great consumers of the output rather than getting confused about the technology or the engineering aspect. Digitization is going to simplify the organization:

a.  Organizations are going to look leaner and simpler.
b.  Processes are going to get less bureaucratic.
c.  Many transactional roles will be eliminated.

At the same time, however, the organization architecture will have greater specialist roles, comprising those who are able to consume and leverage the information better.

**RJ: According to you, what are the core tenets of digital culture? How is it different from the industrial culture?**

**PJ:** According to me these are the core tenets:

1. **Information and Power**: The industrial age was about power, authority and control, which was enforced by the limited access to information based on seniority. In the digital age, information is going to reach people in real-time without necessarily flowing level by level. This is a significant difference between the two periods of time.

2. **Shift from experience to expertise**:  Many of the functions, processes and roles of the digital age would not even have existed a decade ago. Therefore, we will see a culture shift from experience to expertise.

3. **Shift from siloed turfs to collaborative environments**: Digital organizations will have a flatter structure, resulting in faster interfaces. Therefore, the world of collaboration will almost entirely replace the world of siloed turfs and empires. The digital world will be interconnected and mutually dependent. I think that, personally, collaboration and inclusion would become very important.

4. **Reward and appreciation**: A lot of the reward, recognition and appreciation culture that we have will become more real-time. Feedback, performance behaviors, etc. will be addressed immediately. The year-end thing, when you struggle to even remember what really was the episode that the feedback is being based on is redundant. This shift will lend to the culture of greater inclusivity, teamwork, and possibly lead to a culture which is far more responsive and accountable than we may have seen historically.

**RJ: In what ways do you think digital leadership is different from industrial leadership?**

**PJ**: Industrial leadership was a lot about command and control. A lot rested on the amount of grey hair one had. I think a digital leader will have to have a 'let go' style of leadership, one that is inclusive in nature. It is important that a leader in the digital age:

a.   Is more of a coach than a boss.

b.   Learns as much as the perspective he or she may be able to share.

c.   Can be open in his/her leadership style.

It will not be around hierarchy that leadership will work, but around your acceptance by your teams.

Leadership will be a lot more about influence in the digital age. Influence of stakeholders could be within your team, beyond your teams within your enterprise, or even beyond enterprises. Therefore, a person who is open to learn from anyone and everyone at almost real-time speed will be the kind of leader who will survive.

Finally, compared to the earlier world, I think we will need to have leaders who are more about giving than just taking, because the more we give, the more we get. Therefore, leadership in the digital world will also look at their recovery very differently than the old-world leaders recover. This is how, in many ways, leadership styles will change.

# 90-Day Action Plan to Clear the Digital Blur

There are three concrete next steps for clearing the Digital BLUR in your organization

# STEP 1. Conduct Cross-functional Workshops in Your Organization

In this step, try to find answers from leaders and key employees at various levels and functions within the organization to the following question:

## Boundaryless Organizations

- What is the right internal organizational structure that will help our organization become intensely customer-centric, agile in execution and innovative?
- What new competencies should we focus on for the employees across levels to operate in the boundaryless world?
- What enabling cultures should our organization build to thrive in the boundaryless world?
- How will our organization stay relevant in a competitive landscape where new entrants from across industry boundaries threaten our survival?
- How do we manage the change associated with the dismantling of organizational structures from the industrial era?

## Limitless Digitization

- What is our game plan to deal with the explosion of data in our business?
- How do we plan to derive value from existing data?
- What kind of leadership traits are required to drive data-driven decision making in our organization?
- What cultural enablers will we need for our employees to embrace data-driven decision making?

- Are there areas in our business where robotic automation can yield great results?
- How will we manage human-machine confluence?

## Unbounded Innovation

- How will we embrace uncertainties and foster permission-less innovation?
- How do we leverage open source technologies in our business? Are we contributing open source technologies to the community?
- What competencies will we develop in our teams to encourage innovation that goes beyond the current landscape of the business?
- How will our organization become customer-centric and not get bogged down by internal ways of looking at the customer?
- How will we manage the uncertainties involved in the innovation process?
- How do we build a culture that permits failures as part of the innovation process?

## Relentless Iteration

- Does our organization try to maximize customer value over all else?
- Do our teams use the build-measure-learn cycle to validate new ideas?
- What percentage of the teams in our organization are operating in an agile fashion?
- Does our leadership team work closely with management and product builders to make the organization agile as a whole?
- What roles do managers play when teams in our organization are operating in an agile fashion?

# STEP 2. Create an Action Plan

Here is a sample quarterly plan for creating the base for digital transformation of your organization. Please note that the sequence and timelines will depend on the specific context of your organization. It is important to get senior leadership buy-in to create the game plan to clear the Digital BLUR.

| Timeline | Activity | Outcome |
|---|---|---|
| Week 1 | Baseline Current Business Model | Current Business Model articulated in a standardized fashion across business units. |
| Week 2 | Understand BLUR Impact | Conduct research to understand the impact of Digital BLUR on the business and industry. |
| Week 3 | Understand 4 strategic responses | Understand the 4 strategic responses and the LEAPFROG Strategy Framework. |
| Week 4 | Ecosystem as Strategy | Identify Role in the ecosystem, Identify players in the ecosystem, Formulate the ecosystem value proposition. |
| Week 5 | Data as Strategy | Identify the different data layers within the organization, formulate strategy to extract value from the data. |
| Week 6 | Design as Strategy | Create experience journeys for customers and other ecosystem players. Identify strategies for reaching unchartered territories. |
| Week 7 | Agility as Strategy | Identify levers for customer centricity using value canvas and operational agility. Create game changing adaptation through strategic agility. |
| Week 8 | Create Network Canvas | Integrate insights from the strategic responses and capture in the LEAPFROG canvas. |
| Week 9 - 12 | Resolve Digital Fault Lines in Strategy Execution | Create a plan to deal with the fault lines in Execution, Leadership and Culture. |

# STEP 3. Conduct a Digital Readiness Survey Across Levels in Your Organization

The following questionnaire uses a simple formula to assess digital readiness of organization. Strategy, Capabilities and Culture are the three key pillars. Questions have been aligned with the Digital BLUR framework as well.

| Digital Strategy + Digital Capabilities + Digital Culture & Leadership = Results | |
|---|---|
| Mark each of the statements below with a score on a 1-5 scale. 1 being completely disagree and 5 being completely agree. | |
| **Digital Strategy** | **Score** |
| 1 | I believe that my organization's mission and vision align with the digital world. | |
| 2 | We have clear and quanti"able goals for measuring the success of our digital strategy. | |
| 3 | Customer insight actively guides our digital strategy. | |
| 4 | We believe that our competitive strategy leverages digital. | |
| 5 | Senior leadership team is actively involved in sponsoring and executing digital initiatives. | |
| 6 | There is clear-cut ownership and accountability for digital transformation in the organization. | |
| 7 | We dedicate adequate resource to support execution of our digital strategy. | |
| 8 | We feed our lessons from digital execution back into our strategy routinely. | |
| 9 | We manage the co-existence of different business models well. | |
| 10 | We think ecosystems and platforms while creating products and strategies. | |
| **Digital Capabilities** | |
| 11 | We invest in targeted digital education, exposure, experience, enablement at all levels of our organization. | |
| 12 | Every employee understands how their performances ties to corporate digital goals. | |
| 13 | We routinely hire digital savvy talent for critical digital functions within the organization. | |
| 14 | Digital Talent is embedded across the organization. | |

| | | |
|---|---|---|
| 15 | Our organizational structure and processes promote cross-functional collaboration to bust silos. | |
| 16 | Data is shared across the business units for real-time decision making. | |
| 17 | Our organization follows agile practices for product / service development. | |
| 18 | Our organization uses design thinking principles in daily work. | |
| 19 | We have all the digital infrastructure, apps and processes to ful"l the vision and mission of the organization. | |
| 20 | We leverage smart technologies (APIs, Cloud, Mobile) to promote speed and ease of use. | |
| 21 | Digital Technologies are available for frontline staff to make real-time decisions. | |
| 22 | We have teams accountable for the success of various customer journeys. | |
| | **Digital Culture** | |
| 23 | We have digital-savvy leaders who think outside-in. | |
| 24 | Our leaders follow a collaborative leadership style vs. a command-and-control style. | |
| 25 | Our leaders encourage the use of data in decision making. | |
| 26 | We have leaders who believe in design-led innovation. | |
| 27 | Our leaders operate with agility in operations as well as strategy. | |
| 28 | We take measured risks to solve business challenges. | |
| 29 | We clearly communicate our digital initiatives and vision both internally and externally. | |
| 30 | We have a culture that encourages smart failures. | |
| | Total | |

| Rating Scale | |
|---|---|
| 121–150 - Digital Master | 91–120 - Digital Pacesetters |
| 61–90 - Digital Explorer | 30–60 - Digital Rookie |

# Conclusion

Digital BLUR is a real phenomenon impacting many companies and industries. We live in a world characterized by Boundaryless Organizations, Limitless Digitization, Unbounded Innovation and Relentless Iteration. The Digital BLUR phenomenon is triggered by various trends such as connected customers, smart technologies, VUCA environment, great bundling and unbundling of industries and the emergence of a new breed of competitors. Companies need to wake up to this challenge and start adopting four key strategic responses:

- Ecosystem as Strategy
- Data as Strategy
- Design as Strategy
- Agility as Strategy

The overarching transformation that is needed is a journey from being a value chain driven, pipeline business model to a networked business model. To achieve this, organizations can use the 7-step Digital LEAPFROG Process to turbocharge the transformation process. As part of the Digital LEAPFROG process, companies adopt an outside-in approach that is ecosystem centric, use data to enhance value for stakeholders in the ecosystem, employ design to drive adoption and continued growth and demonstrate agility, not just in operations but also in strategy.

To achieve success in the transformation process, companies need to overcome digital fault lines in execution, leadership and culture.

The tension points in execution revolve around structure and talent, process and information, goal alignment and incentives and motivational factors. Organizations need to:

- Devise strategies for attracting and retaining digital talent
- Establish ownership and accountability for digital transformation
- Use the digital operating model framework to minimize friction between existing business and the new digital business
- Use the 3-Box solution for resolving potential conflicts in time, effort and resource allocation

- Align incentives with the success of the digital transformation initiative

Externally, an organization needs to navigate the trade-offs in
- Being open vs. closed as a platform
- Sharing data vs. data protection
- Permissionless innovation vs. precautionary innovation
- Integration vs. standardization in the face of relentless versions of products and services

Leadership takes a completely new twist in the digital age. In the new paradigm, leaders
- Use influence as the key currency in the place of formal authority
- Employ data for real-time decision making
- Think design and customers first
- Operate with agility in both operations as well as strategy

Organizational culture also needs to be rewired in the context of digital
- Boundaryless culture— Teaming is the new way of working
- Data-enabled culture— Debiasing decision making using data
- Design-led culture—Unlocking diversity and inclusion to drive innovation
- Agile Culture—Enabling fail-fast / learn-fast culture

## Ten Rules for Clearing the Digital BLUR

1. Break the reach versus richness trade-off by embracing digital business models.

2. Unlock new opportunity by tapping into the long tail.

3. Build a competitive moat using digital ecosystems that have positive network effects.

4. Act in a boundaryless fashion to leverage underutilized third-party assets.

5. Limitlessly digitize what you can to produce actionable data.

6. Build open systems that connect with external entities. Use the same approach within the organization between teams.

7. Make customer experience the core of your decision-making process.

8. Don't obsess about your value chain, obsess about customer value.

9. Embrace agile ways of working.

10. Learn to manage the now, new and the next and keep producing game changing innovations.

# Acknowledgements

It takes a village to raise a child. One can say the same thing about writing a book. This book would not have reached your hands without the help of many people who have assisted me in the research and development of the concept.

The senior leadership team at KNOLSKAPE—Shobhit Mathur, Vijay Kalangi, Raksha Shenoy, Madan Panathula, Dileep Reddy and Ramya Lakshmanan has been hugely supportive and helped me refine the ideas along the way. The core Digital BLUR development team comprising Nivedita Bhardwaj and Meenal Jain has worked tirelessly to build, learn and iterate on the model. I have benefitted immensely from the research, review, inputs and feedback from Subramanian Kalpathi. Without his help, this book would have taken a lot longer to reach you. I'd like to thank Marieke van Raiij, Sheetal Verma, Sreeram Ramakrishnan for providing timely feedback on the drafts and George Panakal, Amrita Singh, Divya K.R and Sirisha Bhamidipati for creating great frameworks and content around the Digital BLUR framework.

I'd like to thank the clients of KNOLSKAPE who have showered me with insights from various industries and countries across the world. I'd like to thank all the business leaders who have actively contributed during the research and interview process.

I'd like to thank Debarati Sengupta from Wiley for the practical tips and suggestions that helped me at various stages of the book writing process. Hariharan and Vipin from Rezonant and Sandeep Boda and Vinay Bharadwaj from KNOLSKAPE have played a stellar role in bringing the visual elements of the book to life.

This book would not have happened without the constant encouragement from my parents and my wife, Anu and all the KNOLSKAPE employees. My kids, Aadita (9) and Agastya (5) are going to live in a vastly different world in the future. This book is dedicated to them.

# About the Author
## Rajiv Jayaraman

A TEDx speaker and a leading thought leader in the space of digital transformation and learning, Rajiv Jayaraman has keen interest in the psychology of learning, design and technology. He works with CXOs and senior leaders of leading organizations to help them transform talent for the digital age. He trains and coaches senior leaders across many Fortune 500 companies on leading innovation, change and risk. Rajiv has been widely quoted and featured in *Economic Times, Business Standard, Live Mint, CNBC Young Turks, ET Now, Digital Learning Magazine, Entrepreneur*

*Magazine* and Yourstory.in. Rajiv has also been selected as one of India's Top 25 coaches by Marshall Goldsmith, the world's #1 leadership coach.

Rajiv Jayaraman is the Founder-CEO of KNOLSKAPE and serves on its board of directors. He has played a pivotal role in creating an award-winning portfolio of talent transformation products and is responsible for KNOLSKAPE's global business strategy and growth. Under his leadership, KNOLSKAPE has grown into a leading player in the workplace learning space.

Prior to KNOLSKAPE, he worked at Oracle USA in the server technologies division, where he led numerous product development efforts from the ground-up.

An INSEAD MBA, Rajiv earned his bachelor's degree in Computer Science from BITS, Pilani and his master's degree in Computer Science from University of Alabama, Huntsville. He currently lives in Bangalore, India with his beautiful wife and two adorable kids.

 rj@clearingthedigitalblur.com

 @rajiv_jayaraman

# About KNOLSKAPE

KNOLSKAPE

The research in the book was supported by the KNOLSKAPE Insights Center.

KNOLSKAPE is one of the fastest growing experiential learning and assessments companies in the world. Using award-winning experiential products coupled with high-quality expert intervention, KNOLSKAPE helps 300+ global organizations across 25 countries accelerate employee development and become future-ready. Winner of numerous Brandon Hall awards for creating stellar learning experiences, KNOLSKAPE is a Deloitte Fast 500 company in APAC and has been selected as a Great Place To Work in India in 2018.

KNOLSKAPE's Digital Academy, built on the Digital BLUR framework, is being used by Fortune 500 companies across wide range of industries such as energy, banking, pharmaceuticals, aviation and technology. The academy helps accelerate the digital transformation of an organization by focusing on culture, mindsets and capabilities. Visit www.knolskape.com/digitalblur for more information on the Digital Academy.

Visit ClearingTheDigitalBLUR.com to stay current on topics relating to the book.

 @Knolskape

# References

## Chapter 1
### Dial D for Disruption

1. https://en.wikipedia.org/wiki/Blockbuster_LLC
2. https://en.wikipedia.org/wiki/Timeline_of_Netflix
3. https://www.nytimes.com/2006/12/17/jobs/17boss.html
4. http://www.nbcnews.com/id/39332696/ns/business-retail/t/hubris-late-fees-doomed-blockbuster/
5. https://www.cnet.com/news/former-blockbuster-ceo-tells-his-side-of-netflix-story/
6. https://digit.hbs.org/submission/the-rise-and-fall-and-rise-again-of-blackberry/
7. https://techcrunch.com/2007/11/05/breaking-google-announces-android-and-open-handset-alliance/
8. https://www.telegraph.co.uk/finance/newsbysector/mediatechnologyandtelecoms/electronics/10329499/The-rise-and-fall-of-BlackBerry.html
9. https://www.telegraph.co.uk/finance/newsbysector/mediatechnologyandtelecoms/electronics/10329499/The-rise-and-fall-of-BlackBerry.html
10. https://www.fundable.com/learn/startup-stories/amazon
11. http://www.slate.com/articles/business/moneybox/2011/07/readers_without_borders.html
12. https://money.cnn.com/2001/04/11/companies/amazon/index.htm
13. https://www.mlive.com/business/index.ssf/2016/02/borders_5_years_after_bankrupt.html
14. https://www.bloomberg.com/news/articles/2005-06-19/online-extra-pierre-omidyar-on-connecting-people
15. https://en.wikipedia.org/wiki/Amul

16. https://www.statista.com/statistics/263264/top-companies-in-the-world-by-market-value/

17. https://www.wsj.com/articles/SB10001424053111903480904576512
250915629460

18. https://www.scmp.com/comment/insight-opinion/article/1850448/
chinas-digital-monopolies-are-killing-competition-and-need

19. https://www.visualcapitalist.com/chart-largest-companies-market-cap-15-years/

## Chapter 2

**The Four Blurring Lines**

1. https://www.freestylelibre.us/index.html

2. FIhttp://reports.weforum.org/digital-transformation/wp-content/
blogs.dir/94/mp/files/pages/files/digital-enterprise-narrative-final-january-2016.pdf

3. https://www.smh.com.au/business/banking-and-finance/anz-bank-restructure-to-create-150-startups-20170906-gybxr8.html

4. https://www.gartner.com/en/newsroom/press-releases/2017-02-07-gartner-says-8-billion-connected-things-will-be-in-use-in-2017-up-31-percent-from-2016

5. https://www.reuters.com/article/us-emirates-robocop/robocop-joins-dubai-police-to-fight-real-life-crime-idUSKBN18S4K8

6. https://pdfs.semanticscholar.org/6516/c3f2d5c7a33440bccfc45d-988c3088e2d2ba.pdf

7. https://www.salesforce.com/research/customer-expectations/

8. https://www.statista.com/statistics/274774/forecast-of-mobile-phone-users-worldwide/

9. https://www.cnbc.com/2018/02/01/google-ceo-sundar-pichai-ai-is-more-important-than-fire-electricity.html

10. https://www.ericsson.com/en/mobility-report/reports/
november-2017/internet-of-things-outlook

11. https://www.sintef.no/en/latest-news/big-data-for-better-or-worse/

12. https://www.imd.org/publications/articles/is-vuca-the-end-of-strategy-and-leadership/

13. Ibid 2

## Chapter 3

### Boundaryless Organizations

1. https://en.wikipedia.org/wiki/Agriculture_in_India#cite_note-2
2. https://www.itcportal.com/sustainability/echoupal.html
3. https://www.business-standard.com/article/economy-policy/itc-turns-aggregator-with-e-choupal-4-0-to-boost-farm-incomes-117060801198_1.html
4. https://www.theverge.com/circuitbreaker/2017/10/2/16404430/samsung-iphone-x-galaxy-s8-screen-components-money-revenue-display
5. https://hbr.org/1992/05/the-new-boundaries-of-the-boundaryless-company
6. https://www.holacracy.org/
7. https://www.medianama.com/2017/06/223-uber-5-billion-trips/
8. https://www.recode.net/2014/9/8/11630668/uber-adding-50000-new-driver-jobs-a-month-up-from-20000-in-may
9. https://www.upwork.com/press/2016/10/06/freelancing-in-america-2016/
10. https://www.mckinsey.com/business-functions/digital-mckinsey/our-insights/digital-globalization-the-new-era-of-global-flows
11. https://www.kickstarter.com/about

## Chapter 4

### Limitless Digitization

1. https://www.timesunion.com/business/article/GE-using-augmented-reality-to-talk-to-machines-10622203.php
2. https://www.forbes.com/sites/bernardmarr/2017/03/06/what-is-digital-twin-technology-and-why-is-it-so-important/#1b4f57022e2a
3. https://www.ge.com/digital/blog/digital-twin-work-technology-changing-industry
4. http://www.eurekamagazine.co.uk/design-engineering-features/interviews/maserati-has-fused-cutting-edge-digitalisation-methods-with-italian-passion-to-meet-customer-demand/161332/
5. Ibid 2
6. https://en.wikipedia.org/wiki/Global_Internet_usage

7. https://www.forbes.com/sites/bernardmarr/2018/05/21/how-much-data-do-we-create-every-day-the-mind-blowing-stats-everyone-should-read/#7ae8d60f60ba

8. https://www.cnbc.com/2017/08/11/three-square-market-ceo-explains-its-employee-microchip-implant.html

9. https://www.dezeen.com/2017/04/24/biotech-is-the-new-digital-nicholas-negroponte-mit-media-lab-being-material/

10. https://indianexpress.com/article/technology/tech-news-technology/intels-new-bat-sense-device-turns-every-cricket-bat-into-a-smart-one/

11. https://www.pwc.com/ee/et/publications/pub/pwc-cis-wearables.pdf

12. https://www.juniperresearch.com/document-library/white-papers/smart-cities-on-the-faster-track-to-success

13. https://www.mobypark.com/en

14. https://www.ge.com/digital/sites/default/files/Predix-The-Industrial-Internet-Platform-Brief.pdf

15. https://www.siemens.com/global/en/home/products/software/mindsphere.html

16. http://www.brainaryinteractive.com/nao-robot/

17. http://www.moley.com/

## Chapter 5

**Unbounded Innovation**

1. http://fortune.com/2018/03/05/pizza-huts-pie-tops/

2. https://en.wikipedia.org/wiki/Amazon_Dash

3. http://fortune.com/2015/08/25/smart-toothbrush-dental-insurance/

4. https://www.businessinsider.in/19-quotes-that-illustrate-the-unrelenting-genius-of-controversial-multibillionaire-Uber-CEO-Travis-Kalanick/articleshow/47502910.cms

5. https://www.wired.com/2016/08/open-source-won-now/

6. https://www.designorate.com/successful-open-innovation-examples/

7. https://techcrunch.com/2018/07/12/netflix-emmy-nominations/

8. https://bobmorris.biz/clayton-b-christensen-a-book-review-by-bob-morris

9. https://www.forbes.com/sites/oliviergarret/2017/03/03/10-million-self-driving-cars-will-hit-the-road-by-2020-heres-how-to-profit/#6ccec9fd7e50

10. https://www.uber.com/cities/pittsburgh/self-driving-ubers/

11. https://www.sciencealert.com/driverless-cars-could-reduce-traffic-fatalities-by-up-to-90-says-report

12. https://abc7ny.com/science/spacex-proposes-rocket-travel-to-get-around-earth/2467609/

13. https://www.livemint.com/Leisure/RXSIl8TvuVsFPPAKGLarDJ/How-about-Bitcoin-as-a-protocol.html

14. https://www.reuters.com/article/us-banks-barclays-blockchain-idUSKCN11D23B

15. https://www.provenance.org/

16. https://www.forbes.com/sites/suparnadutt/2017/12/18/dubai-sets-sights-on-becoming-the-worlds-first-blockchain-powered-government/#26acf2b8454b

## Chapter 6

## Relentless Iteration

1. https://arstechnica.com/cars/2017/04/formula-1-technology/

2. Ibid 1

3. https://www.forbes.com/sites/stratfor/2017/03/30/the-future-according-to-kevin-kelly/#341aa3a676bf

4. http://agilemanifesto.org/

5. https://hbr.org/2016/05/embracing-agile

6. https://www.forbes.com/sites/stevedenning/2016/09/08/explaining-agile/#2d174369301b

7. Ibid 5

8. http://theleanstartup.com/principles

9. https://www.amazon.in/Blue-Ocean-Strategy-Uncontested-Competition/dp/1591396190

10. https://en.wikipedia.org/wiki/Moore%27s_law

## Chapter 7

### Digital BLUR in the Retail Industry

1. https://www.tacobell.com/stories/tacobot
2. https://en.wikipedia.org/wiki/Amazon_Go
3. http://rejoiner.com/resources/amazon-recommendations-secret-selling-online/
4. https://www.wiley.com/en-us/Digital+Sense%3A+The+Common+-Sense+Approach+to+Effectively+Blending+Social+Business+Strategy%2C+Marketing+Technology%2C+and+Customer+Experience-p-9781119291701

## Chapter 8

### Digital BLUR in the Banking Industry

1. https://www.cbinsights.com/research/report/amazon-across-financial-services-fintech/
2. https://thefinancialbrand.com/66228/bank-credit-union-branch-traffic/
3. https://en.wikipedia.org/wiki/First_Direct
4. https://www.fidor.com/story

## Chapter 10

### Leaping from a Linear to a Networked Business Model

1. https://www.wiley.com/en-us/Business+Model+Generation%3A+A+Handbook+for+Visionaries%2C+Game+Changers%2C+and+Challengers-p-9780470876411

## Chapter 14

### Ecosystem as Strategy

1. https://en.wikipedia.org/wiki/Arthur_Tansley
2. https://www.nokia.com/sites/default/files/files/request-nokia-in-2006-pdf.pdf
3. https://techcrunch.com/2013/06/14/with-waze-google-gets-access-to-social-mapping-data-and-a-possible-lawsuit-from-nokia/
4. https://en.wikipedia.org/wiki/Wikipedia
5. https://www-03.ibm.com/press/us/en/pressrelease/6910.wss

6. https://hbr.org/2016/04/pipelines-platforms-and-the-new-rules-of-strategy

## Chapter 15

## Data as Strategy

1. https://www2.deloitte.com/content/dam/insights/us/articles/3407_2016-Shift-Index/DUP_2016-Shift-Index.pdf
2. https://www.cio.com/article/3207670/big-data/how-netflix-built-a-house-of-cards-with-big-data.html
3. http://uk.businessinsider.com/googles-400-million-acquisition-of-deepmind-is-looking-good-2016-7/?IR=T
4. https://www.mckinsey.com/industries/retail/our-insights/how-retailers-can-keep-up-with-consumers
5. https://www.walgreens.com/topic/promotion/api.jsp
6. https://www.cio.com/article/3003455/apis/apis-have-changed-the-game.html
7. https://www.paypal.com/stories/us/paypal-reports-fourth-quarter-and-full-year-2017-results
8. https://telecom.economictimes.indiatimes.com/news/reliance-jio-crosses-100-million-customers-mark-in-170-days-adding-7-customers-per-second-each-day-mukesh-ambani/57269346
9. https://hbr.org/2015/01/the-strategic-value-of-apis

## Chapter 16

## Design as Strategy

1. https://www.dbs.com/hongkong/newsroom/DBS_HONG_KONG_LAUNCHES_DBS_HOME360
2. https://www.dmi.org/page/DesignValue
3. https://hbr.org/2008/06/design-thinking
4. https://kk.org/thetechnium/better-than-own/
5. https://en.wikipedia.org/wiki/Free:_The_Future_of_a_Radical_Price
6. http://knowledge.wharton.upenn.edu/article/power-by-the-hour-can-paying-only-for-performance-redefine-how-products-are-sold-and-serviced/
7. https://www.juniperresearch.com/analystxpress/july-2017/chatbot-conversations-to-deliver-8bn-cost-saving
8. https://www.marsdd.com/mars-library/case-study-dell-distribution-and-supply-chain-innovation/

9. https://www.nytimes.com/2012/12/01/business/online-retailers-rush-to-adjust-prices-in-real-time.html

10. https://mgt.threadless.com/finding-crowdsourcing-8f707da2b64c

11. https://www.generali.com/media/press-releases/all/2016/Generali-Vitality-better-health-starts-today

12. https://www.genome.gov/27565109/the-cost-of-sequencing-a-human-genome/

13. https://3dprintingindustry.com/news/get-your-moto-on-motorola-ups-the-customization-stakes-16726/

14. https://www.businessinsider.my/wechat-messaging-app-launches-divorce-feature-in-china-2018-5/?r=US&IR=T

15. https://www.deere.com/en_US/corporate/our_company/news_and_media/press_releases/2013/corporate/2013nov14_corporaterelease.page

## Chapter 17

### Agility as Strategy

1. https://techcrunch.com/2012/11/17/heres-how-spotify-scales-up-and-stays-agile-it-runs-squads-like-lean-startups/

2. https://less.works/case-studies/ericson.html

3. https://www.mckinsey.com/industries/financial-services/our-insights/ings-agile-transformation

4. https://www.blueoceanstrategy.com/tools/strategy-canvas/

5. https://www.theatlantic.com/technology/archive/2016/07/ubers-latest-push-toward-driverless-cars/493271/

6. http://theleanstartup.com/

## Chapter 18

### Digital LEAPFROG Framework

1. https://www.mckinsey.com/business-functions/organization/our-insights/safe-enough-to-try-an-interview-with-zappos-ceo-tony-hsieh

## Chapter 19

### Digital Fault Lines

1. https://www.businessinsider.my/marianne-lake-says-jpmorgan-is-a-tech-company-2016-2/?r=US&IR=T

2. https://www.tagheuer.com/en/news/tag-heuer-google-and-intel-announce-swiss-smartwatch-collaboration

3. https://www.mozilla.org/en-US/about/governance/
4. http://news.bbc.co.uk/2/hi/business/1154868.stm
5. http://www.digitalsocialstrategy.org/bac/2016/12/07/is-dominos-a-tech-company/
6. https://techcrunch.com/2016/10/03/walmartlabs-open-sources-the-application-platform-that-powers-walmart-com/
7. https://www.forbes.com/sites/shephyken/2017/07/08/walgreens-at-the-corner-of-technology-and-a-better-customer-experience-cx/#698b338532c9
8. https://marketing.prophet.com/acton/media/33865/altimeter--the-2016-state-of-digital-transformation
9. https://cisr.mit.edu/research/research-overview/classic-topics/enterprise-architecture/
10. https://www.cio.com/article/3218667/digital-transformation/have-you-had-your-bezos-moment-what-you-can-learn-from-amazon.html
11. http://www.3boxsolution.com/
12. https://hbr.org/2013/08/the-innovation-mindset-in-acti-3
13. https://www.businessinsider.com/how-apple-really-lost-its-lead-in-the-80s-2012-12/?IR=T
14. https://3dprintingindustry.com/news/3d-printing-next-five-years-tim-weber-global-head-3d-printing-hp-113255/
15. https://www.forbes.com/sites/quora/2017/06/08/google-wouldnt-negotiate-with-apple-to-keep-maps-on-ios-devices-and-that-was-the-wrong-move/#4805bd2c63a9
16. https://www.reuters.com/article/us-facebook-privacy-tracking/facebook-fuels-broad-privacy-debate-by-tracking-non-users-idUSKBN1HM0DR
17. https://en.wikipedia.org/wiki/General_Data_Protection_Regulation
18. https://www.theverge.com/2017/11/7/16615290/waymo-self-driving-safety-driver-chandler-autonomous
19. https://www.businessinsider.com/android-fragmentation-is-worsening-2017-11/?IR=T
20. https://data.apteligent.com/ios/

## Chapter 21

### Cultural Fault Lines

1. https://www.mckinsey.com/business-functions/digital-mckinsey/how-we-help-clients/digital-culture-and-capabilities
2. https://hbr.org/2013/12/the-three-pillars-of-a-teaming-culture

3. https://www.forbes.com/sites/danschawbel/2017/11/21/
   paul-polman-why-todays-leaders-need-to-commit-to-a-
   purpose/#4f2e70891276
4. https://www.nytimes.com/2018/07/12/world/asia/thailand-cave-
   rescue-seals.html
5. http://www.publicisgroupe.com/en/news/press-releases/publicis-
   groupe-unveils-marcel
6. https://hbswk.hbs.edu/archive/pg-s-new-innovation-model
7. https://en.wikipedia.org/wiki/Ice_Bucket_Challenge
8. https://www.ted.com/talks/wael_ghonim_let_s_design_social_
   media_that_drives_real_change
9. https://www.thehindubusinessline.com/info-tech/on-a-crusade-
   against-online-fake-news/article9669133.ece
10. https://www.cnet.com/news/facebook-sorry-that-balloons-appeared-
   in-indonesia-earthquake-messages/
11. https://www.forbes.com/sites/tomvanderark/2018/04/18/hit-
   refresh-how-a-growth-mindset-culture-tripled-microsofts-
   value/#7ab4c30652ad
12. https://www.mindsetworks.com/science/